What Dreams Were Made Of

# STAR
★★★★★★★★★★★ AMERICAN CULTURE / AMERICAN CINEMA
DECADES

Each volume in the series Star Decades: American Culture/American Cinema presents original essays analyzing the movie star against the background of contemporary American cultural history. As icon, as mediated personality, and as object of audience fascination and desire, the Hollywood star remains the model for celebrity in modern culture and represents a paradoxical combination of achievement, talent, ability, luck, authenticity, superficiality, and ordinariness. In all of the volumes, stardom is studied as an effect of, and influence on, the particular historical and industrial contexts that enabled a star to be "discovered," to be featured in films, to be promoted and publicized, and ultimately to become a recognizable and admired—even sometimes notorious—feature of the cultural landscape. Understanding when, how, and why a star "makes it," dazzling for a brief moment or enduring across decades, is especially relevant given the ongoing importance of mediated celebrity in an increasingly visualized world. We hope that our approach produces at least some of the surprises and delight for our readers that stars themselves do.

ADRIENNE L. McLEAN AND MURRAY POMERANCE
SERIES EDITORS

Jennifer M. Bean, ed., *Flickers of Desire: Movie Stars of the 1910s*

Patrice Petro, ed., *Idols of Modernity: Movie Stars of the 1920s*

Adrienne J. McLean, ed., *Glamour in a Golden Age: Movie Stars of the 1930s*

Sean Griffin, ed., *What Dreams Were Made Of: Movie Stars of the 1940s*

R. Barton Palmer, ed., *Larger Than Life: Movie Stars of the 1950s*

Pamela R. Wojcik, ed., *New Constellations: Movie Stars of the 1960s*

James Morrison, ed., *Hollywood Reborn: Movie Stars of the 1970s*

Robert Eberwein, ed., *Acting for America: Movie Stars of the 1980s*

Anna Everett, ed., *Pretty People: Movie Stars of the 1990s*

Murray Pomerance, ed., *Shining in Shadows: Movie Stars of the 2000s*

What Dreams Were Made Of

Movie Stars of the

1940s

☆☆★★★★★★★★★★★

EDITED BY

SEAN GRIFFIN

RUTGERS UNIVERSITY PRESS

NEW BRUNSWICK, NEW JERSEY, AND LONDON

LIBRARY OF CONGRESS CATALOGING-IN-PUBLICATION DATA

What dreams were made of : Movie stars of the 1940s / edited by Sean Griffin.
    p.   cm. — (Star decades : American culture / American cinema)
    Includes bibliographical references and index.
    ISBN 978–0–8135–4963–7   (hardcover : alk. paper)
    ISBN 978–0–8135–4964–4   (pbk. : alk. paper)
    1. Motion picture actors and actresses—United States—Biography.   I. Griffin, Sean.
    PN1998.2.W45   2010
    791.4302'80922—dc22

                                                                        2010024093

A British Cataloging-in-Publication record for this book is available from the British
Library.

Visit our Web site: http://rutgerspress.rutgers.edu

Manufactured in the United States of America

To Drew Casper, for getting me here

CONTENTS

★★★★★★★★★★★★

ACKNOWLEDGMENTS

★★★★★★★★★★★

First and foremost, thanks are owed to Murray Pomerance and Adrienne McLean, the editors of the Star Decades series, who approached me back in 2007 with the invitation to edit this volume. Since then, they have provided invaluable help and guidance, as individual pieces were conceived and reconceived (I still think a chapter on Bugs Bunny would have been ideal for this volume, but there you go!), as potential contributors came and went, and as deadlines approached and sailed past. I appreciate their patience, advice and—in the case of McLean—specific written contribution to this tome. I also express my debt to all the authors who have lent their expertise and enthusiasm to this endeavor.

I also want to state my gratitude and admiration to a number of people at Southern Methodist University. The Division of Cinema-Television has been of enormous support to me throughout the process. I am privileged to be teaching among so many nationally esteemed colleagues, many of whom are represented in this tome. Whether specifically contributing or not, the SMU community has never ceased to offer inordinate encouragement, advice, and friendship.

Much of the work herein is also indebted to two invaluable research resources: the Margaret Herrick Library of the Academy of Motion Picture Arts and Sciences, and the Constance McCormack Collection of star scrapbooks housed at the Cinema-Television Library at the University of Southern California. Both contain a veritable treasure trove of clippings from trade papers, movie fan magazines, and studio press releases, primary sources that were vital for such a project as this series. I am certain everyone involved herein extends a thank you to the staff at both these institutions.

I have always thought the 1940s to be an undervalued decade in American film history, and so was very pleased when I was invited to be involved in this project. I wanted to try to evoke the uniqueness of the moment as personified by the stars who are specifically identified with the era. A number of them have of course received their own chapters in this collection. Many others did not—Danny Kaye, Jennifer Jones, Alan Ladd, Veronica Lake, Lena Horne, Carmen Miranda, Sabu, Van Johnson, Margaret O'Brien, Esther Williams, Jeanne Crain, Dana Andrews. I hope the ambience of the period that they helped shape still emerges. So, to quote a hit song from the period, praise the Lord and pass the ammunition . . .

What Dreams Were Made Of

INTRODUCTION

★★★★★★★★★★★

Stardom in the 1940s

SEAN GRIFFIN

The 1940s are often conceptualized as a split decade, a temporal "house divided." Most obviously, World War II deftly cleaved the decade in half. Hitler invaded Poland in late 1939, resulting in Britain and France declaring war on Germany. While the United States refrained from entering the fight initially, the pull grew month by month, until the Japanese bombed Pearl Harbor in December 1941. The war then dominated all aspects of American public life for the next few years. Victory came in both the European and Pacific theaters in 1945, and suddenly the country and the entire world had entered a new world order. This postwar era saw a rapid and full-scale revision of life and thought. Not unexpectedly, many hoped to revert quickly to the way things were before the upheaval of the war. Yet major changes in global politics and advances in scientific research also irrevocably altered American life. The onset of the Cold War created a new enemy for the United States, and new fears of internal subversion—which at times veered into a fear of anything that diverged from majority thought. The postwar era was also referred to as the Atomic Age, as humanity started coming to terms with the fact that we could now literally destroy the planet and ourselves. As Jacqueline Foertsch has written, "The momentous events of the mid-1940s are thus pivotal in multiple respects," creating an "impulse to read the 1940s as a decade that is as neatly bisected as it neatly hangs together" (1–2).

It was a split decade for the Hollywood studios as well. Many film history books cut the 1940s in half, regarding the first part as an extension of the classic Hollywood era of the 1930s, and the second part as the start of the post-classical era of the 1950s (Schatz; Lewis; Jewell; Casper). While the studios in wartime had to adjust to the loss of employees to the military, and to stronger involvement (and potential interference) from the federal government, the first half of the decade was generally a high time for Hollywood. With national employment figures suddenly at an all-time high after a decade of economic woes, but with wartime rationing limiting what was available for purchase, everyone went to the movies. Furthermore, the studios had by this time refined their business patterns and the "Hollywood style" of production, resulting in a number of expertly produced, smoothly told, and confidently crafted films. Motion picture theater attendance reached its highest level ever in 1946.

And then the bottom fell out. The federal government's antitrust case, which had been shelved during the war, was revived and in 1948 the Supreme Court decreed (in what became known as the Paramount Decision) that the major studios divest themselves of one arm of their vertically integrated holdings (production, distribution, or exhibition)—signaling an end to the smooth organization of the classical Hollywood system. Furthermore, certain members of the government began training their suspicions on communist infiltration on Hollywood, throwing filmmakers into new panic. Most of all, though, audiences started abandoning film theaters. With the onset of the postwar Baby Boom, many moved to newly formed suburban communities—far from urban centers where most movie theaters resided. Whether in cities or suburbs, Americans also increasingly stayed home to watch the new mass-marketed gadget called television (whose development, like the antitrust case, had been put on hold until the end of the war). As the decade ended, Hollywood was scrambling to figure out how to survive in a very different environment (Dixon).

If the studios felt a sharp divide in the 1940s, it is unsurprising that stars experienced it as well. The war significantly impacted the lives and careers of most stars, and the postwar period brought even more changes. Actors and actresses, like all Americans, were deeply affected by the war. Some men signed up for active duty in the military, such as James Stewart, Robert Montgomery, and Clark Gable. Others were drafted, like Gene Kelly, Victor Mature, and Mickey Rooney. Some, such as (somewhat ironically) Roy Rogers and John Wayne, received deferments and consequently felt certain pressure to explain why they were not "doing their part." Such losses left the studios scrambling to find leading men—resulting in a number of young actors promoted to stardom, such as Van Johnson, Gregory Peck, Danny Kaye, and Alan Ladd. With women only allowed to enlist in women's auxiliary units (the WACs, the WAVEs), actresses did not feel as much pressure to put their careers on hold. Yet female stars did actively participate in the war effort, volunteering at war bond drives, and meeting with soldiers at camps, on USO tours, or at the Hollywood Canteen. Older male stars not eligible for the draft did likewise (Doherty; Dick; Koppes and Black).

In multiple ways, then, stars increased their actual physical presence among the rest of the population, strengthening their connections to the general public. Cheesecake photos and films shipped overseas for screenings in combat zones provided troops with a sense of home and "what they

With many male performers entering the armed services during World War II, Hollywood studios began grooming and promoting a new crop of men. Van Johnson, for example, quickly became MGM's top male star during the war. Collection of the author.

were fighting for." Increased movie attendance further deepened the felt relationship audiences had with stars. Together, these elements created a sense that stars were "just like us," just perhaps a little "more so." As one woman opined at the time, "If your idea of a factory girl is a thin little creature who looks downtrodden and underfed, you're way off the beam, as my chums say. A factory girl in real life looks very much like Brenda Marshall, Anne Shirley, or Betty Grable" (Giles 123).

The major studios had instituted a relatively well oiled system for discovering, grooming, and showcasing talent (as well as controlling it) long before the 1940s, knowing that stars helped market their product. Articles in the industry press indicate that studios began relying more on stars during the decade. Efforts to alleviate pressure from the antitrust case led studios to lessen the amount of block-booking done with theaters, resulting in individual films needing to be able to sell themselves. This often meant employing stars more often in projects (Schatz 103–04). While budgets on average increased during the 1940s partly due to this development, even pictures made at B-studios such as Republic began to rely on stars such as Gene Autry, Roy Rogers, and Judy Canova.

No doubt recognizing their net worth to the studios, stars began to assert greater power. More and more stars finished their studio contracts and became independent artists. This trend had begun by the early part of the 1940s (with the likes of Fred Astaire, Claudette Colbert, Ronald Colman, Ginger Rogers, and Barbara Stanwyck working freelance), but the numbers grew dramatically after the war. New income tax laws spurred individuals to "incorporate" themselves, leading a large number of actors and actresses to set up independent production companies. Stars had greater opportunity to become independent due to a landmark case brought by Olivia de Havilland against Warner Bros. in 1943. The courts decided against the conventional Hollywood studio policy of adding the time an actor was on suspension to the end of the contract period (for stars usually set at seven years), which potentially kept an actor in the studio's control indefinitely. The ruling granted actors the right to refuse roles and to sit out the duration of their contracts (Schatz 206–08).

Thus, as the war ended, stars were finding new power and independence. Independence, though, also meant a lack of protection by the studio against scandal. While valuable contract players could depend upon their studio to help sweep ugly matters under the rug, stars increasingly had to fend for themselves. Headlines about Robert Mitchum's arrest for possession of marijuana or Ingrid Bergman's extramarital pregnancy exemplified a newer "no holds barred" era of star coverage in the press. Most devastatingly, stars found themselves easy targets for communist paranoia in the second half of the decade. Many actors and actresses had looked into socialism or other leftist groups during the depths of the Depression; others had made films or public comments showing support of Soviet Russia as a wartime ally. The House Un-American Activities Committee (HUAC) and various civic groups that sprang up after the war to ferret out communist sympathizers quickly jumped on these factors to accuse a number of people

Olivia de Havilland's successful lawsuit against Warner Bros. helped free stars from inordinate studio control over their careers. As an independent artist in the late 1940s, de Havilland won two Oscars as Best Actress for *To Each His Own* (1946) and *The Heiress* (1949). Collection of the author.

of working to help the Soviet Union undermine American strength. Some stars (such as Gary Cooper, Robert Taylor, and Ginger Rogers) eagerly testified about potential communist influence in the industry. Others (Larry Parks, John Garfield) had their careers destroyed (and sometimes their lives) as a blacklist developed to keep suspects from finding work.

Stars, therefore, like Hollywood and America at large, experienced the 1940s as a split decade. Yet a sense of division has been a key concept to star studies in general. Dyer theorizes how star images are "related to contradictions in ideology. . . . The relations may be one of displacement . . . or of the suppression of one half of the contradiction and the foregrounding of the other . . . or else it may be that the star effects a 'magic' reconciliation of the apparently incompatible terms" (*Stars* 30). Barbara Deming, writing about films in the 1940s, also stressed that "the heroes and heroines who are most popular at any particular period are precisely those who, with a certain added style, with a certain distinction, act out the predicament in which we all find ourselves—a predicament from which the movie-dream then cunningly extricates us" (Deming 2). Many analyses of star images emphasize how performers become stars by somehow embodying (and thus resolving) cultural contradictions.

That Deming writes specifically about the 1940s indicates that the decade was split not just in terms of timeline. Examinations of the decade are often rife with metaphors of ambivalence, divided emotions, and even schizophrenia. Film books about the 1940s stress this duality, often directly in the titles: Deming's *Running Away from Myself* or Dana Polan's *Power and Paranoia*. Even a book about Hollywood studio design in the 1940s touches on this lack of cohesion, describing a tendency to collapse multiple decorative styles into an overarching mélange of tastes (Madelbaum and Myers 25). That Deming began putting together notes for her book *during* the time in question shows that considering this period as dislocated was common then, and not just in hindsight.

The growing interest in psychoanalysis in 1940s America undoubtedly helped spur thought about split personalities and divided desires. Psychological testing in the military rose during the war, most notoriously in an effort to weed homosexuals out of the service. Many in Hollywood also became enamored with Freudian therapy at this time. Conceptualizing the conflict between one's id and one's ego led to a consideration of warring tendencies within the cultural landscape of the period—and there were certainly plenty of "incompatible terms" to negotiate. While World War II is often portrayed as uniting everyone together in a shared goal, plenty of internal disagreement still existed. Until the bombing of Pearl Harbor, the country was locked in vibrant debate between isolationists and interventionists, but fighting the war created its own contradictions. Most centrally, the war was being fought to restore liberty for all individuals, but doing so required people to suppress their individualism and work as part of a team (either in the ranks or on the factory line). Championing freedom also led to much propaganda about America as a land of opportunity for all races and religions. Yet the Zoot Suit riots between white sailors and Los Angeles' Latino population during the war, as well as the number of race riots in cities where factories began integrating their workforce, demonstrated the wealth of prejudice still to be overcome. Women's place in American society was also very ambiguous. Wartime propaganda promoted female strength and capability at traditionally masculine work, while many other aspects of culture (pulp novels and film noir in particular) expressed deep fears about powerful women. Such worries became exacerbated once the culturally enforced unity of wartime ended. Postwar culture became littered with ambivalent antiheroes, and the call for humanist brotherhood after the war was matched by a concomitant growth of existentialist nihilism.

Such emotional dislocation was matched by actual physical dislocation. Men were being drafted and sent to military bases and overseas, and large numbers on the home front moved to industrial centers to work in factories. Integration of women and people of color into the workforce also physically redistributed populations. The federal government also forcibly relocated thousands of Japanese Americans into internment camps. With parents away in the service or working in factories, children were often largely unattended (an issue that was of importance during this period, but has largely been overlooked in subsequent histories of the home front). New housing arrangements, and often housing shortages, were widespread during the war. Such mobility continued after the war, albeit in a different fashion, as thousands abandoned the cities for the suburbs (Polan 254).

Polan and Deming both note the motif of the "wanderer" in films of the period—someone without a home, without direction (see, in particular, Polan 264–71). Home itself becomes a site of ambivalence and duality. While a number of films glorify the American home—particularly nostalgic representations of America at the turn of the century—the shadowy apartments and mansions found in noir, gothic romances, and wartime spy thrillers present home as entrapment and danger. Certain films encapsulate both emotions, such as Alfred Hitchcock's *Shadow of a Doubt* (1943), Vincente Minnelli's *Meet Me in St. Louis* (1944), or Frank Capra's *It's a Wonderful Life* (1946). For male veterans attempting to adjust to a civilian life that no longer felt comfortable, as well as women feeling constrained by a concerted effort to place them back into the domestic sphere after the war, home was an increasingly complex environment.

Stars, therefore, may have provided an anchor for audiences feeling cut adrift from everything they had known before. Certain stars seemed present to address each of the contradictory set of values or emotions listed.

Brazilian "bombshell" Carmen Miranda became an iconic figure of the Good Neighbor Policy, singing and dancing in musicals of the 1940s. While presented as comically outrageous, her stardom celebrated cultural outreach between the United States and nations south of its border. Collection of the author.

Some performers even founded their stardom on divided selves: Danny Kaye constantly played dual roles, and Lon Chaney Jr. was forever typecast as the Wolf Man. The prevalence of star couples also suggests the divided self: Abbott and Costello, Bob Hope and Bing Crosby. Individual stars such as Carmen Miranda, Sabu, or Lena Horne acknowledged racial and ethnic diversity, but often within a certain comfort zone for white audiences. Others helped negotiate the thorny issue of individualism versus working as a unit. For example, male stars such as John Garfield, James Cagney, and Errol Flynn regularly played self-centered guys learning to be part of a team.

Various female stars became prominent by balancing elements of self-assertiveness with conventional female glamour—whether the gumption and gams displayed by Betty Grable and Rita Hayworth, the grace yet grit of Greer Garson, or Jennifer Jones's ability to be both earthy and innocent (in different proportion depending on the role). Representative of the interest in psychoanalysis, a number of actresses starred as characters with fragmented psyches: Bette Davis in *Now, Voyager* (1942), Ginger Rogers in *Lady in the Dark* (1944), Joan Crawford in *Possessed* (1947), Gene Tierney in *Leave Her to Heaven* (1947), Olivia de Havilland in *The Snake Pit* (1948). Female stars such as Veronica Lake, Lana Turner, Lauren Bacall, and Barbara Stanwyck also delved into the duplicitous figure of the femme fatale common to noir (Renov).

The most emblematic stars of the decade, though, were the actors who crafted images of weary souls, cynical about the world but upholding a sense of morality and justice nonetheless. Deming's analysis of the decade's films reveals the prevalence of disenchanted heroes who take up the war effort, yet often with a semi-suicidal sacrifice implicit. She connects these figures to "tough guys" after the war actively courting the ultimate disinvestment of death. Whether crusading in the cycle of social problem films that developed during the postwar period or wading through webs of intrigue in noir thrillers, leading men (John Garfield and James Cagney again, but also Robert Mitchum and Dick Powell, among others) doggedly carried on in their missions, even though they were not certain of victory, or even survival (Naremore; Palmer). Nowhere is this more evident than in the rise to popularity of Humphrey Bogart, whose star image perfectly demonstrates the dualities of the era, and who stands as probably the most iconic star of the entire decade. He and others gave voice to the dis-ease many seemed to feel at the time, yet these stars appeared to hold seemingly opposite aspects together and resolve the tensions, at least for the duration of each performance.

In various ways, the stars discussed in this volume negotiated the unstable, ever-shifting terrain of the 1940s and helped audiences do the same. Certain stars are emblematic of the decade. The comic duo of Abbott and Costello, as David Sedman describes, shot to stardom in a series of military farces that helped prepare a still wary American public for entrance into another war. Their slide after the war and rebound toward the end of the decade by uniting with various iconic horror figures is an almost perfect mapping of how many stars had to reconfigure their careers across this period. Similarly, Hannah Hamad details how Greer Garson became the queen of the MGM lot in the early 1940s, supplanting Greta Garbo, Joan Crawford, and Norma Shearer, but then found it difficult to adjust to post-war tastes. The 1940s also saw the rise of the pinup, and Adrienne McLean examines the two most famous ones: Betty Grable and Rita Hayworth. McLean shows how the two, in different ways, counterbalanced the overt objectification of their bodies with expressions of female independence. While such a balance fit the "Rosie the Riveter" era of the war, it became more problematic afterward. McLean details how Grable began to fade in popularity toward the end of the decade and Hayworth became the source of scandal for asserting what was considered a bit too much independence in her affair with Aly Khan. Robin Blaetz describes how Ingrid Bergman was also punished by Hollywood for her extramarital relationship with Italian director Roberto Rossellini. Having become one of the most respected and in-demand stars of the mid-1940s, Bergman's story provides a stark picture of how quickly fortunes could change during this era.

As mentioned, Humphrey Bogart has become symbolic of 1940s Hollywood, precisely for his ability to straddle categories and attitudes—arguably American cinema's first antihero. Rick Worland describes Bogart's path from villain in supporting parts to existential romantic figure. Part of that transition happened through the chemistry the actor found with Ingrid Bergman in *Casablanca* (1943), and then in his films with Lauren Bacall. Worland also examines the rise of Bacall, who developed a female persona that matched Bogart's sense of strength yet cynicism. Ed Countryman's chapter on John Wayne suggests many parallels between Wayne and Bogart. While Wayne is often regarded as an uncomplicated icon of American masculinity, Countryman shows how often Wayne played characters who were just as world-weary and emotionally isolated as Bogart in his westerns and war films of the 1940s. The personae of singing cowboy stars Gene Autry and Roy Rogers are considered usually in even more simplistic terms than Wayne. Ed Buscombe, though, displays how each, in his own way, mediated between city and county and between tradition and modernity.

Charlie Keil's examination of Katharine Hepburn and Cary Grant along with David Lugowski's discussion of Claudette Colbert, Ginger Rogers, and Barbara Stanwyck are reminders that performers who rose to prominence in the 1930s had to negotiate the ever-shifting terrain of the 1940s as well. Both authors describe the personae that had served each of these stars earlier, and then show how those images were altered to maintain popularity both during the war and afterward. In particular, the female stars in various ways domesticated their images—or played characters punished for their independence and strength. Grant's image, though, as Keil points out, also felt pressure to become more "ordinary." The emphasis on stars as not much different than the average Joe or Jane trails through many of the analyses in this volume. Nowhere is this more apparent than in the popularity of Mickey Rooney and Judy Garland during the decade. My overview of their careers shows how audiences liked to perceive them as "ordinary Americans" or average teenagers, even though it was plainly obvious how extraordinarily talented they were. That both had troubles balancing that sense of ordinariness and extraordinariness in the latter half of the 1940s matches up with the experiences of many of the other stars investigated herein.

In sum, the 1940s were—for the United States, for Hollywood, and for its stars—exhilarating and frightening, filled with potential and uncertainty: the best of times and the worst of times, but always (as Bogart's Sam Spade intones at the end of *The Maltese Falcon* [1941]) what dreams were made of.

I
Abbott and Costello
Who's on First?

DAVID SEDMAN

Up from the deeps of bedizened burlesque, and toting all the gags
mellowed in the memories of that medium and the medicine shows
before it, Bud Abbott and Lou Costello have spiraled in two short years
and seven quick pictures from nowhere on the screen to the Number
One spot among the Money-Making Stars.
—William R. Weaver, *Motion Picture Herald*, 26 December 1942

Bud Abbott and Lou Costello were undeniably the most
prolific comedic actors of the 1940s. In that single decade the comedians
appeared in more than two dozen films, as well as performed live on

---

Bud Abbott and Lou Costello portrait, c. 1944. Collection of the author.

stage, broadcast multiple radio shows, appeared on Broadway, and made numerous fund-raising tours to sell U.S. war bonds. Their slapstick routines and flawless comedic timing captivated audiences and helped catapult them to fame far beyond the burlesque shows in which they began their partnership.

In contrast to some Hollywood stars of the era who tried to maintain some degree of privacy in their lives, Abbott and Costello chose the path of all-out publicity to further enhance their reputations. Consistent exposure was the guiding force in building their public image and promoting them as the country's preeminent comedy team. Publicity experts, as well as the duo's film studios (Universal and MGM) and broadcast networks (NBC and ABC), went to considerable effort to ensure that the public knew what Abbott and Costello were up to personally as well as professionally. Abbott and Costello's onscreen and offscreen pursuits were covered regularly throughout the 1940s by the major Hollywood columnists, including Hedda Hopper, Wood Soanes, Sheilah Graham, and Jimmy Fidler. The sheer volume of their appearances in films and broadcasting led to consistent coverage by fan magazines such as *Photoplay*, *Screenland*, *Motion Picture*, and *Movie Story*. Beginning in 1948, they even had their own monthly comic book. The pair granted scores of interviews to the press and enjoyed performing for reporters while relating colorful stories about their days on the burlesque circuit prior to hitting it big.

★★★★★ The Abbott and Costello Story

Bud Abbott was born in 1895 to parents working in the circus. He left school at fourteen to work at Coney Island, which led to jobs in the theater and vaudeville. He married burlesque dancer and comedienne Betty Smith in 1918 and began producing touring shows. By the mid-1920s, Abbott had become a highly regarded straight man on the burlesque circuit.

Lou Costello was athletic as a youth and excelled in basketball and boxing at school. His athletic skills were put to good use when he was hired as a stuntman in Hollywood in the late 1920s. When that failed to provide a steady income, Costello decided to become a performer in burlesque. Like Abbott, he was also married to a burlesque dancer, Anne Battler. As a result, Abbott and his wife would cross professional paths with Costello and his wife while touring the country. Abbott and Costello worked together for the first time in 1935 and became a comedy team in 1936, with Abbott playing the part of the straight man and Costello delivering the punch lines.

The comedy pair's humor was anything but subtle. As Abbott put it, "There are only two types of comedy: there's the topical such as Jack Benny and Bob Hope do, and there's the old-fashioned corny comedy from the 'burley' houses—and that's us" (Frank Daugherty, "Comedy as Comedians See It," *Christian Science Monitor*, 17 October 1941, 14). Abbott explained that their approach to comedy was based on two-man comic strips such as *Mutt and Jeff*. From the newspapers came their formula: "Right then an idea was born, why couldn't we be animated comic strips?" (*Hold That Ghost Show Showman's Manual*, 1941).

Abbott and Costello's rise as a team was rather rapid by show-business standards. They secured an agent and manager, Eddie Sherman, and were represented by Sam Weisbord of the William Morris Agency. Within three years of debuting the new formula on the burlesque stage, they received their first national exposure on radio's "Kate Smith Hour" as guest performers in 1938. Their popularity grew, and they continued on as "Smith Hour" regulars for the next two years. This led to roles in a 1939 Broadway musical, *The Streets of Paris*, for which they received rave reviews. Hollywood scouts soon recognized their stage presence and visual humor, and the bid was made.

In 1940, Universal Pictures signed the comedy team for the musical *One Night in the Tropics* (1940), designed primarily as a showcase for its star, Allan Jones. Abbott and Costello would be supporting characters and, supposedly, perform one comedy bit. The duo's first filmed scene was what was to become their signature skit, "Who's on First?"—the baseball-themed routine that had captivated audiences on the burlesque circuit. The news from the set was that Abbott and Costello's comic timing was so stellar that they might be headliners on film and certainly deserved more exposure in *Tropics*.

Universal was confident enough in the duo's appeal that it directed its newsreel division to highlight them in coverage of the film's world premiere in July 1940. The studio moved the scheduled October opening of *One Night in the Tropics* from New Orleans to Lou Costello's hometown of Paterson, New Jersey, where Costello was performing a benefit to help raise funds for his church. Universal took no rental fees for the opening, and the publicity continued with the town declaring it "Costello Day" as its native son broke ground on the site of the new Saint Anthony's Church.

The Abbott and Costello publicity effort would continue unbridled throughout the decade. Their success encapsulated the American dream, a storyline that would only escalate thanks to the star-making publicity machinery of 1940s Hollywood.

★★★★★ **Early Publicity in Hollywood**

"Publicity," Lou Costello said. "We're always reading things we didn't do."
—Frederick James Smith, *This Week Magazine*, 28 September 1941

In the late 1930s, Abbott and Costello gave the impression that their earliest professional meetings occurred in 1929. They told of their struggles together until being discovered in 1938. The team reportedly could make as much as $100 a week during the 1930s (Frank S. Nugent, "Loco Boys Make Good," *New York Times Magazine*, 24 August 1941, 112). In the embellished story, the comedy duo met their spouses simultaneously at an unspecified performance after separating the dancers during a "backstage squabble" (Dee Lowrance, "Hollywood Finds a New Team," *Washington Post*, 1 June 1941, L1). In a nationally syndicated column, Dale Harrison's "New York," Costello punctuated the story by saying that the newfound female acquaintances were plied with the invitation, "Let us all go forth to a lunch wagon and partake of some rare delicacies—hamburgers with onions, let us say" (*Reno Evening Gazette*, 12 July 1939, 4). From there, Costello said it was true love and both were married. While this account was not quite accurate in its timeline, the populist storyline would play well to an America that had suffered through the Depression years. For Universal Studios, having signed the duo to star in two low-budget B-comedies following *One Night at the Tropics*, the rags-to-riches theme was too good to pass up.

Universal's publicity was based upon the theme that the team began its professional alliance in 1930, with success following many years of financial deprivation. The studio's bio, sent out to both the press and fans, began, "Bud Abbott and Lou Costello in 1940 celebrated their tenth year as partners and their second year as partners with money in the bank" (*Abbott and Costello–Biography*, News Release, 1940–1942). Articles in the press that echoed the Universal bio were commonplace in the early 1940s. Wood Soanes, in his nationally syndicated column, wrote that the comic pair "had been turned away from the studios and been kicked around generally" ("Curtain Calls: Miracle of Abbott, Costello Told," *Oakland Tribune*, 25 August 1941, 14). *Movie Album* wrote, "The death of vaudeville hit the boys hard, and they were playing for peanuts" prior to getting into movies ("Fun for Your Money," 1941, 30). In the pages of the *Movie-Radio Guide*, Abbott and Costello's struggles were said to have occurred after the "1929 era," where "for seven years they kicked about 'small time' and offered their act for free to passers-by in Times Square." The publication awarded the duo its "Stars of the Year" award because "never has there been such an utter phenomenon as the team of Abbott and Costello" ("Stars of the Year: Abbott and Costello," 12–18 July 1941, 8).

The comedy team's leap from obscurity to stardom is generally told in fan magazines and newspapers as that "one big break" where "dame fortune smiled upon" them. One could easily point to the team hooking up with manager Eddie Sherman and getting William Morris representation from Sam Weisbord as their biggest breaks. Television producer and director Bob Banner, who directed the TV biopic *Bud and Lou* (1978) and also once worked with the boys in live television, said that "Sherman ran their lives" and was responsible for virtually all their professional dealings (personal interview, 14 June 2007). Of Weisbord, Norman Brokaw, the founder and chairman of William Morris, said, "We get the talent in the right venues; that's what we do and that's what Sam could do" (personal interview, 15 June 2007). The notion of a singular big break is a moving target because the story as told by Abbott and Costello themselves incorporates several "one big break" themes.

One story the pair liked to tell was that Jesse Kay of the Roxy Theatre gave them their biggest break by moving them out of small-time appearances and to a much bigger presence on the stage of the Roxy. Another of their oft-told stories is that Harry Kaufman gave them their break by putting them in the Broadway version of *The Streets of Paris*, which legitimized their stature beyond the burlesque circuit. Another undeniable big break was that Ted Smith, Kate Smith's manager, saw the pair live and was convinced by Weisbord and Sherman to feature them as guests on "The Kate Smith Hour." The guest spot proved so successful that it turned into nearly a hundred consecutive guest spots on Smith's show. And again, another big break came when producer Jules Levey wanted them for a supporting role in Universal's *One Night at the Tropics*.

Despite the fact that the team's success revolved around a series of major breaks that occurred in a timeframe between roughly 1937 and 1941, Abbott and Costello would generally concentrate their success on one big break as opposed to a series of breaks, apparently to make the storyline more approachable to their readers. That big break varied from interview to interview. Yet one of the lesser-told storylines of their fame in Hollywood was their pairing with producer Alex Gottlieb in 1940 for their first starring role in Universal's *Buck Privates* (1941). Although rarely focused on publicly, it would be a milestone in the team's professional history.

Gottlieb was a reporter who became a publicity director in live theater in the 1930s and moved on to publicity and advertising jobs in the film industry, after which he began writing for both radio and film. With this diverse background, Universal hired him as a producer for *Buck Privates*. Much like RKO's Wheeler and Woolsey and Fox's Ritz Brothers films made in the 1930s, Gottlieb said his goal was made clear by the head of Universal with the Abbott and Costello comedies: "Do anything you want with them, just make the pictures and don't spend too much money" (Furmanek and Palumbo 43).

Gottlieb's frugality and efficiency was embodied on the set. Moreover, it led to a large profit potential and a model for virtually every Universal Abbott and Costello film to follow. The formula was rather straightforward: shoot the project quickly while allowing the comedy team to fulfill its radio commitments and live touring schedules. The key was to get as much in one take as possible. This method only worked because Abbott and Costello frowned upon multiple takes and eschewed most rehearsals. Their enormous talent for performing comedy bits flawlessly on the burlesque stage translated well to the medium of film where they could perform their scenes in a time-efficient manner. While most films of the period would take several months to shoot prior to their post-production editing, *Buck Privates* was shot in about twenty shooting days covering four weeks, including a break at Christmas. Within three weeks of wrapping its shooting schedule, the film was edited, given its premiere, and released as a B-picture which, like any such B-film, was designed to play with A-films as the lower half of a double bill.

Buck Privates is fairly typical of most of Abbott and Costello's films in which they work in comedy bits from their live act. The boys play Slicker Smith and Herbie Brown, tie salesmen struggling to make ends meet, either looking for a better job opportunity or becoming entangled in some comical scenario not of their own making. Peddling their wares from the street with no small amount of hucksterism, Slicker and Herbie also must stay one step ahead of the police. One fateful day, the boys elude the police by entering a movie theater. While there, they sign up for what they think is a drawing for a prize, only to find out that the theater has become an army recruiting center and that they have unwittingly volunteered for the army. This turn of events allows Abbott and Costello to perform a comedy routine from their stage act known as "The Drill," in which the boys deliver a staggering array of jokes and sight gags. As straight man, Abbott's Slicker barks out "Order arms," to which Costello's Herbie responds with "I'll have a cap gun." This basic formula would repeat itself throughout much of the Abbott and Costello oeuvre of the 1940s.

In their first starring film roles, Abbott and Costello delighted audiences. Gottlieb and company had delivered in a big way, as *Buck Privates* would become Universal's biggest grossing film in 1941, taking in $4 million at the box office (which was more than the year's most talked-about film, Orson Welles's *Citizen Kane*). Reviews were stellar. *Variety* noted that the film "has a good chance to skyrocket the former burlesk and radio team of Bud Abbott and Lou Costello into topflight starring ranks" (5 February 1941, 12). There was a word of caution in the *Dallas Morning News* review, however: "Unless they are badly messed up by corny handling, they will take a place among movie greats" (John Rosenfeld, "Ladeez and Gen'mun, Abbott and Costello," 6 April 1941, 6:1). The concern voiced by the Dallas critic and a number of others centered on the longevity of comedy teams in general. In the 1930s, teams such as Wheeler and Woolsey and Olsen and Johnson had simply run out of good quality scripts. As a result, the shelf life of comedy teams in Hollywood tended to be rather short. The publicity savvy of Gottlieb came to the fore, however: he declared that he had writers working on some ninety-two stories that would keep Bud and Lou busy until the year 1983.

The success of Abbott and Costello's first film was a pleasant surprise and, at the same time, a missed opportunity for Universal. Because *Buck Privates* was released as a B-film, the lion's share of the profits went not to the studio but to the movie theater exhibitors. It was something of an embarrassment that a film the studio had pegged as a B-film outgrossed all of the more prestigious films that it had released as A-pictures. Universal quickly realized the financial error it had made and sold the team's second starring film, *In the Navy* (1941), as an A-picture.

★★★★★ **Giving the Public What It Wants**

> Sure we know it's low comedy that we do, but that's apparently just what the public wants. . . . 100,000,000 Americans can't be wrong.
>
> —Lou Costello, qtd. in *Hold That Ghost*
> *Showman's Manual*, 1941, 1

In the two-year period 1941–1942, Abbott and Costello starred in a staggering eight feature films. They filmed five to six days a week, and, on Sundays, they were also regular performers on "The Chase and Sanborn Hour" radio show starring the venerable ventriloquist Edgar Bergen and his dummy Charlie McCarthy. This was said to be by design, as Universal publicity noted that Bud and Lou "have a dread of inactivity, real or anticipated. When a variety man is not busy, he is out of work and out of pocket. In a decade of vaudeville, night club engagements, tent shows, tabloid tours, and revue assignments, Abbott and Costello were never at liberty" (*Who Done It? Showman's Manual*, 1942, 2). Scripts for the comedy team were prepared while one film was in release and another was being

Abbott and Costello's humor was anything but subtle; here the pair yuck it up for publicity shots on the set of *Keep 'Em Flying* (1941), one of four service comedies made by the team during the 1940s. Copyright 1941, Universal Pictures, Inc.

shot. As Costello said, "If you don't have a good picture ready to show right now, you're a dead duck" (Don Reeve, "Rumors on Set of Killers," Universal Studios News Release, 1 March 1949, 1).

Three of their eight films, *Buck Privates, In the Navy,* and *Keep 'Em Flying* (1941), were service comedies that played well as America entered World War II. In her nationally syndicated column, Hedda Hopper called Abbott and Costello "the first cinematic heroes of the present war" ("Balmy

Biographies!," *Washington Post*, 17 June 1942, 14). Some articles attributed the success of these service comedies as the team's sole reason for becoming breakout film stars. "Loyal Americans and excellent citizens, Bud and Lou hate and despise Hitler, but had it not been for him and that atmosphere," a 1942 *Liberty* magazine cover story noted, "Abbott and Costello would probably still be playing some four-a-day grinder" (Frederick Van-Ryn, "Abbott, Costello, and Hitler," 23 May 1942, 21). Twice in 1942, Abbott and Costello would prove their loyalty by engaging in cross-country tours raising money for the war effort.

Following *Pardon My Sarong* (1942), the team decided to tour to buy a bomber to knock out Hitler. Undersecretary of War Robert Patterson suggested that the tour be revised to raise money for the Army Emergency Relief Fund. The comedy team's connection to the public was never made clearer than when they had no problem raising their targeted goal of $500,000. After shooting *Who Done It?* (1942), Abbott and Costello toured seventy-eight cities in thirty-four days and raised a staggering $85 million for war bonds and stamps (*It Ain't Hay Showman's Manual*, 1943, 3).

The combination of radio, burlesque tours, war bond tours, populist marketing, and approachable humor led the public to feel extremely close to the comedy duo. Children, in particular, had no reservations about approaching them for special requests. One such example occurred on their cross-country tour. On a stop in Omaha, a twelve-year-old named Jerry Young sneaked into their hotel and offered Abbott and Costello seventy cents to perform at a benefit being held in the child's backyard. After an appearance in nearby Lincoln, the comedy team honored their commitment to the youth, helping him raise some eighty dollars. The exploits of Costello, Abbott, and Young made national headlines and their show was even captured in an issue of *True Comics* ("Jerry Young Presents Abbott and Costello," December 1942, 52–53). On another stop, some boys requested a cheering-up gift to a local orphanage, and Costello soon sent a case of gum to the children there.

For Universal, the embedding of its star comics in public service announcements and newsreels, as well as promoting the boys' great service to the country on their fund-raising tours, was pure gold. In a report of its own war effort carried in the *Film Daily Yearbook* of 1943, Universal explained how the studio worked closely with the Navy and War Departments on two Abbott and Costello service comedies. The publicity department's copy was well rooted in patriotism: "Long before Pearl Harbor, Universal pictures went on alert. *Buck Privates* starring that indefatigable pair, Abbott and Costello, broke the ice for a steady flow of productions keyed to the war effort before and since that fateful December 7" (Alicoate 232).

In 1942, the comedy pair toured seventy-eight cities in just over a month and raised $85 million for the war effort; this photo taken by a fan in the crowd of an event in September 1942 demonstrates the magnitude of the event. Collection of the author.

In the years 1941 through 1944, Abbott and Costello placed in the Top Ten of the annual *Motion Picture Herald* Exhibitor Poll each year, including a first-place finish in 1942. The *New York Times* called them the "best and most promising clowns to hit the screen in ten years" ("Low Comedy of a High Order," 15 June 1941, X3). In an article explaining why Abbott and Costello were "slap happy," the pair felt their stock had risen to the point that they valued their gags—which they willed to their sons, Bud Jr. and Lou Jr.—at $100,000,000 (*Movie Life Yearbook*, "Why Abbott and Costello are Slap Happy," 1943, 92).

But despite their number one status at the box office, their incredible good will from the American public, and their continued presence in live shows, radio broadcasts, and films, trouble was just under the surface. The quickly produced films that were once seen as box office security were becoming too similar. These films, which had thin premises even by Abbott and Costello standards, began receiving fewer positive reviews. For Universal, the films were profitable and allowed the studio to finance more prestigious films during a period in which it was trying to recast itself as a serious movie studio. But Abbott and Costello did not sit back quietly and let this happen; they began to use the press to complain about the ongoing film production system of the 1940s. This led to favorable press coverage in their support. An example can be found in a 1942 issue of the fan magazine *Hollywood*:

> When Hollywood wants to get rid of a player, it uses its own peculiar process that works like slow poison. Poor stories, typed roles, unsympathetic parts, too much publicity. . . . Right now, the most flagrant case of killing players is going on with Abbott and Costello. They're new in Hollywood. They don't know how the subtle, slow killing works. They're being shoved into one picture after another. . . . Every critic in the country is crying out against the treatment they're receiving. But they're a couple of geese who are laying golden eggs. Yet, their studio insists upon feeding them material that is better suited for the scrap heap. "They're giving us five dollar stories," they complain bitterly, "but what can we do about it?"
>
> (Gene Schrott, "How Hollywood Kills Its Stars," July 1942, 25)

Universal was aware of the concerns and countered such articles in the publicity material it sent to motion picture exhibitors. In the 1942 showman's manual for *Who Done It?* the studio highlighted the fact that it was the boys' ninth comedy in two years. It commented, "All this talk about the boys making too many pictures and thereby recklessly spending their box office value seems to be just that—talk." Despite the publicity effort and the financial success of each Abbott and Costello film, many reviewers directed their critical barbs not at the actors but toward the film studio for the shortcomings that were apparent in the films. A *New York Times* review of the comedy team's film *In Society* (1944) demonstrates the focus of the problem for Universal:

> Probably no other comedy team in pictures has been so sincerely and enthusiastically supported by screen observers and critics generally. Whatever criticisms have been leveled, they have been pointed, not at the comedians, but at their vehicles. This almost universal loyalty from the press springs from the personal warmth of the comedians themselves plus a deep faith, on the parts of most critics, in the real comedy potentialities of the two men. Thus we find a team generally accredited with having all the qualifications of a long-enduring comedy and money-earning combination being bled white, so to speak, in pieces beneath their abilities. . . . *In Society* will undoubtedly make money for the studio, too. But what will they do for Abbott and Costello? That's the thought for today.
>
> (Paul P. Kennedy, "Abbott-Costello, Inc.," 24 August 1944, X1)

Many Hollywood columnists credited Deanna Durbin and Abbott and Costello with saving Universal Studios from financial ruin. But, by the end of the war, even Universal had to rethink its handling of its top-drawing stars, as its comedy team would drop off the list of the top ten money-making stars for three consecutive years, 1945 through 1947. In the marketing of comedy teams, Hollywood had found it difficult to resurrect a comedy team's act once it began to fade at the box office. As such, Universal had a challenge ahead of it.

★★★★★ Refreshing the Act

Although enormous profits continued to be derived from each Abbott and Costello film, problems began to exist for Universal in the marketing of the duo. Universal had built an image based upon a couple of regular Joes who had struggled together since the beginning of the Depression and who were enormously patriotic during World War II. But once both the war and the Depression had ended, the studio had to face the fact that what it had was a very rich but aging property. Critics complained about the studio's handling of its stars, but if there were any question about the comedy team being well compensated for its endeavors, a Treasury Department report put an end to it. For the 1943 tax year, the Treasury Department listed Abbott and Costello as the fourth-highest earners in the country, at $424,320 ("Film Magnate Again Tops U.S. Personal Income List," *Dallas Morning News*, 13 December 1945, 6). (Abbott and Costello had the distinction of being the only unrelated taxpayers in the country considered as a pair.) The next year, the Treasury Department listed them as the highest salary earners of 1944 with $469,170, just ahead of the combined salaries of Universal's chairman of the board J. Cheever Cowdin and Universal executive producer N. J. Blumberg ("Abbott, Costello Top Big Pay List," *New York Times*, 7 January 1947, 27).

To combat the potential for the public viewing its underdogs, the "Mutt and Jeff" comedy duo, as getting too big for its britches, Universal publicity sent out a press release that explained how Abbott and Costello spent their money. Said Abbott and Costello:

> Well, we give each of us $234,535. Then each one of us gives Uncle Sam $175,000. Then we toss most of the remainder into the foundation. Then we spend a little bit on our families, and, if there's any left over, we go out and buy a new shirt or a pair of socks. . . . Just shows what success can do for a couple of guys—it makes paupers out of them!
>
> (qtd. in Don Reeve, *Buck Privates Come Home*,
> Universal Studios News Release, 16 February 1947, 1)

The publicity material added that Bud and Lou were known as "soft touches for any worthy cause." When they heard of a child who needed life-saving surgery, they paid all expenses, "all of this without the benefit of publicity," according to a Universal press release (Reeve, *Buck Privates*

Abbott and Costello were recognized as among Hollywood's most generous stars; here they pose with Father Bernard Hubbard (a.k.a. the "Glacier priest") as Bud and Lou reportedly give up their personal 16 mm film library and projectors for the sake of America's "entertainment starved troops" in the Aleutians. Collection of the author.

Come Home, 1). In another instance, an Oklahoman in need of an iron lung was sent the medical item, and Bud and Lou paid all related costs. The comedians helped acquire a "new wonder drug" known as penicillin to save the life of a two-year-old ("Ethel Powell Gives Rare Drug to Boy," *Case Grande Dispatch*, 24 September 1948, 8). Even Abbott's own restaurant, The Stagedoor, was a haven for people who needed a meal or a job. Said to lose about $50,000 per year, the restaurant, Abbott claimed, was purchased and operated to help those in need. "For years," he said, "I walked the sidewalks without the price of beer in my pocket. I finally made enough money to buy a place" where he and some selected patrons who were less fortunate could "receive a free meal" (Don Reeve, "Bud Offered $75k for His Restaurant," Universal Studios News Release, 23 February 1949, 1). Abbott said he would put old-time friends who found themselves out of work on his payroll as assistant managers at his restaurant. This theme of helping out the less fortunate extended to the movie sets, according to Lou's daughter Chris. She explained that it was not uncommon for Costello to "support the underdog" and provide accommodations for cast and crew that the studio would not fund. In one instance, Costello used his own money to buy air-conditioned trailers for co-stars because Universal would only provide flimsy tents (personal interview with Chris Costello, 21 May 2007).

One reason that Abbott and Costello earned as much as they did was because of their grueling schedule, which included their weekly radio show, films, endorsements for products ranging from antacids to car batteries, and personal appearances. The sheer amount of time spent together took a physical and mental toll on both. Lou Costello was diagnosed with rheumatic fever that took him out of work for parts of 1943 and 1944. Further bad news came in 1944 when Costello's infant son, Butch, drowned in the family swimming pool. Even though Costello, in show business tradition, continued with his professional duties the night after learning of Butch's death, the event obviously changed Costello forever. He would create a foundation devoted to building a youth center in Los Angeles for underprivileged children.

The team faced further unfortunate events at this time. Alex Gottlieb, who had produced eight of the team's comedies, left Universal for Warner Bros., and his understanding of how to handle the team was to be sorely missed. Each of the next three Abbott and Costello films—*In Society* (1944), *Lost in a Harem* (1944), and *Here Come the Co-eds* (1945)—would have different producers, each with only middling success. Meanwhile, in Washington, D.C., some criticism was leveled at the nature of the war bond sales effort. Treasury Secretary Henry Morgenthau criticized a press release from

Universal's publicity department lauding Abbott and Costello's war bond efforts. Morgenthau said that entertainers should not exploit bond sales for personal publicity. He commented, "I have been watching this sort of thing and will check it still more closely" ("Scores Publicity for Bond Sellers," *New York Times*, 16 July 1942, 11).

Finally, in 1945, rumors of a split between Abbott and Costello were becoming rampant. A national column by Elizabeth Poston suggested that the team was finished. In the article, Costello said there was no reconciling his differences with Abbott: "I've tried to keep the team together, but Abbott and his advisors have been hitting me time and again below the belt" ("Funny Man Lou Costello Bares an Old Feud with Bud Abbott," *The Oklahoman*, 22 July 1945, 9). Other gossip columns echoed that the split was either imminent or had already taken place.

One of the earliest internal memos at Universal dealing with such concerns suggested changing the duo's bio to say that their initial performance together occurred in 1936 rather than in 1930. In a January 1947 memo, publicity chief Maurice Bergman wondered if the studio were to alter their timeline up and accordingly promote the team's tenth anniversary that "we might freshen the boys up a bit," especially if "it is a fact." Indeed, Universal moved up the anniversary, and their future communications cited 1936 as the year the team first appeared in vaudeville acts together, at a Chicago theater. As a result, Abbott and Costello had two twelfth anniversaries, one cited in the publicity materials for *Rio Rita* (1941) (*Rio Rita Showman's Manual*, 1941, 4) and another in a Universal press release picked up by a number of newspapers (Don Reeve, "Bud and Lou Celebrate Their 12th Anniversary," Universal Studios News Release, 27 September 1948, 1).

Many articles in the early 1940s referenced the boys' propensity for playing rummy on the set with each other. This masked the reality that they were well known among insiders as big-time gamblers in poker and horse racing. As a result, they became involved with non-Hollywood businessmen, which in one case led to a legal battle. The team was subpoenaed and forced to testify in a trial involving a nightclub owner and poker acquaintance to whom the comedians had paid $85,000 in a four-year stretch ("Abbott and Costello Subpoenaed," *New York Times*, 21 March 1947, 28). This not only was their first widely reported negative publicity but also the first indication of their financial liabilities. The financial woes would mount by decade's end to the point that Costello faced tax liens from the Internal Revenue Service ("Costello, Flynn Faced by Income Tax Liens," *Cedar Rapids Times*, 21 September 1949, 18) and Abbott was forced into bankruptcy during the 1950s. Universal's publicity department was also concerned about the impact the gambling-related trial might have on its stars. At the time of the trial, it issued a press release: "Costello has never taken an alcoholic drink nor a smoke, they gambled for money just once in films but then didn't hold their winnings. Neither has knowingly broken a law." In an almost hopeful tone, the release continued, "Few other fun-maker pairs have held on to box office potency through as many pictures as Abbott and Costello. . . . Bob Hope and Bing Crosby are still going strong but have not approached Abbott and Costello's 20 vehicles" (Harry Friedman, *Wistful Widow of Wagon Gap*, 6 June 1947, 1).

The most aggressive publicity campaign was associated with the Lou Costello Jr. Youth Foundation. The actors personally funded $400,000 for a community space for underprivileged children in Los Angeles, which opened its doors in 1947. Costello also produced a film short, *10,000 Kids and a Cop* (1948), that would be shown in movie theaters across the United States to spotlight the project. Columnist Jimmie Fidler wrote that despite the fact that the pair would never win Academy Awards, they should receive "an even more enviable award. They're neither child psychologists, 'welfare workers' nor reformers—just good Americans who saw a job to do and did it" ("Costello's Charity Going Strong," *The Oklahoman*, 22 May 1947, 11). In another column, Fidler noted that they "deserve an extra deep bow" for donating all proceeds from one of their films to the foundation, and appealed to other stars to donate to the cause. "I want to wonder a bit about the apathy of other in-the-money stars who seem strangely disinterested in the magnificent job that these two comics are doing" ("There Oughta Be a Law," *The Oklahoman*, 11 November 1947, 13).

In hoping to refresh the act, Universal also heeded advice from its stars and from the industry and raised the bar on the first two postwar Abbott and Costello films, *Little Giant* (1946) and *The Time of Their Lives* (1946). A top-rated director, William A. Seiter, was brought in to direct *Little Giant*, working from a script that downplayed gags and slapstick. In the publicity material for the film, Seiter said that "an artist must grow or fall into a decline. And since there seemed no further room for improvement in the established technique of Abbott and Costello, it followed a new prescription was indicated" (*Little Giant Showman's Manual*, 1946, 5).

Both films broke the established formula of Bud as straight man, Lou as funnyman, and scenes built around comedy bits from the team's stage act. *The Time of Their Lives* best reflects the new approach, featuring Costello as Horatio, an eighteenth-century tinker hoping to marry a housemaid. His rival is Abbott's character, a butler named Cuthbert. Horatio and the housemaid's mistress are mistaken for traitors and shot to death by the army. The story moves to the twentieth century where the ghosts of Horatio and his fiancée's mistress are trying to clear their names. Abbott, in a dual role, portrays a psychiatrist who is a descendant of Cuthbert. What makes this film different is that Abbott and Costello's characters share dialogue in just one scene early in the film. Not one Abbott and Costello routine from their live act is included in the film. Abbott would get a chance to play a comic character instead of the usual straight man. Further, the production costs for *The Time of Their Lives* were the highest yet for an Abbott and Costello picture. The studio brought in director Charles T. Barton, who would direct the team in its next eight features. The *Hollywood Reporter* wrote of *The Time of Their Lives*, "Something new is being offered by Abbott and Costello. . . . Long specialists in the borrowed and the blue, Bud and Lou had their first whirl at situation comedy in *Little Giant*, and they came out so well that Universal really throws the book at them. . . . By long odds, it is the best A&C show to date" (16 August 1946).

Universal International (Universal having merged with International Pictures in 1946) tried to upgrade Abbott and Costello pictures much as they were trying to move up into the upper echelon of film studios. In a press release, Universal International Pictures noted, "This is part of the studio's plan to stress that Abbott and Costello are now playing characters in well-formulated stories, rather than in loosely contrived farces" (Universal Studios News Release, 4 June 1947, 1). When the box office results did not pay off, the comedy team went back to familiar turf, doing a sequel to *Buck Privates* entitled *Buck Privates Come Home* (1947). The boys reprised their roles from the earlier film, now having returned from their tour of duty in World War II. Playing familiar characters allowed the comedy team to return to the straight man and funnyman formula associated with their earlier, more successful films.

Their follow-up film, *The Wistful Widow of Wagon Gap* (1947), also found the team returning to their familiar formula, as Bud and Lou played Duke Egan and Chester Wooley, traveling salesmen who are wrongfully charged with murder in a financially strapped Montana town. The scenario has many comic scenes, including a revised routine from one of their earlier movies. By film's end, not only are Duke and Chester cleared of the charge, but Duke's claim that the town would be saved financially if the local judge married the "wistful widow" turns out to be true. Audiences welcomed the familiarity of *Buck Privates Come Home* and the *Wistful Widow* judging by their success at the box office. This return to form for Abbott and Costello led the studio to sign a new deal with the team that would call for two low-budget films per year.

Costello exploited columnist Sheilah Graham in helping to secure yet another new contract with Universal International. "Lou Costello had coffee with me at the U.I. Café and sprung the bombshell that directly [after] he finishes his current *Mexican Hayride* [1948] he'll stage another fight to pry himself loose from the studio. Lou says he's not getting enough money" ("Hollywood in Person," *Dallas Morning News*, 2 July 1948, 17). Clearly, Graham felt burned in a subsequent column pertaining to UI's new contract with the comedy team. She wrote, "If Lou Costello ever complains again, I'll have no sympathy for him! His new percentage deal, based on returns of recent pictures, will give him and partner Bud Abbott $1,000,000 for two pictures—which makes them top earners in Hollywood" ("Hollywood: Good Deal for Abbott and Costello," *Dallas Morning News*, 26 May 1949, 4).

★★★★★ Abbott and Costello Meet Profits at Decade's End

The formula for the Abbott and Costello films in the late 1940s was straightforward: keep the productions cheap, produce them quickly, and hold advertising costs low. Abbott and Costello would receive bonuses for films that came in under budget. UI treated its Abbott and Costello films like a property akin to a B-series and, as a result, the advertising and marketing budgets were minuscule, often one-tenth the amount of other comedy films. The advertising agency that handled many of Abbott and Costello's films wrote a memo in 1947 to the head of UI, William Goetz, which pleaded, "Could you possibly use your influence to get Abbott and Costello to start mentioning on their radio program . . . their forthcoming picture *Buck Privates Come Home* . . . in view of the fact we have no national advertising on this picture . . . most of this success is in their hands" (19 February 1947, 1).

The studio's reliance on the Abbott and Costello series to maximize profits is also seen in its use of the team-up concept in which the duo was paired with some other property owned by the studio. Universal utilized the characters associated with its successful horror series of the 1930s and 1940s to create new genre-bending films. For example, *Abbott and Costello Meet Frankenstein* (1948) was one of UI's highest earning films of the year. The film starred Bud and Lou as Chick Young and Wilbur Gray, well intentioned but bumbling railroad baggage clerks. Two crates headed for Mac-Dougal's House of Horrors that contain the remains of Frankenstein and Dracula are mishandled by the clerks. The clerks are then forced to go to the House of Horrors where a mixture of comedy and thrills await them, including meeting up with the Universal Studios monsters Frankenstein, Dracula, and The Wolf Man.

The financial success of *Meet Frankenstein* paved the way for *Abbott and Costello Meet the Killer, Boris Karloff* (1949), *Abbott and Costello Meet the Invisible Man* (1951), and *Abbott and Costello Meet Dr. Jekyll and Mr. Hyde* (1953). With a profit and speed mentality combined with fairly predictable storylines, UI had virtually ensured that Abbott and Costello would earn neither an Oscar nomination for their work at the studio nor the critical attention Universal International had contemplated for the pair just a few years earlier. But what it did find was a business plan for financial success at a time when studios were beginning to worry about the impact of television on their profits. The studio would replicate its production model with the highly profitable "Ma and Pa Kettle" and "Francis the Talking Mule" films in which the characters' names were also placed in the title to sell the films to theaters and audiences alike.

Abbott and Costello's resurgence at the box office was demonstrated in their return to the top ten, according to the Exhibitors Poll; they finished third in both 1948 and 1949. These were the team's first top ten appearances since 1944. In terms of their standing in the community, Abbott and Costello were viewed as two of Hollywood's "Ten Best Citizens" according to *Modern Screen* magazine. The Lou Costello Jr. Youth Foundation helped lead to a 40 percent decrease in juvenile delinquency on Los Angeles's east side ("Hollywood's Ten Best Citizens," February 1950, 73). From the theater owner's standpoint, a *Life* feature crowned the comedy duo as the champs at the concession stands. "Their comedies sell more popcorn than anyone," said one theater owner ("Popcorn Bonanza," 25 July 1949, 41). This fact was not lost on UI, which decided to use the item in their trade advertisement for one of their features (David Lipton, memo to Hank Linet, 25 July 1949, 1).

Though shooting twenty-five feature films in the 1940s, not one Abbott and Costello movie during this period was shot in color. The decade opened with Deanna Durbin and Abbott and Costello keeping the lights on at Universal Studios and, by decade's end, Hedda Hopper noting that films such as *Abbott and Costello Meet Frankenstein* made "everyone at Universal-International happy because the Abbott and Costello pictures plus Ma and Pa Kettle pay the salaries" ("$4.5 million for A&C Meet Frankenstein," *Pittsburgh Press*, 25 January 1949, 17). While critics still complained about Universal's treatment of the decade's busiest and most bankable stars, director Charles Barton held a different view. He explained that a number of radio comics had tried to make the transition into films but not all succeeded. "Who made

Bud and Lou?" Barton asked. "It was the studio in back of them that said we'll gamble on them" (Furmanek and Palumbo 32).

Despite the smiles within the studio's accounting office, rumors of Abbott and Costello's breakup were still active at the end of the decade. In Harold Swisher's United Press Radio Feature, "In Movieland," Abbott said, "I hear the rumor is out again that Lou and I are breaking up. Please help us deny it. We've been together 13 years day and night. We'll continue to be a team for many years to come. Sure we have squabbles. What partners don't?" (18 July 1949, 1). There was a need to quash such rumors; UI itself may have contributed to the problem by suspending the duo just before the end of 1949. The studio said it was "just a technicality" so that Universal would not have to pay the stars' $6,500 weekly salary while Costello recovered from a prolonged illness ("Costello Illness Cited in Suspension of Duo," *Cedar Rapids Times*, 22 December 1949, 3). Despite the suspension, Abbott and Costello were poised to start the 1950s in strong form with projects already lined up. The boys had signed to do their first European comedy tour, rumors abounded that the pair was being courted to do television, their radio series continued, and there seemed to be no end in sight for the Abbott and Costello films. Press agent Joe Glaston and the boys believed that his clients' biggest moneymaking film would be *Abbott and Costello Meet Hopalong Cassidy* if the money could be raised for the production (*Cedar Rapids Gazette*, 1 September 1949, 24).

UI addressed the breakup rumors head-on with a press release suggesting that the two had a lifetime contract that prohibited either from appearing without the other. The contract would run for as long as the two were physically able to continue their careers together. "I have a copy in my safe at home," Abbott said, "and Lou has a copy in his safe" (Reeve, "Rumors on Set of Killers," 1). The comedians ended the 1940s looking forward to the decade ahead and hoping for new and improved professional opportunities. Costello said, "Comedians like Danny Kaye and Red Skelton get color and good stories, and girls like Esther Williams in their pictures. We're third on the box office list, a bigger draw than any of them. But we've never done a color picture: we've never gone on location, and instead of Jane Russell we get Patricia Alphin. From now on we're going to give the fans more" (Patricia Clary, "Costello, Well Again, Thinner Than Bud Abbott," *Cedar Rapids Gazette*, 7 September 1949, 13). For the comedy team that had shot more than two dozen features, starred in hundreds of hours of radio shows, and made countless personal appearances during the 1940s, as well as perfecting one of comedy's most enduring sketches in "Who's on First?," giving the fans more would be a daunting task.

★★★★★ Postscript: Bud and Lou after the 1940s

As they entered the 1950s, Costello's prediction of the team's starring in its first color film came true but it would not be backed by Universal. Instead, Abbott and Costello independently financed their color feature *Jack and the Beanstalk* (1952). They appeared on television semi-regularly as hosts on twenty episodes of the "Colgate Comedy Hour" in 1951, and in two seasons of their own situation comedy, "The Abbott and Costello Show" in 1952 and 1953. Unfortunately, the added exposure of television did not help their longevity as a team. When Abbott and Costello's status as the most sought-after comedy pair was taken over by Dean Martin and Jerry Lewis, the team's descent was almost as rapid as its rise to stardom.

Abbott and Costello finished 1951 with their seventh top ten ranking in the *Motion Picture Herald* exhibitor's poll, behind Martin and Lewis. Less than four years later, in 1955, Abbott and Costello found themselves without a studio movie contract when Universal could not reach an agreement with the two comedians. The team made what would be its final film together in the independently produced *Dance with Me, Henry* (1956). The absence of a regular film, radio, or television series contract meant that the Hollywood fan magazines provided scant coverage of the pair during the mid-1950s. For a team that depended on maximum exposure, the future looked dim. Meanwhile, bad financial news came when, in 1956, at a most inopportune time, the IRS forced each of the stars to pay back taxes. The financial liabilities resulted in tremendous loss of their assets, including their homes and their film rights. The team even lost its comic book deal when the publisher, St. John's, discontinued the comic line in September 1956. When news of their split as a team was announced in 1957, neither the fan magazines nor the general press gave the story much prominence. The comedians, known for feuding away from the cameras, continued to have moments of bad blood. Abbott sued Costello for $222,000 in 1958 over a dispute concerning the amount of money Abbott earned on the situation comedy earlier in the decade ("Bud Abbott Sues Costello Over Pay," *The Oklahoman*, 12 March 1958, 2). Abbott would retire temporarily from show business until his less-than-stellar return in the 1960s, while Costello died in 1959 just after completing his only solo comedy, *The 30 Foot Bride of Candy Rock* (1959). Yet the pair received perhaps its most prized recognition when the Baseball Hall of Fame placed their gold record of the skit "Who's on First?" in a permanent exhibit. Said Costello, "This is better than winning an Oscar" ("Baseball Skit in Shrine," *New York Times* 30 May 1956, 16).

2 ★★★★★★★★★★★★

Gene Autry and
Roy Rogers
The Light of Western Stars

EDWARD BUSCOMBE

Friends have learned to tolerate my apparent obsession with the western movie (they don't any longer call them "cowboy films" when I'm around). Even so, there were some sniggers when I said I was trying to write something about singing cowboys. "You mean Roy Rogers?" they'd say with a laugh, scarcely bothering to disguise their disdain. "Do you really like that stuff?"

Gene Autry portrait, c. 1942; Roy Rogers portrait, c. 1944. Both photos collection of the author.

33

Such an apparently simple question raises a lot more questions in turn. First, there's the assumption that in order to write about something you have to actively enjoy it. Perhaps only people who aren't film studies academics (normal people, if you like) believe that. They think that film criticism or film history is a sort of cheerleading activity. You write about things to convey your enthusiasm and hopefully to convert others to your enthusiasm. There's nothing wrong with that, of course, and I've done it myself. But that's not why I am writing this piece. I really don't mind if not one reader is inspired to watch a Gene Autry film. I don't want to turn anyone into a fan. I'm not really a fan myself. What I'd like to do is try to understand something that was once a considerable phenomenon in the cinema, something too big to be ignored, though mostly it has been.

I was a fan once. When I was very young, I was passionate about Roy Rogers. In the small town in the west of England where I grew up, the local picture house—called, with a deplorable lack of ambition, The Cinema—ran double bills that changed twice a week, and as likely as not a singing cowboy western would make up one half of the bill. There must have been plenty of Gene Autry films on offer, but my memory is that whenever I pleaded with my mother to be allowed to go to the pictures for the second time in a week, it was always because there was a new Roy Rogers film I simply had to see.

My brother and I preferred Roy because, first, his films also featured George "Gabby" Hayes, whom we much preferred to Gene's regular partner, Smiley Burnette. I guess we just thought he was funnier, though actually I now think I prefer Smiley. Gabby is just, well, too gabby. Also, Gabby was relentlessly misogynistic, whereas Smiley was always mooning after girls, which we didn't approve of. (I feel differently now.) Second, it was our feeling that there was more action in Roy's films, more chases on horseback, more fistfights and gunfights. And the action (you could hardly call it violence) was just a little more realistic in Roy's films. Most important, Roy didn't sing as much. At least that's what we thought. In fact, further research shows that both Gene and Roy sang five or six songs each per film. For us that was five or six too many. We liked the films because they were westerns, not because they were musicals. But while I suspect most small boys at the time shared our views, the music that Roy and Gene made was immensely popular with older audiences, and it's clear that both performers regarded themselves as singers who acted, not the other way round. In his autobiography, *Back in the Saddle Again*, Autry put it thus: "Music has been the better part of my career. Movies are wonderful fun, and they give you a famous face. But how the words and melody are joined, how they come together out of air and enter the mind, this is art. Songs are forever" (Autry 18).

★★★★★ The Careers: Stardust on the Sage

Gene and Roy (it seems natural to refer to them in that friendly manner; they encouraged that kind of identification) had a lot in common; in many ways they were mirror images of each other. Both came from humble backgrounds. Gene Autry was born in rural Oklahoma in 1907 (originally named Orvon Grover Autry). His education was limited; at age seventeen he got a job working on the St. Louis–San Francisco Railroad. In his early twenties he combined railroad work with singing on local radio shows, and by 1929 he had begun a successful recording career, though his family was too poor to buy a phonograph on which to play his records. It's hard to imagine that degree of poverty now; in 1932 Autry's mother died of pellagra, a disease caused by malnourishment. (His father was constantly in and out of jail for petty frauds.) In 1931 Autry moved to Chicago to appear on the highly popular "Barn Dance" show put out by radio station WLS. It was at this point that Autry began dressing in western style and was billed as "The Oklahoma Yodeling Cowboy," his style of music owing much to the "hillbilly" yodeling songs of Jimmie Rodgers.

In 1934 Autry was taken to Hollywood and signed by Mascot Pictures to appear in a couple of westerns starring Ken Maynard. Mascot was almost immediately taken over by Republic, who would produce almost all of Autry's early films. His role in these first films, *In Old Santa Fe* and *Mystery Mountain*, was mainly to sing, while Maynard supplied the action. Though Autry's acting was stiff and awkward, the popularity of his singing was not in doubt, and when Maynard left the company Autry was offered the starring role in *The Phantom Empire* (1935), a serial that was a bizarre hybrid of the western and science fiction genres. The film was enough of a success for Autry to be given his first starring role in a feature western, *Tumbling Tumbleweeds* (1935), in which Autry sings in a total of nine musical numbers. In subsequent films that number was trimmed to half a dozen, but otherwise the format was to vary little over the next twenty years. During that time Autry made some ninety films, which up until 1948 were distributed by Republic and thereafter by Columbia.

Roy Rogers was born Leonard Slye in Ohio in 1911. Like Autry, his parents were poor and he had minimal schooling. His family moved to California in 1930, and Roy got work as an itinerant fruit picker. He joined several short-lived musical groups before helping to found in 1934 the Sons of the Pioneers, who would eventually achieve great and lasting success. By this time he had changed his name to Dick Weston, but when he was signed by Republic in 1937 the studio renamed him once more, and Roy Rogers was born.

Though he had several bit parts, largely uncredited, with the Sons of the Pioneers, Rogers's big break came in 1938. Gene Autry was in the middle of a bitter dispute with Republic, essentially about getting a bigger share of the spoils from his growing movie popularity. As a means of putting pressure on Autry to settle, Republic head Herbert J. Yates offered a contract to Rogers, whose first feature, *Under Western Stars*, was released in 1938. Though Autry soon returned to the fold, Rogers was enough of a success for Yates to keep him working, and the careers of the two singing cowboys continued in tandem for some years.

When the United States entered World War II, Autry enlisted in the Army Air Corps and spent the war years flying planes, his film career suspended. Rogers, on the other hand, stayed behind in Hollywood. There are different accounts of why Rogers did not join the military. In his autobiography, *Happy Trails*, he says that he was too old for active service; he would have been thirty when war was declared (Rogers and Evans 71). But another version was that he was kept out by chronic arthritis (George-Warren 224). However this may be, Autry's absence provided Rogers with the perfect opportunity to leap ahead in the popularity stakes, and in 1943 he topped the list of western stars performing best at the box office.

Autry resumed his Hollywood career in 1946 and thereafter he and Rogers vied for the number one spot. The following year Autry left Republic and his remaining films were to be produced by Columbia. Both Rogers and Autry were alert to the coming appeal of television, and each tried to prevent Republic selling their old films to TV, because such screenings would affect the box office for their current theatrical releases. At the same time, each was anxious to begin production of his own television show, and screenings on TV of their old films damaged the prospects for this. Eventually these disputes were settled and the two stars made the transit from cinema to television. Autry's final feature film, appropriately titled *Last of the Pony Riders*, was released in 1953. "The Gene Autry Show" first aired on television in 1950. Roy Rogers's last leading role in a western was in *Pals of the Golden West* (1951); "The Roy Rogers Show" premiered on television the same year.

★★★★★ The Films: Happy Trails

Not surprisingly, in view of the fact that Rogers was groomed as a replacement for Autry, their films were similar in many respects. Budgets were tight; Republic's boss, Herbert Yates, didn't like to throw his money around. The films generally ran just over an hour. The formula was arrived at very early, and scarcely deviated in twenty years of production.

In his autobiography, Autry describes it thus: "1) a decent story; 2) good music; 3) comedy relief; 4) enough action, with chases and fights; and 5) a little romance. And always we played it against the sweep of desert scenery, mountains and untamed land, and an ocean of sky" (Autry 39).

From the sound of that summary, one might suppose that the films made by the singing cowboys closely followed the recipe for westerns that had been laid down almost from the beginning of cinema: an entertaining tale of the frontier, with glorious western scenery, and plenty of action, with the only variation being the addition of songs integrated into the diegesis. But in fact the differences from the standard A-feature western as it had become codified by the mid-1930s are as striking as the similarities.

In the films of Autry and Rogers the stories follow a basic pattern. The motor that drives the plot is usually some kind of criminal activity. Bad guys are trying to cheat or strong-arm some nice, ordinary folks out of their rightful possessions, often a ranch, a mine, or some kind of business. Gene or Roy comes to their rescue, convincing the victims of his honesty of purpose, winning their trust, and eventually defeating the villains with a combination of ingenuity, good sense, and a little forceful physicality. The films eschew the historical themes and narratives that commentators have seen as the essence of the western genre, lacking the mythical dimension the western has frequently exhibited. Manifest Destiny, the winning of the West, the conflict of civilization and savagery—none of these plays a large role. Instead of dealing with such grand themes as the Indian Wars, building the transcontinental railroad, or westward migration, singing cowboy films are concerned with problems of a more contemporary nature. As Peter Stanfield has shown, there is a considerable affinity between their actions and the ethos of Roosevelt's New Deal (Stanfield, *Horse Opera* 144). Small farmers and ranchers are often the victims of crooked bankers or lawyers from the city. Roy or Gene is successful in defending them because the hero is very much an ordinary man, not possessed of superhuman qualities, and with only one exceptional talent—a pleasing singing voice.

The west of Gene and Roy has largely been settled; it's not really a frontier world at all. Indians scarcely exist. The films take place in a curious never-never land that mingles past and present. Many iconographical trappings originating in the western's historical roots are present onscreen: Gene and Roy appear on horseback (Autry on Champion, Rogers on the equally famous Trigger), dressed in a stylized version of western costume (wide-brimmed hat, fancy shirt, embossed gunbelt and six-shooter, cowboy boots). But the stories are not usually set in the historical past. The milieu they inhabit is recognizably modern, replete with radio, telephones, cars,

Roy Rogers with his trusty equine sidekick, Trigger, c. 1941. Collection of the author.

and even airplanes. Thus the films are able to deliver many of the traditional pleasures of the western (fistfights and gunfights, chases on horseback) while at the same time the stories are more closely related to a
contemporary everyday world.[1]

Under Fiesta Stars (1941) is representative. It has a present-day setting.
Gene is left a half-share in a mine by an elderly man who had been his
mentor. The man has been employing local men ruined by the dustbowl,
many of them Mexicans. Unfortunately, the other half of the mine has been

left to the man's niece, Barbara (Carol Hughes), who simply wants to sell her share for as much money as she can get. She hires a couple of shyster lawyers, who in turn pay some hit men to dispose of Gene. In a confrontation, Gene tells her off for being mercenary, and she counters by calling him a cheap rodeo rider. But eventually through the sheer goodness of his personality Gene wins her over to his way of thinking and the bad guys are routed. The mine can continue to fulfill a socially useful purpose.

In *Silver Spurs* (1943), Roy's employer owns a large ranch where oil has been discovered. Legal complications mean he is unable to sell it, but his widow could. Some crooks from the big city hatch a plan to marry him off to a pretty newspaper reporter. He is then shot and Roy is framed for the crime. But eventually Roy unmasks the crooks, having first won over the reporter to his side. At the end Roy and the girl plan to set up a cooperative oil company to benefit all in the community.

One curious feature of the narratives is that almost invariably the character that Autry plays is named "Gene Autry." Rogers, too, is more often than not playing a character named Roy. This further removes the story from any historical referent, serving instead to blur the line between a fictional world and the world outside the movies, in which Gene Autry and Roy Rogers are real people. The films thus become something resembling the stars' personal appearances or their radio shows, expressions not so much of a recognizable western milieu as a continuation of their life as showbiz personalities.

In the A-feature western of the 1940s we find an increasing concern with issues of masculinity, focused in particular on the nature and consequences of violence, the need for a man to stand up and be counted, and to overcome whatever doubts he has about his courage and commitment. This is the era of the so-called "psychological" western, in which the troubled hero broods upon his fate, often suffering from the burden of some emotionally crippling incident in his past. The hero's personality is often dominating, harsh, even bitter. Frequently condemned to live on the margins of society, he shoulders a heavy burden, and the forces he pits himself against are merciless. Gene and Roy have undergone no such psychological traumas. Invariably sunny and serene in their disposition, they never doubt themselves, nor suffer anxiety about what to do next. Their way forward is always clear, and they integrate easily into the world they inhabit. Instead of an aggressive masculinity, they display a genial and friendly manner, kind to children, animals, and women.

Occasional musical interludes are not unknown in the A-feature western. One thinks of the stars of *Rio Bravo* (1959) singing "My Rifle, My Pony, and Me" together in the jailhouse. But such numbers are not an essential part of the film's appeal. With Autry and Rogers, their fame as singing stars was what made their films viable. The western musical, such as *The Harvey Girls* (1946) or *Calamity Jane* (1953), is a special case, a separate subgenre. The music of such films does not have a specifically western style. Instead, it comes out of the American stage musical tradition, the show-business world of composers such as Cole Porter, Jerome Kern, and Irving Berlin. The plots of these musical films center around a romantic relationship, as in nonwestern musicals, whereas in the singing cowboy films, as we shall see, romance is incidental.

The singing cowboys' musical style originates in what was later to become country music, at that time still labeled "hillbilly" music. Autry early modeled himself on Jimmie Rodgers, whose distinctive style of "blue yodeling" gained him a large following in the South in the 1920s. Rodgers's songs are plaintive, sometimes scabrous laments for a rambling, restless life, full of brushes with the law, drinking bouts, and women who played fast and loose with his affections. Rodgers had nothing of the cowboy about him; Peter Stanfield's thesis is that this music lent itself to adaptation to a western idiom because the cowboy was a similarly restless roamer. But in transposing the music from south to west, Autry, a key player in this process, effaced the "overt racist or class connotations of the hillbilly," as well as repressing the "black heritage apparent in so much early country music." Repackaging the popular music of the south into a cowboy format gave it nationwide popularity, and cleaning up the sexual frankness of the hillbilly tradition made it more suitable for a public medium such as the radio, upon which so much of the economics of popular music depended at that time (Stanfield *Horse Opera*).[2]

There's little to choose between the singing styles of Autry and Rogers. Both of them were hugely popular as recording artists as well as movie performers, and Autry in particular had some breakout numbers that took him beyond the limitations of his cowboy persona. "Rudolph, the Red-Nosed Reindeer," released in 1949, reached the top of both the country & western and pop charts in *Billboard* magazine. In the first year the song sold two million copies, and sales reached twenty-five million over the next forty years. But in terms of their movies, both Rogers and Autry remained comfortably within their niche market. True, Roy Rogers had occasional parts in bigger movies, appearing alongside Bob Hope in *Son of Paleface*, a comedy western of 1952. But this was a rare excursion outside the self-contained world of the singing western.

Although, as I have said, romance is not a major element within the films, it does feature prominently in the songs that Autry and Rogers sing.

Gene Autry with guitar, c. 1941. Collection of the author.

Bells of Capistrano (1942) is typical. Two of the five songs that Autry sings are romantic ballads ("Forgive Me" and "At Sundown"). A third song, "Fort Worth Jail," is more in the Jimmie Rodgers tradition, a lament about falling foul of a treacherous girl and landing in prison. The fourth song, "In Old Capistrano," celebrates the musical vitality of the Mexican town where some of the action is set (the Hispanic southwest, on both sides of the border, is a persistent leitmotif in the films of both Autry and Rogers). This film

Gene Autry and Smiley Burnette frame a War Bonds poster in *Bells of Capistrano* (1942), Autry's last film before entering the armed forces. Copyright 1942, Republic Pictures, Inc.

was Autry's last before enlisting in the military, and so it concludes with a patriotic musical finale entitled "Don't Bite the Hand That's Feeding You," an exhortation to love America or leave it:

> If you don't like your uncle Sammy,
> Then go back to your home o'er the sea.

But this is a rarity. Despite Hollywood's major effort to play a part in World War II, Rogers and Autry largely ignore it in their films, even though they are set in the present. Other cowboy stars wrestled with Nazi or Japanese aggressors, but *King of the Cowboys* (1943) is unusual in having Roy Rogers battling against saboteurs who are attacking American government property on behalf of unspecified foreign powers.

Comedy was an integral part of the films' appeal. The comic sidekick is a stock figure in the western, and not only in the films of singing cowboys. Character actors such as Walter Brennan, Arthur Hunnicutt, and Jay C. Flippen were the comic foils of such as John Wayne and James Stewart in A-feature westerns. Autry's habitual companion was Lester "Smiley" Burnette, a large, rather shapeless man who was a talented musician and songwriter. Though he occasionally appeared with other stars (he briefly accompanied Roy Rogers when Autry was having his dispute with Republic), Autry remained loyal to him and gave him a part in his very last picture. Burnette's character was usually named "Frog" Millhouse; much of the humor revolved around Frog's rarely successful attempts to ingratiate himself with ladies. By contrast, George "Gabby" Hayes, apparently offscreen a highly intelligent and refined individual, cultivated the persona of a crabby old misogynist in the scores of films he made with Rogers.

Both actors thus provided a foil for the stars they worked with, throwing into relief, either through their lack of success with women or a lack of interest in them, the appeal of both Autry and Rogers to the female audience. As Autry observed, the films required "a little romance" and invariably they featured a pretty girl, who would be gently drawn into the star's orbit, without his seeming very actively to woo her. There was rarely an embrace, even in the last scene; as Autry remarks in *Back in the Saddle Again*, "Small boys . . . hated it" (Autry 55). However, Stanfield is of the view that the chasteness of Autry's films owes as much to the fact that women made up a large part of the audience (as they did for hillbilly songs on the radio) (Stanfield, *Hollywood* 96). He calls Autry's sex appeal "neither threatening nor overtly physical"; instead, to his female fans he offered "a reassuring image of fantasized romantic involvement that transcended the desires of the body" (Stanfield, *Horse Opera* 100). Autry's interest in the female lead is more of a kindly, even fatherly one, displaying a solicitude for her welfare and a determination to look after her interests, rather than any overwhelming passion.

Stanfield also believes Autry's "dandified" appearance is aimed at women. Certainly some explanation would seem to be required for the extreme elaboration of the costumes worn by Autry and Rogers. There's really nothing to compare in other cinematic genres of the time, certainly not in the A-feature western, to the fancifulness and sheer splendor of the highly colored shirts with "smiley" pockets and their elaborate stitching and piping, or the hand-tooled boots embellished with motifs of sunsets and cactus. In 1936, by which date he was an established star at Republic, Autry spent $500 on customized cowboy clothes, a considerable sum at the time, but "an amount that was to triple over the next two years" (George-Warren 157). Shirts came from Rodeo Ben in Philadelphia, western-style suits from Nathan Turk in the San Fernando Valley, and boots from the Lucchese company of San Antonio (George-Warren 158). Empirical evidence of the gender breakdown of the audiences for singing westerns is hard to come by, nor do we know much about the particular satisfactions the audiences

derived from their experience, but it's hard to disagree that the stars' sarto-
rial displays were designed primarily to appeal to women.

On the other hand, the "action, with chases and fights" that Autry lists
as a necessary part of the formula was presumably not aimed at women.
Elsewhere he specifically identifies his female audience as requiring a
restraint on violence: "We toned down the gunplay, as it became more obvious that women made up nearly half of my audience" (Autry 51). But it
couldn't be dispensed with altogether. Fighting and other kinds of physical
struggle have, of course, been an essential component of the western genre
from the beginning. The West was always wild and needed taming.
Whether it was the physical obstacles to settlement, the challenge posed by
vast distances, by mountains, rivers, and deserts, the resistance of those
people who were already in occupation (principally of course the Native
Americans), or the lawlessness inherent in a frontier setting, the hero was
obliged to pit his body against the forces that stood in his way.

By the end of the 1940s, the A-feature western was becoming increasingly "realistic" in its depiction of violence. Anthony Mann's films of the
1950s such as *The Man from Laramie* (1955) depict brutal beatings and show
the pain of gunshot wounds. In the 1960s the Italian spaghetti western and
films like Sam Peckinpah's *The Wild Bunch* (1969) presented elaborately
choreographed orgies of gunfire. The action in the films of Autry and
Rogers is, by contrast, almost entirely unaccompanied by pain or blood.
Usually there is a gunfight, but rarely does anyone get hit, let alone killed.
Gene and Roy do not engage in the single-handed ritual duel in the street
that was a stock situation in the western from earliest days (it is a feature,
for example, of Owen Wister's highly influential novel of 1902, *The Virgin-
ian*). To do so would set them up as killers. By contrast, in their films gunfights are usually communal affairs, with Gene or Roy joining in as people
blaze away in all directions.

There's often a fistfight, and Rogers's films were perhaps more energetic
in this respect, but again no one seems to get seriously hurt. Chases are virtually obligatory. Repeated time and again is a scene in which a child or,
more frequently, a young woman is marooned on a buckboard with a runaway horse. Gene or Roy gives hot pursuit, usually leaping from his own
mount onto the seat beside the terrified woman just in time to prevent her
plunging over a precipice.

Despite what Autry says, spectacular scenery, the glory of so many
classic westerns, is not much in evidence. It is really only the titles of the
films that call attention to location, evoking as they do the "land of enchant-
ment," an image the Southwest had constructed for itself in the early years

of the century as a means of building up its tourist appeal (see Buscombe). The titles of films such as *Sunset on the Desert* (1942), *Ridin' Down the Canyon* (1942), *Heart of the Rio Grande* (1942), and *Call of the Canyon* (1942) summon up a spirit of place that usually has no realization in the actual narrative. Budgets didn't allow for outdoor shooting in exotic locations. Most of the films look to have been shot in typical Californian scenery not too far from the Hollywood studios: hilly rather than mountainous, with a few scrubby trees. Some of Autry's later films went a little further afield, as far as the Alabama Hills, an area of round, bulbous rocks near Lone Pine in central California, between Death Valley and Mount Whitney, where Budd Boetticher filmed with Randolph Scott in the later 1950s. But one could never say about the films of either Autry or Rogers that the landscape became thematized, part of the meaning of the film, as it does in the films of John Ford or Anthony Mann.

So much for the similarities between the two cowboy stars. What of their differences? I happen to prefer Autry's singing voice; I find it warmer and more melodious, but this is of course a subjective judgment. Possibly Rogers is a better actor. In time Autry's acting became adequate to the rather modest demands placed upon it, but he never lost a certain stiffness. Rogers is also better looking, perhaps; Autry's face, with its slightly lumpy nose, is rather homely compared to Rogers' striking high cheekbones. The fights in Roy Rogers's films also have a slightly harder edge. Stanfield says that Republic deliberately tried to play up the differences, that Rogers was perceived more as an actor and Autry as a singer, quoting the trade paper *Exhibitor*: "Republic decided Autry should be its singing buckaroo, [and] that Rogers should be its action caballero" (Stanfield, *Horse Opera* 95). Autry's personality in the films is more genial than that of Rogers, adopting a somewhat protective attitude to young women, children, and his comic sidekick. Nat Levine, who originally signed Autry up for Mascot, said that "he lacked the commodity necessary to become a Western star—virility!" (George-Warren 134). But this is a very narrow view of the genre, showing an inability to see what gave the singing cowboy his special appeal.

★★★★★ The Personae: Don't Fence Me In

In terms of their offscreen personalities, the differences between the two stars are more marked. With the active encouragement of Herbert Yates, Autry cultivated a clean-living and morally upright image, as articulated in "The Cowboy Code," which laid down the ten commandments for a western hero:

1. A cowboy never takes unfair advantage—even of an enemy.
2. A cowboy never betrays a trust.
3. A cowboy always tells the truth.
4. A cowboy is kind to small children, to old folks, and to animals.
5. A cowboy is free from racial and religious prejudices.
6. A cowboy is helpful and when anyone is in trouble he lends a hand.
7. A cowboy is a good worker.
8. A cowboy is clean about his person, and in thought, word, and deed.
9. A cowboy respects womanhood, his parents, and the laws of his country.
10. A cowboy is a patriot.

(Hurst 168)

Additionally, in the films neither Autry nor Rogers smoke, drink, or cuss. This somewhat prudish list of moral prescriptions is adhered to in Autry's films, as in Rogers's. Its tone suggests it was written with an eye to the parents of their younger patrons, assuring them that their children would come to no harm watching these films. For Autry, things were not quite the same in real life. As Holly George-Warren makes clear in her biography, in later life Autry had a considerable drinking problem, and indeed he admits to it in his autobiography. George-Warren also details a series of romances that Autry had both with groupies and with co-stars, including a lengthy and serious affair with leading lady Gail Davis. Rogers, on the other hand, was converted to evangelical Christianity by his co-star and later wife, Dale Evans, and thereafter insistently promoted religion and clean living in his personal appearances, for example insisting on singing a religious song at the 1952 World Championship Rodeo in Madison Square Garden. (Autry, by contrast, states in *Back in the Saddle Again*, "I'm not a devoutly religious man" [Autry 34].)

In later years Autry achieved spectacular success as a businessman. He was quick to identify the opportunities for merchandizing that his stardom presented, and a stream of products gained his endorsement. Many were aimed at his younger fans: breakfast cereals, with Autry's smiling face on the packet offering assurance of the goodness contained within, as well as children's clothing, toys, and comics, and everyday household items such as bedside lamps and towels. Rogers, too, exploited these commercial possibilities, later lending his name to a chain of fast-food outlets. But Autry also expanded his activities into other spheres of activity, owning several radio stations, a TV station, and a television production facility, as well as the California Angels baseball team, a hotel, and ranches, all of which made him into a very wealthy man.

Roy Rogers, Dale Evans, and Gabby Hayes in publicity photo for *Yellow Rose of Texas* (1944). Copyright 1944, Republic Pictures, Inc.

Both Rogers and Autry ploughed some of their wealth into the building of a museum, but the differences between the two institutions are instructive. Autry's museum was constructed in Griffith Park, Los Angeles, in 1988. Originally named the Museum of Western Heritage, it subsequently amalgamated with the Southwest Museum of the American Indian and now, under the title of the Museum of the American West, forms part of the Autry National Center. It is both a museum of the history of the west, with exhibits of artifacts from the classic period of white expansion in the nineteenth century, and also a museum of representations of the West, with several works of art by western painters such as Albert Bierstadt and Frederic Remington, as well as a wide range of western movie costumes, memorabilia, merchandizing, and such. The museum has a research center, produces publications, and regularly mounts special exhibitions and other events. Without question it is the premier museum of the western movie.

Roy Rogers's museum was originally in Victorville, out in the California desert a hundred miles or so from Los Angeles. While the Museum of the American West is relatively restrained about Autry's contribution to the history of the western, Rogers's museum was focused almost entirely on Roy himself. Props from his films, posters, guns, and saddles that he owned lined the walls. Trophies from Roy's hunting expeditions in Africa were proudly displayed. Roy's horse Trigger was stuffed and mounted, and you could see Roy's customized car, decorated with Winchester rifles and with the horns of a longhorn cow mounted on the front. There was even a section devoted to the scholastic achievements of Roy's children.

The Roy Rogers museum, now the Roy Rogers–Dale Evans Museum, subsequently migrated to Branson, Missouri. I haven't visited it in its new site, but I think one can assume it remains pretty much the same. For someone like me, Autry's museum has a far greater appeal, with its much wider range of material, the greater quality of the exhibits, and its support for scholarship. It takes the western seriously. For example, the DVDs of Autry's films available from the museum present versions of the films restored with the assistance of the UCLA Film Archive. Too many of Roy Rogers's films are available only in dim and fuzzy versions taken from old prints made for television screenings and consequently edited down and missing some of the songs.

There's a temptation to read these differences back into the movies themselves, to see Autry's films as more significant than Rogers's, despite the manifold similarities. Peter Stanfield's two books dealing with singing cowboys treat Autry as a much more significant figure than Rogers. Stanfield is particularly interesting on the way in which the musical interludes in Autry's movies are integrated into the narratives, providing a level of complexity, of self-reflexivity, that is rarely present in Roy Rogers films. For example, in *Oh, Susanna!* (1936) Gene finds himself in jail, having been mistaken for a killer:

> To prove he is Gene Autry he has to sing before a group of his radio fans, who have been invited to the jailhouse. Unfortunately for Gene, his voice was damaged earlier in a fight. Saving the day, Smiley steals a phonograph and an

Autry record that some old-timers on a street corner were listening to and secretly plays it under the jailhouse window. Gene lip-synchs and convinces the audience of his "true" identity.   (Stanfield, *Horse Opera* 108)

The effect of this is to "authenticate" Autry as a successful recording artist and not merely a performer in the movie. "Gene Autry," the star of the film, is both actor and singer in the movie, but has another dimension outside the movie itself. There is nothing quite like this degree of narrative complexity in Rogers's films.

But ultimately the resemblances between the two stars' films outweigh the differences. Both constructed a world that, in its characters and predicaments, appealed to small-town and rural audiences, while remaining self-contained, almost hermetically sealed, and separate from the A-western. Rogers's and Autry's films force us to reconsider our definitions and understanding of the genre.

NOTES

1. It's true that several of Roy Rogers's early films had a historical setting, with Roy sometimes playing actual historical characters, as in *Young Buffalo Bill* (1940) and *Young Bill Hickok* (1940). It may be that this was part of an attempt by the studio to differentiate the two stars and give Rogers a unique selling point. But this was soon abandoned and thereafter Rogers's fictional world was, like that of Autry, the world of the present.

2. George-Warren (115) says that early in his career Autry recorded some obscene songs, though of course they were never publicly released.

3 ☆☆☆☆☆☆☆☆☆☆☆

Ingrid Bergman
The Face of Authenticity in the Land of Illusion

ROBIN BLAETZ

The story of Ingrid Bergman, the Swedish actress who starred in fifteen films in the 1940s and won one of the three Oscars for which she was nominated during that decade alone, has become known as a subset of the story of independent producer David O. Selznick. While Selznick, who distributed his films through United Artists during this period, did indeed work hard to get Bergman to Hollywood after seeing her in the Swedish version of *Intermezzo* in 1936, his authorship of her personal and professional life may not have been what it has seemed to scholars

Ingrid Bergman portrait, c. 1943. Collection of the author.

searching to explain the striking Bergman career. A line in film scholar Robin Wood's careful evaluation of Bergman's persona in relation to her work with Alfred Hitchcock typifies the mindset. He writes of Selznick's "decision *not* to remold her features or glamorize her (and of her own resistance to such a process)" (312). Framing Bergman's decision parenthetically is symptomatic of the discourse that has developed around her career. In an interview later in her life, Bergman spoke of her initial refusal to change, claiming that Selznick "was so surprised by this approach that he accepted it" (Kobal 472). I suggest that Selznick was not the engine of Bergman's career but its caboose, so to speak, and that the well-known dramatic story masks a more complicated and culturally significant one.

It would be a mistake to assign any sort of authorship role to Bergman herself; she would most likely have failed to understand the concept. I suggest that, instead, Bergman might best be seen as a professional woman who was not unlike the multitude of women who worked to support World War II in factories across the United States. Film historians have been far more likely to approach Bergman in relation to Greta Garbo because they were both Swedish (Wood 311), and several have described her as the anti-Garbo because she was neither mysterious nor typically glamorous. While this analogy has a certain superficial logic, it comes from a narrow view of U.S. society at the time. The country was filled with first- and second-generation Scandinavians and Germans whose cultural presence and influence were pervasive. Investigation in the archives shows that Bergman was in reality only briefly compared to Garbo, with whom she had next to nothing in common. Instead, with only the slightest attempt at contextualization, Bergman can be seen as a woman who had a particularly strong passion for her chosen career but whose career was not her life; indeed, she lived a life that was no more or less complicated than that of many women. The difference between Bergman's life and the lives of other working women of her time was that everything she did was watched and shaped retrospectively so as to benefit the studios that employed her. When Bergman's life overflowed the bounds of any story that Hollywood was permitted to tell—through her abrupt departure from her family in the United States in 1949 and subsequent child with Italian director Roberto Rossellini—the Bergman story became the tale of shock and betrayal that operates predominantly today.

When Bergman's story is disentangled from Selznick's, a different reading emerges. Bergman turned out to have been the person she said she was, which might be best conceptualized as *captured* rather than authored by the myriad publicity that followed her career. She was, one might say, authentically what she was constructed to be. The professionalism, the generosity, the simplicity, and the all-important wholesomeness have proven to be real. I would argue with those who claim that naturalness is necessarily as constructed as glamour. Of course makeup is used to alter the effect of the lights in a photographic medium, but that is not the same thing as artificially creating naturalness. In positing the latter, women are essentially defined as nonexistent, as Galateas waiting for their Pygmalions to enliven them.

The problem for the studios and for all those who have described Bergman's affair with Rossellini as a scandal lies in the definition of wholesomeness. For Bergman and, I would argue, for women across the United States, to be wholesome did not exclude sexuality and self-determination. It is only a patriarchal notion of women as virgins or whores that enable a reading of Bergman's actions in the late 1940s as an irredeemable betrayal. In fact, women everywhere may well have quietly applauded her actions, seeing for the first time and in contrast to the sultry Lana Turners or saccharine June Allysons of the day a complex woman who was wholesome and sexual, good and independent. In the following pages, I investigate Bergman's career just before coming to the United States as well as her work in Hollywood through the 1940s. As attention to the enormous amount of publicity surrounding Bergman's affair and subsequent second marriage attests, Bergman's fans were certainly surprised but were not, I imagine, appalled. Bergman's choices about the way she lived her life were less scandalous than they were revelatory and prescient in relation to gender roles. I intend to tell her story so as to situate her as an unclaimed iconic figure in the history of mid-twentieth-century feminism.

My particular approach to Bergman's career during the 1940s reflects Richard Dyer's simple observation that it is impossible to know what any star meant to people at a given time in the past. All one can do is tease out the variety of meanings that may have been present, using the evidence that remains (*Stars* 74). While many scholars have undertaken this task, few have looked at the nature of the film industry in Sweden that gave rise to Bergman's character and career, and fewer still have situated Bergman in relation to other working women of her time. I argue along with Joanne Meyerowitz that the late 1940s and early 1950s were not the simplistically conservative years that popular history has come to assume. Women in this period continued to work in the public sphere (albeit in typical female jobs), gaining confidence and profiting from increased competence and a rising feminist consciousness (Meyerowitz 4). The reduction of Bergman's career to a melodramatic scandal is of a piece with conceptualizing women during the postwar period as contained and invisible. In fact, Bergman can be seen as having left the realm of stardom altogether at the end of the 1940s. As Dyer reminds us, stars are acceptable to the degree that they have no real institutional influence or power (*Stars* 7). While the censure that accompanied the birth of the Bergman-Rossellini baby was far weaker than film history has led us to believe, the fact that Bergman was denounced on the floor of the U.S. Senate indicates that a serious breach had occurred in the status quo concerning the natural place of women (Crawford Dixon, "Saint or Sinner," c. 1949–1950, 59, 80).[1]

An examination of the discourse around Ingrid Bergman when she first arrived in the United States reveals that she was anomalous on every level, particularly in relation to her home life and maternity. The seven thick scrapbook volumes documenting her career in the Constance McCormick Collection reveal the process through which the Swedish actress, whom Selznick called his "Nordic Natural," was created as an image. The perpetual cataloging of the famous unshaped eyebrows, the lack of makeup and lipstick, the simple hairstyle, the flat shoes was meant to stun the fans with the paradox that this woman looked like a movie star without any effort. The very existence of this impossible and almost magical feat was fraught with danger, and the studios worked continually to ameliorate the risk with numerous text-rich articles. Instead, Bergman's rejection of the feminine masquerade with its cosmetics and excessive style of dress calls into question the proper place of women. The independent and professionally ambitious Bergman apparently did not need the approving gaze of her fans. Moreover, Bergman was often shown with her friends, many of whom were male, without makeup, and she dressed plainly, laughing and smoking without regard to how she appeared ("Ingrid Bergman Takes a Short Holiday from Hollywood," *Life*, c. 1943–1945).

Faced with this lack of acquiescence and the inevitable instability that it caused, the studio quickly produced a list of attributes that were repeated compulsively throughout the 1940s as a way to attempt to create a star image from a set of shifting personal characteristics. The love of ice cream, the punctuality, the frugality, the rapid walk, the efficient packing, the eagerness to please—all repeated in article after article and all meant to substantiate the studio commodity called the Nordic Natural. While film history indicates that the stunning revelations of 1949 were almost fatal, an examination of the enormous amount of press material around the events shows that interest was high but condemnation low (*Stromboli* [1949]).[2] Is it impossible to believe that many female fans would have loved not Selznick's image of the almost childlike, housewife Bergman but what they had perhaps seen under the surface all along—a woman like themselves who found the strength to free herself from the strictures of patriarchal marriage?

☆☆☆☆☆ Bergman in Sweden

A brief look at Bergman's life and career in Sweden provides a platform from which to investigate Bergman's unusual career and persona in the United States in the 1940s. The outline of Bergman's life story was told repeatedly, and its multiple losses proved a valuable counterweight against unconventional behavior (for example, Ida Zeitlin, "Ingrid Bergman," *Modern Screen*, August 1943). Bergman was born in Stockholm in 1915 to a German mother and Swedish father, who was a photographer and amateur filmmaker. Friedel Adler Bergman died when her daughter was three and Justus Bergman died in 1927 after raising his only child on his own. Bergman lived with an aunt for several years before the latter died with Bergman standing at her side. Sent to live with yet other relatives, Bergman finished school and was accepted, against her family's wishes, into the Royal Dramatic Theater in Stockholm in 1933. She appeared briefly in a film in 1932 and in *Munkbrogreven* in 1935, which led to a contract with Svensk Filmindustri and the end of her formal theatrical training. In the course of appearing in nine more films before leaving for Hollywood, Bergman married a dentist named Petter Aron Lindstrom eight years her senior in 1937 and bore a daughter just over a year later. Bergman came to the United States in 1939 to star in a remake of *Intermezzo*, the 1936 film that had made her the most popular actress in Sweden.

Bergman's experience as an actor in Sweden (and briefly in Germany in 1937 in *Die Vier Gesellen* with Carl Froelich) could hardly have been more different than what she faced in Hollywood. As is well known, the U.S. star system was put into place in the early 1910s through a publicity stunt involving the Biograph Girl (Dyer, *Stars* 9). Sweden, on the other hand, had a strong theatrical tradition from which many film actors were drawn. Perhaps due to the much smaller size of all the pertinent institutions or because of a greater tendency for cross-pollination across the arts, actors moved across genres relatively easily (Johansson 58). This is not to say that film was considered the equal of other arts in Sweden, but simultaneous appearance in film and theater by trained actors was quite different from the U.S. situation, in which it was rare. Whereas a star such as Ginger Rogers only appeared in musicals and light comedy in the 1930s, Ingrid Bergman moved from *Walpurgis Night* (1935), in which she plays the ethically sound child bearer in a film about abortion and the low Swedish birthrate, to *Intermezzo* (1936), in which she survives her adulterous affair to become a professional pianist, to the melodramatic *A Woman's Face* (1938), in which Bergman wears truly grotesque facial makeup to play a twisted soul. The point is that she was an actor and she appeared in as many interesting roles as she could find. The roles were not considered contradictory but simply different and the logical range for an actor of Bergman's skill (Hedling, "European" 191). Ironically, the only photographs of Bergman from her Swedish years that appear to have been published in the United States come from films in which she wore glamour makeup. Rather than asking where the images are that show her in *A Woman's Face*, scholars have concluded that Bergman was glamorous in Sweden, which is used to prove that her naturalness in the United States was artificial (see Wood 312). In addition, the films of the 1930s were not remotely vehicles for any one star, but thematically complex, often daring works of art intended to speak to contemporaneous concerns in a country that was fully aware of the rapidly approaching World War II (Gelley 29).

Perhaps the best-known attribute of the Swedish cinema, particularly in the silent period, was the use of landscape. The great directors Victor Sjöström and Mauritz Stiller developed the Swedish cinema as a blend of studio photography, in which actors embodied and drove the narrative line, and location shooting, in which long takes of Sweden's dramatic expanses of mountains and sea were used to suggest emotional complexity (Hedling, "Welfare" 181). The expressive use of the world in tandem with narrative action had no counterpart in U.S. commercial cinema. Whereas much of U.S. film in this period was fairly close to filmed theater, with the all-important close-ups that distinguished the medium, Swedish cinema had developed into a distinctive art form. The dominant use of landscapes, objects, and lighting to telegraph emotion in an expressionistic mode made the actor less important and the close-up unnecessary. The film *A Woman's Face*, which was directed by Gustaf Molander, is typical of the films in which Bergman acted in the 1930s. I do not use the verb "to star," even though Bergman plays the titular character, because the film is an ensemble performance. Bergman's face is made up into a twisted grimace that is the result of a childhood burning accident, which has left her hunched over as if tormented into the life of greed and cruelty that she has chosen. Although a doctor has repaired her face by the end of the film, there are no searching tight shots that might signal understanding and there is little resolution in either human relationships or plot lines. The only memorable close-ups in the film are photographs of World War I soldiers with hideously disfigured faces seen in a book in the doctor's office. The audience is never given the sense of access to Bergman's character that would give the illusion of know-ing her, which would then, in turn, lead to the idolization of her as a star (see Dyer, *Stars* 16).

Given the enormous differences between the two film industries, par-ticularly regarding the place of the attractive female actor, it is no surprise that Bergman was not allowed to act in *A Woman's Face* when it was remade in the United States in 1941. Joan Crawford, who played complicated, hard, often psychologically twisted characters, was given the role because it did not interfere with the star persona that had been constructed around her. Although Bergman had no way of knowing it when she arrived in Holly-wood, she would have to fight to play anything but pretty, nice victims whose gift for self-sacrifice allowed men to do what they had to do. The fact that she did insist on practicing her craft as she had been trained to do out-side the capitalist mode of standardization made her seem capricious in Hollywood. In an irony that followed Bergman throughout the 1940s, her attempts to do well in Hollywood by extending herself and taking chances were antithetical to the system in which she was expected to maintain the iconographic continuity through which she was sold in both her roles and her life.

★★★★★ Bergman Comes to Hollywood

The second of the four phases into which Robin Wood divides Bergman's career can be divided in half, following the Swedish period of 1934 to 1940 and preceding the Rossellini period from 1950 to 1955, and then the final period that included work around the world in film, theater, and television and that ended with her death in 1982 (310). The first half of the 1940s, in which the studios worked on the star persona, concluded with *Spellbound* in 1945, and the second, in which the fragile persona evaporated under the pressure of a lived life, ended with Berg-man's departure from her family, the Hollywood film industry, and the United States.

The vehicle that brought Bergman to Hollywood held within it seeds that sprouted throughout her career. *Intermezzo* had been made in Sweden in 1936 and was remade in an all but identical copy in the United States in 1939. Bergman plays a brilliant pianist whose talent and charm lead her into an affair with her young pupil's violinist father, with whom she travels around the world giving concerts. When he is drawn back home, she bravely and amicably leaves to pursue her career in Paris. As one might expect, Joseph Breen was not at all pleased with this conclusion and he wrote several letters in 1938 requesting that the Bergman character not be allowed to succeed but instead, as he wrote in one, *"lose out"* on the scholarship to pay for her adultery (*Intermezzo* [1938]). While reviews of the film make no mention of what the industry felt to be scandalous, the studios were unsettled enough to create and widely disseminate a document called "A Portrait of the First Lady." This six-page, double-spaced list by the man who became Bergman's agent and good friend, Joseph Henry Steele, combines a remarkable number of random characteristics along the lines of the first, "She is currently addicted to singing 'Don't Fence Me In' if no one is within earshot" to "She can outwalk anyone in Hollywood in speed and distance" to "She never wears earrings" (Bergman folder). The list itself is fascinating as an amalgamation of observations that the writer himself clearly cannot (and one senses, would rather not) turn into a coherent product. Yet certain items in the list are repeated to a degree verging on absurdity in the fan magazines throughout the 1940s in the attempt to control the discourse around Bergman. While the items on the list are more or less true, one imagines, the repetition of certain things (such as her love of ice cream) was most likely meant to divert attention from aspects of the roles she was playing that contradicted the Nordic Natural persona. Yet I would argue that Bergman's fans would not have had any trouble accepting the discrepancy between her offscreen life and that of, for instance, a nineteenth-century prostitute in *Dr. Jekyll and Mr. Hyde* of 1941 (see Gelley 40). Further, I would suggest that this discrepancy may well have been the source of her popularity.

The publicity of the 1940s continually marvels at the fact that Bergman was not a star in the mode of what Daniel Boorstin might call a "pseudo-event," at the same time that it awkwardly tries to shape a trademark out of her complex set of characteristics (see Dyer, *Stars* 14). Try as they might, the studios could not flatten her into the person featured in her second film in Hollywood, the insistently titled *Adam Had Four Sons* of 1941. Bergman plays a radiant young woman who begins as the governess for a charmed family consisting of Adam, his wife, and his four sons and ends up married to Adam after a series of disasters. Bergman's character verges on the saintly; she is the wife's best friend, the sons' hero, and the father's savior. Her dazzling but down-to-earth competence and charm are only matched by her almost masochistic capacity for self-sacrifice. When the film appeared, the press stressed Bergman's family and roots. One caption under a photograph says, "Nordic—But Nice," while an article says: "She's committed the Hollywood faux pas of being ecstatically married. . . . Has a blond daughter . . . [and] has no maid, no car, doesn't own a lipstick. She likes to wash dishes, has a complexion like Shirley Temple and bites her nails."

After saying that Hemingway, Spencer Tracy, and the like think she is great, the article continues, "Ah, but ask the man who owns one. . . . Dr. Lindstrom says she's the most wonderful woman in the world and the most beautiful" (*Motion Picture* and *Modern Screen*, c. 1941–1942).

Film history has for the most part ensconced Bergman in this persona of the acquiescent Swedish wife/mother and used it to create the story of the Rossellini affair as a scandal. The fact that most people identify *Casablanca* (1943) as Bergman's signature role is proof of the dominance of this particular version of the 1940s career. *Casablanca* features a woman whose sexuality is entirely offscreen and in the past, but whose luminous face and radiant smile inspire men to do well and to do good. She is in the background, inactive, statuesque, lovely. Robin Wood is surely thinking chiefly of this film when he writes that Bergman's main attributes are being nice and being a lady, and that they are used to contain her irrepressibly healthy sexuality, which is ultimately more threatening than the much more common surface masquerade of mere sexiness (312–13). However, *Casablanca* was but a second thought when it was made, while all of Bergman's energy was directed toward *For Whom the Bell Tolls* (1943). In this Oscar-nominated film that was intended to be and publicized as her breakout role, Bergman plays an adventurous, highly emotional, openly sexual woman. The press around Bergman at this time struggles to continue the domestic story. One awkward series of photographs declares that she spoke with Gary Cooper about "her madness for Rocky Road ice cream" and with Cedric Gibbons about the dress that Pia wore at her fourth birthday party (Ida Zeitlin, "Ingrid Bergman," *Modern Screen*, August 1943). The non-sequiturs distract the reader momentarily, but deliberate scrutiny of the biography and the fan material up to the middle of the decade leaves the reader with a firm sense that Bergman actually did not like to entertain at home, did not dress up, and loved to work. In short, while the press worked hard to contain Bergman through the discourse of the family, it was impossible to portray her as a conventional "lady" when she was a hard-working, self-disciplined, professional actor. Other film historians, including James Damico, maintain that Bergman was seen as a lady despite her racy roles because the discourse asserting her thespian skills served to defuse and neutralize them (249). The more the studios played the professionalism card, the more justified they were in continuing to claim that Bergman was a simple ice cream–loving wife and mother. I find the crux of the Bergman image at this time in a photograph in the *Los Angeles Times* on 4 April 1943. A group of famous actresses is seen sitting at the Hollywood Bowl, waiting for the appearance of Madame Chiang. While most of the women work to attract

Bergman as the innocent yet sensual Maria in *For Whom the Bell Tolls* (1943), a performance that earned her first Oscar nomination. Copyright 1943, Paramount Pictures, Inc.

the camera in dramatic hats and elaborate jewelry, Bergman sits hatless,
wearing a dark, unadorned jacket, looking out of the field of action. Not to
be forgotten is the fact that Bergman was known for filming with her 16 mm
camera and was often photographed looking rather than being observed
(for one example, see *Movie Stars Parade*, May 1944, 30).

A more typical photo shoot of this period shows Bergman visiting a
Minnesota farm (*Look*, 6 April 1943, 27–29). Dyer notes that Bergman was

never photographed engaged in traditional leisure activities but largely at work, engaged in sports, or with friends (*Stars* 42). Because she had already proven herself, so to speak, in producing Pia, Bergman had earned the right to be coded in ways usually reserved for men. Unlike the attributes of femininity, which can only be said to worsen and decrease in value with time, Bergman was seen as more fully human and thus permitted to change and develop (see Stacey 225). It is not hard to imagine that a star who dressed functionally, behaved modestly, and worked diligently during World War II might have appealed to a nation forced to conserve and sacrifice at all levels. She does not offer the mask of glamour but a safer kind of escapism based in a sense of camaraderie, only slightly elevated by studio lighting. Joe McElhaney writes about how the camera rather obsessively investigated the healthy eroticism located in her famous smile as both an investigative tool of the supposed naturalness and as a means of containing the tall, physically imposing woman, especially when her co-stars were shorter than she was (2). The close-up is used with particular insistence in *Dr. Jekyll and Mr. Hyde*, which is famous for the fact that Bergman fought to be cast as the prostitute with the juicier role, as opposed to the bland fiancée. After this early film, Bergman was perceived as a wife, a mother, an athlete, an actor, and a normally sexual woman, terms that are only contradictory within a narrow, patriarchal definition of femininity. Bergman's potential appeal to women in particular is simple to understand; she was more like them than she was dissimilar in ways that played themselves out throughout the 1940s in a magnified but not categorically different way.

Bergman's performance as the prostitute Ivy in *Dr. Jekyll and Mr. Hyde* must at first have assured studio executives that they had been right in trying to cast Lana Turner in the role. Where they would have expected the seductive gazes and vamping for which Turner was famous, Bergman was all smiles, hugs, and open invitation. When Mr. Hyde loses his ability to turn back into Dr. Jekyll, this particular version of the story makes some sense. The man is livid that the woman lays claim to her own sexuality rather than playing the object of his desire, and he turns her into an increasingly passive slave before killing her in frustration. What seems to drive him mad is her cheerful independence; she creates none of the anxiety that would make her appear in patriarchal logic to deserve the castigation. What makes matters worse is that she accepts her punishment as if willingly paying the price for crossing gender lines and enjoying her desiring self. In the slightly later *Gaslight* (1944), Bergman is given the role that most embodies what Ora Gelley calls her dominant trope of "eroticism and suffering" (31). The film is close to unbearable to watch; the sadistic

Bergman won her first Academy Award for *Gaslight* (1944), one of the most masochistic characters she ever portrayed. Copyright 1944, Loew's, Inc.

attempt of the husband to convince the masochistic Bergman character that she is insane is unrelenting. Only at the very end of the film, when a detective has convinced her that her husband is only after the family's hidden jewels of which she had been unaware, does the character react. Pretending actually to be insane, she threatens the bound and tied husband for less than a minute of screen time. Given the strength and competence that real women were displaying during this wartime period, it is hard to imagine that many fans enjoyed this film. In fact, the press around the film in 1944 to 1945 avoids actually discussing it, turning instead to rehashing bits of the list that deal with Bergman's family and her simplicity.

Bergman's next film appears to be an about-face, with *The Bells of St. Mary's* (1945) offering the role of a robust, athletic, elegant nun. Yet once again, the story both flaunts and reins in the Bergman energy and radiant smile. Bergman is thoroughly wrapped in the full regalia of a nun through-out the film yet teaches one boy how to box and plays baseball with other children. She brings the film to life as a counter to Bing Crosby's smarmy double entendres. In the end, the Bergman character is neither killed nor driven insane but is dismissed from her job. Unhappy at first, she bursts into the trademark smile upon learning that she has tuberculosis, which the Crosby character had hidden from her but which oddly reassures her. Damico describes this sort of surrender moment, in which Bergman holds back her emotions and then finally unleashes them, as her dominant mode. However, where he believes that audiences perceived the passion to be related to spiritual moments, at the fore of films such as *The Bells of St. Mary's* and, later, *Joan of Arc*, I imagine that women who were losing their jobs at the end of the war might have read the scenes differently (Damico 250; see Blaetz 135). Following Adrienne McLean's work on Bergman and Rita Hayworth ("Cinderella" 164), I think it very likely that Bergman's life, the richness of which was the obsessive target of the studio's press corps, combined with the relentless attacks on her in her films, would have cre-ated a sympathetic character whose rebellion at the end of the decade would have been greeted not with wrath but with a silent cheer.

The next two films that Bergman made in 1945 were covered in the press with material about what seem to have been unusually popular tours to entertain the U.S. troops abroad. Given the insistence on Bergman's Everywoman status in several articles, it is interesting that she played the most brazenly and happily sexual woman of her career in *Saratoga Trunk* in 1945 (*Movie Star Parade*, May 1944, 55). The complex narrative, set vaguely in nineteenth-century New Orleans and Saratoga Springs, positions her as an independent woman who has returned to redeem her mother's reputa-tion and find a wealthy man to marry. Of particular note is an astonishingly erotic point-of-view tilt from the Bergman character's gaze, up from Gary Cooper's crossed cowboy boots to his unabashedly desiring eyes at their first meeting. The rest of the film is filled with their sexualized horseplay, which ends with Bergman abandoning her plan to find a rich husband. Also in this film one finds, not for the first time, the admiring older woman who gains secret satisfaction by abetting the plans of the Bergman character to get what she wants outside of society's bounds.

With *Spellbound* (1945), Bergman first worked with Alfred Hitchcock in a role that relates in intriguing ways to her other roles in the same year and to the second half of Bergman's principal Hollywood period. Moving from playing a nun and then a flagrantly sexual single woman, Bergman appears on screen first in eyeglasses and a doctor's loose white jacket. She is a woman immersed in her work and rather than being associated with insanity herself, she is called upon to help a traumatized man. When the Gregory Peck character first appears, the screen is filled with the trademark soft close-ups of Bergman's smiling face indicating her desire for him. Yet for the first time, this energy is made therapeutic rather than being either closely observed or attacked. It seems no accident that the man's difficulties are connected with the returning shell-shocked soldier motif. Bergman's working woman, wearing the eyeglasses that signify an active agent, is permitted a socially beneficial use of her libidinal energy. Accompanying the excellent reviews of the film are several signed pieces about Bergman that begin a shift in tone. Rather than the usual references to ice cream sundaes, Bergman is quoted as saying that she does not "believe in Fate or Luck. According to my philosophy, one works for what one gets. Neither the supernatural nor the seer interests me, I have no faith in either one" (Alice L. Tildeslley, "This Is Ingrid Bergman," *Movieland*, April 1945, 28–29). For reasons relating to the war and most likely to Bergman's ever greater expressions of independence and increasing trips to New York for work on the stage (particularly for *Joan of Lorraine*, which opened in 1946), the simplistic Nordic Natural persona was gradually abandoned by the studios.

★★★★★ Approaching Sainthood

In 1946, Bergman is described as a "mature, happy, intelligent human being" who dislikes "the slickness of Hollywood films, cares little for money or billing" and who is bored with playing women in love (*Movieland*, October 1946, 69). While articles about her in fan magazines continued apace, they relied ever less on photographs, which were replaced by well-written and remarkably long essays. The infamous list was mostly abandoned and replaced by signed articles that explored the complexity of a lived life, with one bearing a title surely meant to reassure the studio heads, "There's Only One Bergman" (Jack Sher and John Keating, *Screen Guide*, c. 1946–1947). The events of Bergman's private life at this time were echoed throughout the United States as men returned home from war to women who had been running lives that were both domestic and public with confidence and success. While no one can know what transpired in the Bergman/Lindstrom marriage, the impression gleaned from the various Bergman biographies is that although the alliance was ending in the middle of the decade, Lindstrom refused to consider divorce (Joseph H. Steele, "The Bergman Love Story," 38–39, 94–95, and Arthur L. Charles, "Dangerous Paradise," c. 1949–50). Bergman apparently began an affair with photographer Robert Capa in Paris in 1945, followed by close friendships with musician Larry Adler and director Victor Fleming. Perhaps more important is Bergman's growing dissatisfaction with the nature of her work in relation to the postwar world. The three key films of this period, *Notorious* (1946), *Arch of Triumph* (1948), and *Joan of Arc* (1948), in relation to the plethora of publicity material intended to control the lucrative star, present a clear picture of the trajectory that led to Bergman leaving the United States for Italy in 1949 to make *Stromboli* with Rossellini.

In 1946 Bergman made her second film with Alfred Hitchcock. *Notorious* is considered by many to be her best work and, not coincidentally, the film in which the director helped her to refine her acting style (Gelley 32–33). Although directors had always been drawn to recording Bergman's radiant smile in close-up, the use of this particular shot distance in *Notorious* is almost self-reflexive in its ubiquity. In relation to this technique, Bergman tended to do less with her face and allowed the lighting and juxtaposition of shots to signify her more complex character. However, the plot of the film (and the events of Bergman's life) are relevant as well. Her role in the film is the rather wild and overtly sexual daughter of a wartime traitor; she pays for his misdeeds by serving her country as a spy in the form of a prostitute. Bergman's character marries a German to gather information even though she has fallen in love with the U.S. agent who is her contact. Poisoned by the end of the film by her suspicious mother-in-law, Bergman is on the verge of death when she is saved by the U.S. agent, who carries her ravaged body out the door of her home in her bathrobe.

The publicity during this period is of a piece with the film's narrative project of controlling the independent woman. In April 1947, an essay called "The Truth about Ingrid" appeared (Robbin Coons, *Movieland*, April 1947, 34–35). The essay is unlike anything that had come before; Bergman is described as having a bad temper, getting colds, and arguing with her directors. Other articles in this period reveal that she actually does smoke and drink and that she eats too much (*Modern Screen* and *Photoplay*, c. 1946–1947). As if on cue, Bergman next appeared in *Arch of Triumph* in the least typical role of her career to date. In this Lewis Milestone film, Bergman plays a Parisian woman in shock at the death of her lover, wearing obvious lipstick, a cocked beret, and resembling a 1940s femme fatale with an intense stare and catatonic air. She is rescued by a doctor, who is operating clandestinely during the war and whose sole desire is not to help her but to kill the Nazi who tormented him in prison. By the end of the film, we are on familiar ground. The character, presciently named Joan, has been shot by a jealous boyfriend and lies immobile in bed, dying in extreme close-up with her face once again radiant in surrender.

The combination of her character in *Arch of Triumph* and the increasing reports of Bergman's affairs led to a series of incongruous publicity texts. An odd and often quoted petition signed by twenty-one crew members on the film reads as follows: "We have just learned that the Hollywood woman's press club has selected Ingrid Bergman as the most uncooperative actress of the year stop This is not true stop She is the most cooperative of actresses stop. . . ." (Lewis Milestone collection, *Arch of Triumph*). At the same time, the *Los Angeles Examiner* featured a comic book–style drawing of Bergman as the "Never, Never Girl," in which she is described as never playing cards, never wearing earrings, never eating raw onions, and never having hobbies, superstitions, sisters, or the measles ("Ingrid Bergman: The 'Never, Never' Girl!" *Los Angeles Examiner,* c. 1946–1947). This first evidence of the press having fun with the absurdly simplistic Bergman persona indicates that the façade was cracking. As the decade moved to an end, the photograph of Bergman most often used is one that won an award for the photographer, in which she wears her Parisian low-life costume with a cigarette dangling from her lips. *Time* magazine published the photo but still hoped to deny the evidence, saying that Bergman manages "to look like a woman who could never understand Ingrid Bergman" (*Time,* c. 1947–1948).

In his discussion of the Bergman persona, Damico channels the studio heads of the late 1940s, noting their rants about her "obstinacy, her chronic restlessness, her compulsive eating." He quotes Capa, who said that she is "tied up in a million knots," and a producer who accused her of being "a very selfish, self-centered woman" (248). Indeed, by this point in her career Bergman was no longer fully cooperating with the publicity machine. While she had always lived her life as she pleased, her choices were no longer as easy to cover and she seemed to care little if she were condemned for living as an independent professional woman. The press made one last attempt at closing the lid by finding the apparently long lost Swedish photographs of Bergman on her wedding day and as a young actress and mother ("the missing Bergman pictures!") and ever more frequently publishing

Bergman in *Joan of Arc* (1948), a project she had worked toward since she arrived in Hollywood. Copyright 1948, Sierra Pictures, Inc.

photos of Bergman with her husband (*Modern Screen,* c. 1948–1949). The studios did their part in moving *Joan of Arc* forward so that Bergman could play the part that she had come to Hollywood to play almost ten years earlier and continue to explore the role that she had recently finished on Broadway in Maxwell Anderson's *Joan of Lorraine.*[3] An editorial in the *Philadelphia Catholic Standard* may have most clearly articulated the desires of

Hollywood at this point: "It is Joan herself that we see, not Ingrid who has disappeared" (7 January 1949).

The publicity around *Joan of Arc* was extensive, with both *Look* and *Life* giving the film lengthy cover stories (20 July 1948 and 14 November 1948, respectively; see Blaetz 128–34). Like many actors, Bergman had spoken often about her interest in playing Joan of Arc. While one can never know just what about the fifteenth-century figure has inspired any one person, it seems clear that women are attracted by the freedom and independence of a fearless young girl and find the end of her story unfortunate if accurate. (Male directors, on the other hand, seem to rush through the life story to get to the burning.) Film historians who connect this role to Bergman's part in *The Bells of St. Mary's*, since both women are celibate Catholics, have clearly not seen the films. Unlike the lively Sister Benedict, Bergman's Joan and the film itself are pious and naïve to a fault. At every moment of anomalous female behavior, a booming voice of God narration straightens out the story. In the end, the voice tells the viewer that the eroticized, beautiful, suffering Bergman, chained to a stake as she dies, is living her "greatest triumph."

I propose that a slightly earlier scene in the film, in which Bergman comes to understand her fate, offers a clearer picture of what she may have meant to U.S. women at the end of the 1940s. She is dressed in black, leaning against a dark background in an unusually long take of a high-angle close-up that isolates her tear-stained face as the very image of suffering. While the film participates in the punishing of the woman who has dared to cross gender lines—the driving force in the vast majority of films about the heroine—it uses the story for its own contemporaneous ends. Joan's death is equated with the sacrifices that U.S. women were making as soldiers were returning to their jobs at home after the war. The film suggests that female heroism in 1948 entailed a return to the domestic sphere and the end of action in the world. Bergman's final film before leaving for an extended period in Europe was her last project with Hitchcock, *Under Capricorn* (1949). It is little wonder that this role is unknown; Bergman plays yet another oppressed woman, made to feel insane by a maid in pursuit of her husband. Considering her interest in leaving Hollywood altogether, it is remarkable that she was able to play one more adorably pathetic, passively wounded victim, and it is just that the film is ignored.

★★★★★ **Revelations**

Much has been made of Bergman being inspired by the Neorealist cinema of Roberto Rossellini in the mid-1940s and then volunteering to act in his films. Less known is Bergman's longstanding regret that she had left her native country on the eve of World War II and failed to participate in the response to it as a European (Gelley 29; Kobal 461–63). What she saw in Rossellini's films was real engagement with not only the harrowing problems of a country at the end of a war but with the cinema as an art form. In her first film with Rossellini, *Stromboli*, Bergman is given the space and time to register her involvement with the world and with the other characters in the film. She is shot wearing her own clothes, without artificial lighting, in long takes in long shot, and for the first time appears to author her own physically strong performance. In a later interview with Oriana Fallaci, Bergman said, "In a certain way Roberto was the instrument of my flight, the consequence of a deeply matured tiredness. For years I had dreamed of escape. . . . In Hollywood I felt locked in a prison. . . . The only talk I could hear was talk about money and career" ("Ingrid Bergman," *Look*, 5 March 1968, 28).

The fact that the studios could no longer control the story when Bergman left the United States in 1949 and gave birth to a baby a year later only increased the sense that she was just what she said she was, that she was authentic. McLean notes that Bergman refused to participate in the studio's attempt to integrate the Rossellini scandal into her star discourse ("Cinderella" 172). The attempt itself indicates the sea that separated Bergman from Hollywood at this point in her life. In the end, Bergman's actions at the close of the 1940s were no different from anything else that she had done in her career. What had changed was Hollywood's ability to impose its version and, after the initial surprise, U.S. culture's growing inability to impose restrictive social roles on women. McLean notes that eight out of ten of the 30,000 to 40,000 letters received around the time of the baby's birth were positive and supportive of her courage ("Cinderella" 180), and the press soon began to express the sense that Bergman had been true to herself as always. I would add that every baby that she added to her eventual total of four most likely helped to smooth over the shock of a woman who claimed sexual desire for herself and lived her life with self-determination. Film historians have given too much credence to the actions of Senator Edwin Johnson, who reviled Bergman on the floor of the U.S. Senate for an hour, in evaluating Bergman's star persona (Damico 243). Johnson may have been the voice of patriarchy, like the voice of God narration in *Joan of Arc*, but he was surely not the voice that was thrilled to welcome Bergman back to Hollywood with an Oscar for *Anastasia* in 1957.

Following Bergman's productive career in Italy, where she made five films with Rossellini, she continued to work in film, theater, and television in Europe and the United States for the rest of her life. In the very last year of her life, suffering from the cancer that killed her at the age of sixty-eight, she played Golda Meir for a television movie. In her interview with Fallaci, she said the following: "I had a very special place in the heart of the Americans. And I didn't know why at that time. I understood later that my success was a woman's success more than an actress's success. They were so used to the European prima donnas, those who break mirrors to get things, and wear jewels even in bed, and walk holding a tiger by the leash. They were intrigued, then conquered by the Swedish girl who had arrived with a child and a suitcase. Women, I think, liked me before men. And men identified me with their wives, their mothers, their sisters" ("Ingrid Bergman," *Look*, 5 March 1968, 26–28). Bergman was indeed prescient in assuming that she was good enough without the accoutrements of femininity and that she had the right to children, work, and authentic love. In discussing her life as a professional woman, she states what U.S. women may have seen in her career all along. She says, "I've never built my career on beauty and youth. It can't last" (Kobal 461). The journey from the masochistic close-ups of her lovely, suffering face that characterized her early films to her incarnation of the aged Israeli prime minister charts the course of women's sense of identity over four decades of U.S. history.

NOTES

1. Many of the popular sources both studied and cited in this article are from the Constance McCormick Collection of star scrapbooks housed at the Cinema-Television Library, University of Southern California; there are seven scrapbooks for Bergman. Incomplete textual citations are from a CMC scrapbook.

2. Any textual citations with an incomplete reference refer to folders about Ingrid Bergman in the Margaret Herrick Library of the Academy of Motion Picture Arts and Sciences in Beverly Hills.

3. As early as 1940 and regularly throughout the decade, Bergman asserted her desire to play Joan of Arc (with the last of the three opportunities being Rossellini's *Giovanna d'Arco al rogo* in 1954). See Dora Albert, "Bergman Is Back!," *Screenland*, April 1940, 62–63.

4 ☆☆☆☆☆☆☆☆☆☆

Humphrey Bogart and Lauren Bacall
Tough Guy and Cool Dame

RICK WORLAND

Although the thriving Hollywood studio system of the 1940s produced hundreds of movies featuring dozens of popular stars, Warner Bros.' Humphrey Bogart, typically imagined with fedora and trench coat, cigarette dangling from his lip, may have been the decade's most emblematic star—the thoroughly contemporary man. Bogart (1899–1957) had been paying dues onscreen since 1930 and made notable movies in the

Humphrey Bogart portrait, c. 1941; Lauren Bacall portrait, c. 1944. Both photos collection of the author.

fifties before his untimely death, but the forties saw the apex of his commercial and artistic success. Midway through the period, he met and married an actress half his age, Lauren Bacall (b. 1924), his sultry co-star in *To
Have and Have Not* (1944) and soon integral to the Bogart legend. This was
but the start of her distinguished career, one happily still unfolding at the
time of this writing more than sixty years later. Bogart's output in this
decade included at least six efforts—*The Maltese Falcon* (1941), *Casablanca*
(1942), *To Have and Have Not*, *The Big Sleep* (1946), *The Treasure of the Sierra
Madre* (1948), and *Key Largo* (1948)—that were not only hits at the time but
are still commonly cited as among the best American movies. These rich
and engaging pictures—three not coincidentally featuring Bacall—epito-
mized Bogart's popularity in the 1940s and laid the foundation for his rise
to cultural icon by the early 1960s.

Typical of the studio system, the jewels appeared within a steady work-
load in which Bogart, like many major stars, often made three pictures
annually. All contributed to his forties star image: tough yet vulnerable,
laconic but wry, urban prole and democratic everyman. Arriving in Hollywood near the end of the studio period, Bacall made only five movies
before 1950, four with Bogart. Director Howard Hawks, who discovered
her, claimed he sought to create "a girl who is insolent, as insolent as Bogart, who insults people, who grins when she does it" (McBride 100).
Though this was not Bacall's typical persona beyond her two Hawks/Bogart
outings, it initiated a long and far more varied career. Still, in the latter half
of the forties, while Bogart remained a movie star, "Bogie and Baby"
became a phenomenon once the public responded in delight to their
romantic and sexual chemistry, overwhelming *To Have and Have Not*. The
roles they played and the images they projected separately and together
reflect the evolution of the Hollywood industry and its changing place in
American culture during this crucial decade.

Bogart's star-making performance as a doomed gangster in *High Sierra*
(1941) neatly bridged the first and second decades of his career. Through
the combination of a talented actor's ambition and studio design, Bogart's
hardened crooks of the thirties were reshaped into sympathetic and compelling figures. At just this point the war began, his cool strength enliven-
ing some of the conflict's most enduring Hollywood artifacts. Shortly before
Pearl Harbor, his new image helped define the hard-boiled private eye in
The Maltese Falcon, and then varied it after the war as *The Big Sleep* was ex-
tensively reworked to add interplay with Bacall. Moreover, that genre's
importance in feeding the diverse streams of what we now call film noir
soon granted the star roles that not only undercut heroic authority but also

revealed its obverse in movies such as *Dark Passage* (1947) and *Dead Reckoning* (1947). These major strains of Bogart's persona often intermingled with complex and always engaging results.

☆☆☆☆★ From Duke to Earle

That Bogart's first movie released in the forties was *Virginia City* (1940), a western starring Errol Flynn, tells us everything and nothing about his career to this point or what he would soon become. As in his only other Warner Bros. western, *The Oklahoma Kid* (1939), Bogie projects a sinister, big-city toughness, looking as out of place in a cowboy hat as fellow gunslinger James Cagney, though that quintessential urban ethnic star of the thirties could at least draw on his dancer's grace to sit atop a horse comfortably. For contemporary audiences, the familiar aspect of Bogart's roles was that he played the outlaw, the bad guy fated to be gunned down by the stars. No matter that these climactic shootings took place in the rocky desert or a saloon rather than the whisky warehouse or prison yard. Once again he was billed second or third behind the major stars, playing a violent, small-time crook.

In 1934, after struggling for four years in small parts at Fox and other studios, Bogart had left Hollywood in frustration and returned to the New York stage. There he landed the role of gangster Duke Mantee in the Broadway production of Robert E. Sherwood's *The Petrified Forest*. Slouching yet tense, wearing beard stubble and a cold, hard look, his entrance was reportedly electrifying. When Warner Bros. sought to make a movie version in 1936, Leslie Howard, star of the play, insisted, against some resistance, that Bogart reprise Mantee. The movie proved a success and the actor's strong notices won his first long-term contract with the studio (Sperber and Lax 44–47, 50–53). Despite getting his break in a prestige movie where he played a complex character, Bogart was quickly typecast as a ruthless gangster and killer who could be slotted into most any crime story regardless of merit or budget.

Still, over the next four years, Bogie's career trajectory was typical for a second-rank contract star—lead roles in B-pictures (such as *Isle of Fury* [1936] and *Crime School* [1938]); plum supporting parts in prestige efforts (*Dead End* [1937]); and lots of character work in assorted genre movies including westerns, social problem pictures (*Black Legion* [1937]), woman's pictures (*Men Are Such Fools* [1938]), and (rare for Warner Bros.) a horror film (*The Return of Dr. X* [1939]). The premise of this system was that if you persevered and honed your craft, you would be ready if called upon to star in an A-picture. Before this happy circumstance occurred with *High Sierra*, Bogart wasn't always a crook or killer but he played this part often and never completely shook the image. Instead, through the films subsequently tailored for him, Bogart skillfully deepened and adapted that criminal tough guy into a sympathetic, world-weary figure able but never eager to use violence. Add the romantic attention of Ida Lupino, Mary Astor, Ingrid Bergman, or Bacall and a fascinating star emerged.

Bogart's supporting part as a struggling independent trucker in *They Drive By Night* (1940) made a crucial contribution to his impending breakthrough. As usual, George Raft, Ann Sheridan, and Ida Lupino were all billed ahead of him. Raoul Walsh helmed a generally typical Warner Bros. social problem film, the hard-edged and unsentimental kind at which the studio had excelled since the early days of the Depression. Raft worked hard and dreamed big for himself and younger brother Bogart, whose self-effacing character had more modest dreams of a home for a wife he adored. Even when he tilts into anger and apathy after a crash that costs him an arm, the movie stays rooted in the hard times still not quite ended. Bogie's tragedy is only marginally worse than the everyday misery of those around him, like dead-end diner waitress Sheridan or fellow driver Roscoe Karns, the smiling king of every pinball table along the highway but just another anonymous loser in the economic game. "These fellows are the Okies of the trucking business," the *Brooklyn Eagle* observed (Herbert Cohn, "Grown-Up Films Arrive at N.Y. Strand and Roxy," 29 July 1940).[1]

Audiences were lured by an advertising campaign pushing sex: "*They Drive By Night . . .* and *anything* can happen at night!" winked many ads; or, "What do you think happens when George Raft meets Ann Sheridan? Well, it does!" The social problem formula often included sensationalism and tawdry sex, yet promotion emphasized the latter to the point of distorting the plot to pair Bogart with Lupino's character: "Yes! It's true. George Raft tangles with Ann Sheridan who out-claws Ida Lupino who turns on Humphrey Bogart." No, it isn't. They never even have a scene together, yet ads picture Bogie kissing Lupino or lighting her cigarette off his. Even without a gun or snarl this time, Bogart was a familiar face and could not be simply left out even while playing a secondary part.

Yet Bogart's professionalism did not go unnoticed as it indicated his range. In a glowing review, the *Hollywood Reporter* observed: "George Raft and Humphrey Bogart, always two tough guys in any picture, are still tough, but they are given some softness in their roles in this show, and to fine effect. Both of them handle their new touches excellently and we believe audiences will rally plenty of praises for their performances" (9 July

1940). Such reviews on top of a solid record helped boost Bogart into *High Sierra* after Raft refused the part—that and the timely parting between Warner Bros. and one of its major stars of the thirties, Paul Muni, who angrily quit the studio in July 1940 because they wanted another Scarface rather than his dream project of a Beethoven biopic. Bogart had already seen the potential of *High Sierra*'s Roy Earle for his career and actively sought the part—his familiar gangster figure but one with the shrewd mind of Duke Mantee plus the crucial benefit of audience sympathy. Others already agreed.

With Muni gone and highly positive trade reviews in for *They Drive By Night*, S. Charles Einfeld, director of advertising and publicity for Warner Bros., set to work crafting the studio's newest star. Writing to his associate Martin Weiser on 17 July 1940, Einfeld momentously ordered: "I want you to give the utmost concentration to the building of Humphrey Bogart to stardom in as quick a time as possible. Bogart has been typed through publicity as a gangster character. We want to undo this." Lest we assume a cynical publicity apparatus could make a gullible public accept anything, Einfeld recognized that the actor's recent work helped make this a natural progression, citing the depth and variety of Bogart's roles in *Dark Victory* (1939), *It All Came True* (1940), and the new trucker picture: "In 'Dark Victory' he showed a type of sex appeal that was unusual and different from that of any other actor on the screen today." Weiser's marching orders were clear: "Sell Bogart romantically. Sell him as a great actor. . . . This is one of the most important jobs you have before you in the next few months."[2] Fresh from her scene-stealing triumph in *They Drive By Night*, Ida Lupino got top billing over Bogart in *High Sierra*, but it was the last time anyone ever did. As the tough but vulnerable Marie, who abandons the two "boys" fighting over her as she is drawn to the mature authority of Bogart's Roy Earle, Lupino was the first of several strong, savvy women who would both soften and amplify his romantic appeal in movies to come.

As Einfeld had directed, the *High Sierra* press book took the offensive, shifting Bogart's image to emphasize his superior acting. An advance feature prepared for newspapers began, "Humphrey Bogart is strictly a nonconformist. Up to now his life has been a constant fight against doing the expected thing. . . . He likes to play 'hard guys' but not cardboard caricatures of gangsters. He insists they be believable, three-dimensional personalities." Moreover, *High Sierra* is positioned as a prestige picture built on Bogart's performance by evoking recent award-winning adaptations of John Steinbeck: "Earle has an earthy, believable quality about him. . . . In fact, Bogart would have liked to have played Tom Joad in 'The Grapes of

Wrath' or George in 'Of Mice and Men.' He believes that the contemporary scene is the most interesting source of dramatic material" (*High Sierra* Press Book 9).[3] Another item claims Bogart's preparation includes study of real criminals: "Bogart says that the practice of many underworld characters of speaking out of the corner of their mouths is based on the fact that men who have served time in prison [that is, like Roy Earle] get in the habit of conversing that way to keep guards from seeing them talking." Convenient how the actor's observation meshes perfectly with his own typical speaking style in assorted roles before and after this one. Other publicity items point up the romance with Lupino and note that Joan Leslie "figures prominently in a brief but important episode that helps set up the human side of the character Bogart plays."

Raoul Walsh introduces Roy Earle as he is released from prison, looking aged with whitened temples and gaunt features yet still confidently hooking his thumbs in his waistband to hitch up his pants, one of Bogie's stock gestures. But after a long jail stretch, he doesn't yearn for a bottle or a woman but instead heads to the nearest public park where a smiling walk among trees and sunlight signals his soul's liberation. Roy Earle is at heart a man of the soil, a Jeffersonian yeoman, revealed when he makes a sentimental journey to his lost family farm and points the new owner's son to the sweetest fishing spot in the creek. In Huck Finn overalls and straw hat, the smiling boy mirrors Roy as a child. The fictional Earle was the last of the grass-roots gangsters like "Pretty Boy" Floyd, Bonnie and Clyde, and Ma Barker—heartland criminals made into romantic outlaws by the combination of hard times ("You from the bank?" the farmer asks nervously when the stranger appears) and J. Edgar Hoover's media-crafted counter-myth of the heroic G-man. Roy, we learn, had once run with John Dillinger, the badman brought down by the FBI in Chicago in 1934, just outside a theater showing a gangster movie with Clark Gable; and he seethes when a rabid press dubs him "Mad Dog" Earle after the hotel robbery in which he kills a deputy. As Bogart had modeled Duke Mantee's wardrobe on photos of Dillinger, so history, myth, and Hollywood were converging and reflecting each other here.

But Earle remains a hard and dangerous man, memorably shown when he warns the nervous hotel clerk, inside-man of the heist, about the price of ratting by telling of another crook who talked too much. Fixing the clerk with a stare, Roy explains how a gangster cradling a tommy gun in his lap "just touched the trigger a little and the gun went [tap-tap-tap]," he says drumming index and middle fingers on the gun case, "and the rat fell out of his chair." The bullet-spewing weapon that fires just three lethal rounds

The love of a strong woman (Ida Lupino) makes gangster Roy Earle put away his gun in *High Sierra* (1941), the role that made Bogart a major star. Copyright 1941, Warner Bros. Pictures, Inc.

parallels the controlled violence behind Roy's terse account. The star's physical transitions drive the characterization. At Earle's most criminally professional, Bogart tends to keep his arms straight to his side and his shoulders hunched forward to convey wariness and coiled strength—the basic ticks he had used as Duke Mantee including the lowered jaw and hard stare of his wide, dark eyes. But in the poignant or romantic scenes with the crippled girl to whom he is drawn or similarly relaxed moments with Lupino, Bogart adopts the mannerisms we know from his most famous roles—the comfortable slouch punctuated by reflexive lifts of his shoulders, the teeth-baring grin, and dry laugh. He varies these modes throughout this, one of his most intense and convincing performances. When a police sniper finally shoots Roy Earle off a mountain ledge, even a weeping Marie and a whimpering terrier clinging to the body can't reduce it to melodrama.

On the edge of this breakout at the end of 1940 (*High Sierra* had been enthusiastically press-screened prior to its general release in January of the new year), the fan magazine *Modern Screen* lavishly profiled Bogart in an article "Bad Boy Makes Good." The molding of the star's offscreen image first took a common tack, stressing that the movie tough guy is a thoroughly ordinary fellow, one who enjoys a steak, likes to sail and take photographs, and is happily married to his third wife, Mayo Methot. She accompanies him to the interview and is pictured on the first page posing in a lawn chair with their dog, while in a larger image Bogie prepares to snap a photo. (Never mind that they were already widely known in gossip columns as "The Battling Bogarts.") But the story's more important aim was separating Bogart's new star image from Paul Muni's persona.

The writer claims that "wags are now calling him Humphrey 'Weisenfreund' (Muni's real name). Wig manufacturers and purveyors of false beards, egged on by pranksters, are sending him samples of their wares. Everyone's wondering if he's going to start stealing Muni's stuff" (*Modern Screen*, December 1940, 32). The story makes clear that Bogie will be his own man—nothing like the now implicitly hammy Muni whose act may have depended too heavily on props and costumes, his dismissal sealed by unmasking even his Jewish surname. Against such evident calculation, Bogart points to the fallibility of his own career hunches: "Why, I'm the guy who thought 'They Drive By Night' would be a lousy picture and the script for 'The Roaring Twenties' was no good!" (32–33). Still, publicity versions of the actor's "real" life cannot stray too far from the onscreen persona without a confusing dissonance. The contrast with the theatrically large (and feminized) Paul Muni and his beloved biopics is further amplified by assurances that Bogart will not only continue to play but be a contemporary tough guy because he has done so seemingly all his life: "I never played theatre as a kid, and I didn't like boys who did. They were sissies."

As the new decade began, screen detectives like Charlie Chan (Fox), Sherlock Holmes (Universal), and Boston Blackie (Columbia) were flourishing in the lowly series format. *The Maltese Falcon*, directorial debut of *High Sierra* screenwriter John Huston, was an A-picture, albeit a modestly budgeted one elevated by casting and treatment. Rotund Sydney Greenstreet got a Best Supporting Actor nomination but Mary Astor, Peter Lorre, and Elisha Cook Jr. prove equally vivid foils for Bogart's Sam Spade in performances that seemed to bring out the best in all. Warner Bros. had already filmed Dashiell Hammett's 1930 novel twice, grabbing its mystery plot and neglecting the book's sharp and witty dialogue—the feature Huston's script emphasizes. In a crime movie with little action and few locations, Bogart and the ensemble cast shine in scenes where every exchange between characters is a wary dance of gambits, insults, and lies alternately couched in tough talk and wry sophistication. A production less about "the stuff that dreams are made of" than the joy of performance itself ("the play's the thing" might have been a more pertinent Shakespearean quote) often finds the actors struggling to contain their obvious delight with the material and each other. Nominated for Best Picture, *The Maltese Falcon* cemented Bogart's stardom and launched Huston's long directing career.

Roy Earle had humanized Bogie's gangster but he was still a killer. In the star's first major outing as the hero, he remains dangerous and not completely sympathetic, a cunning shamus often only a bit more trustworthy than the pack of thieves and killers out for the black bird. Some ads indeed announced, "'Killer' Bogart, a guy without a conscience . . . Moves in on Mary Astor, a dame without a heart!" closely describing both characters. Spade admits to an affair with his late partner's wife and itches to be rid of her as easily as he orders Miles Archer's name taken off what is now the door of his office alone. Ultimately honest, Bogart's Spade carries a streak of sadism, too. He clearly enjoys hitting Lorre's fey Joel Cairo ("When you're slapped, you'll take it and like it") and baiting Elisha Cook's Wilmer with homosexual taunts, though subdued here by the Production Code.

What of selling Bogart romantically? Some publicity shots and poster images depict him pointing two guns and then with his hands closing around Astor's neck: "He's a killer when he hates. And even more dangerous when he loves." The plot reveals Brigid O'Shaughnessy to be a murderer and perhaps the worst of the villains, but it remains startling to see Bogart about to strangle a woman. The press book, however, devotes a full page to answering a key question for exhibitors, "Do tough guys have sex appeal?" then readily responding, "Bogart's screen love life proves they do." Shots of Bogie and recent leading ladies ring the page emphasizing his "rough and ready approach," though his manner is varied to appeal broadly: "In this clinch with Mary Astor . . . Bogart proves there's nothing wrong with his kissing technique"; "in 'High Sierra' he lands Ida Lupino . . . with his tough but tender love-making"; "in 'They Drive by Night' his light o' love was gentle Gale Page," etc. Finally, above a small cartoon of a postman burdened by a huge sack trailing hearts and tagged "Humphrey Bogart," the copy asserts, "Although his approach to love-making is seldom gentle, he has made love to some of the screen's most glamorous ladies. . . . Do they love it?" As proof the company claims, "Over 75% of Bogart's fan mail, which is among the heaviest at the Warner Bros. studios, comes from women."

★★★★★ *Aux Armes!*

Even setting aside the landmark *Casablanca*, Bogart enjoyed perhaps the most interesting and varied onscreen enlistment of any major

star of the World War II years. Besides moving from isolation to commitment at Rick's Café Americain, then doing it again between sexy banter
with Bacall in *To Have and Have Not*, Bogart's battles with the Axis spanned
the conflict: reprising and spoofing his gangster roles while foiling German
saboteurs in New York in *All Through the Night* (1942); going undercover
from the army to fight Japanese plotters in *Across the Pacific* (1942); sailing
against U-boats in *Action in the North Atlantic* (1943); commanding a tank in
North Africa in *Sahara* (1943); and finally becoming a Free French airman
in the convoluted *Passage to Marseille* (1944). The star's newly refined image
synchronized with the historical moment. Tough guys were plentiful, but
Bogart's particular mixture of strength and cool confidence, his ironic
humor, and courage without bravado would be recognizable and, for American moviegoers, welcome responses to the immensity of global war.

Pearl Harbor and the rapid collapse of U.S. forces in the Philippines sent
Americans into shock that only began to lift after the first victory over the
Japanese navy at Midway in June 1942. As fascist expansion reached its
height, public fear and suspicion fed an outpouring of frantic, paranoid
movies about spies, saboteurs, and fifth columnists loose on the home front.
(The Japanese American internment in March was the tragic manifestation
of this panic.) The cycle encodes a paradoxical sense that a helpless America
was crawling with enemy agents yet shows them easily thwarted. Bogart
entered the fray in *All Through the Night*, an oddball blend of gangster and spy
adventure with comedy, action, and a couple of songs. An almost palpable
sense of experimentation appears here and in other fifth column movies
whose clashing mix of tones and genres bespeaks near total uncertainty
about how to treat the onset of war. Bogie's mob stumbles onto a Nazi cell
led by Conrad Veidt and Peter Lorre scheming to blow up a battleship in New
York harbor. The film features corny Runyonesque dialogue and well-staged
fights, including one between Bogart and a Nazi on a shadowy freight eleva-
tor that would impress in a straight crime drama. In all, a lot of talent is on
display in a strange yet well-received effort that affirmed Bogart's new status.

The press book assured exhibitors, "With Bogart in your billing you've
got the male star at your theatre that says 'excitement' more than any other
name in Hollywood. 'Maltese Falcon' proved that conclusively as anything
further we can say." Once more, ads depicted "'Killer' Bogart" clutching a
pair of .45s, this time with a smile to signal a spoof and because now "He's
gunning after the Gestapo!" The *Philadelphia Inquirer* called the premise "an
irresistibly funny idea and the [audience] laughed itself hoarse over it yesterday" (22 January 1942). Yet attesting to the star's broadening appeal, the
Lincoln Journal and Star's strong review noted that previously "it has always

been as hard in Lincoln to arouse much interest in Humphrey Bogart as a star as it is possible to put magnetism into many others of the same, or even lesser importance. Bogart is of the hard-bitten, up-from-the-slums school, and that may be the reason for his lack of acceptance in the Midwest where the slums are not a big factor of community life" (15 February 1942). The *Los Angeles Examiner*'s Dorothy Manners called Bogart "a weakness of mine— and a couple of million other women," indicating that Einfeld's romantic pitch was succeeding (16 January 1942). Bogart took the fight to the enemy in another concocted fantasy, Huston's *Across the Pacific*, about a Japanese raid to destroy the Panama Canal, this time played straight. Posters depict Bogie delivering a satisfying punch to a Japanese gunman, and although the movie portrays a fully assimilated Nisei as a traitor, it treats Imperial naval officers without condescension as dangerous opponents. In reuniting Bogart with Mary Astor and Sydney Greenstreet in an exotic (studio-built) locale, it looked ahead to *Casablanca*'s combination of wartime romance and intrigue.

While some studio movies that inspired cult-like devotion in later years like *The Wizard of Oz* (1939) or *Citizen Kane* (1941) were not so well received in their day, *Casablanca* was a critical and commercial hit from its first press screening to its national release and Academy Award for Best Picture. Some accounts have suggested the deeply satisfying film was a happy accident, but *Casablanca* was a studio product in the best sense of the term, the harmonious blending of resources and professionals doing some of their best work. Though the film has a distinctive look, a bit misty and soft-focus to suggest idealization and memory rather than gritty immediacy, most remembered are the performances by Bogart and a great cast and a tightly constructed and eminently quotable script. This despite, or perhaps because, six different writers labored to turn an unproduced play into an A-picture; veteran producer Hal Wallis assigned writers to aspects of the story in which they specialized: Phillip and Julius Epstein spun the witty lines, making Bogart's insolence endearing in its direction toward the vain and cruel ("I do [know who you are], you're lucky the bar's open to you"; "Are my eyes really brown?"). Casey Robinson (*Now, Voyager* [1942]) punched up the romantic scenes. Howard Koch worked on the timely political material that in recent decades has been downplayed in favor of celebrating the movie as the apotheosis of the Bogart image or even Old Hollywood itself (Harmetz 35–60). This may account for its lasting appeal but for viewers in 1942–1943, *Casablanca*'s particular mediation of the war experience was its central feature.

The invasion of North Africa on 8 November 1942 fortuitously publicized the movie because when it opened for a limited release in New York on Thanksgiving, Allied forces occupied the Moroccan city. "The Army's got

Casablanca—And so have Warner Bros.!" cried press books with joy. Even more fortunate for the studio, the movie's general release on 23 January 1943 coincided with the Casablanca conference between Roosevelt, Churchill, and de Gaulle. But such historical coincidence would have been meaningless without a powerful and moving film, the first shaped for Bogart rather than handed to him after bigger stars refused. Tough yet vulnerable, cynical yet honest would be central to this role. The female lead of the play *Everybody Comes to Rick's* was a shady American divorcee named Lois, but the European Ilsa Lund, played by the shimmeringly beautiful Ingrid Bergman, allowed their romance to allegorize the moment—Rick Blaine was America, the wounded idealist who would do right for Ilsa, Victor Laszlo, and himself despite his misery. Before lamenting "all the gin joints in all the towns in all the world," with tears glistening, Rick's famous drunk scene has him asking, "If it's December 1941 in Casablanca, what time is it in New York?" "My watch stopped," Sam (Dooley Wilson) replies, drawing together Rick's bitter memory of lost love and the national halt at the war's outbreak. "I'll bet they're asleep in New York. I'll bet they're asleep all over America." Many wartime movies contain clumsily inserted and delivered propaganda while Rick's many denials—"I stick my neck out for nobody," "The problems of the world are not in my department," "I'm the only cause I'm interested in"—grew from the character and only made the audience long for the decent man to act for the larger good. The existential sadness in Bogart's eyes conveyed how Rick finally accepted that for all life's pain and disappointments, there were still values worth fighting for, sacrifices worth making. "Ilsa, I'm no good at being noble . . ." No, he's great at it.

Every aspect of Bogart's now perfected star image—strong, tender, cool, a man of action—appeared in the climax, no less effective dramatically for having been hard to achieve. The Epstein brothers, Koch, and Wallis all contributed to the ending, which contrary to many reports always included some version of Lois/Ilsa leaving with Laszlo. Above all, the war required sacrifice. Everything had to be done right here, however. In one filming of the final confrontation with Major Strasser (Conrad Veidt), Bogart ad-libbed the line, "Alright, Major, you asked for it," pulling his gun and firing. It's a traditional western showdown but an ideological problem for the film. Rick has just become a reluctant hero and as much as he detests the Nazi, he couldn't shoot first and preserve his recouped stature. Among Hal Wallis's final instructions to director Michael Curtiz was to retake this shot without the dialogue (which survives in the film's original theatrical trailer) and establish that Strasser draws first (Harmetz 238). Rick's confident stroll into the fog with Captain Louis Renault (the invaluable Claude Rains) to join a

Free French garrison anticipated Bogart's subsequent war pictures where he donned a uniform for combat; all were well made and successful productions, but none attained the lasting stature of *Casablanca*.

Bogart had joined the navy near the end of World War I, and was now too old for the military, so he could make macho war films without risk of the muttering directed at other male stars who stayed home. Upon release of *Action in the North Atlantic*, the *New York Herald Tribune* described his service, even noting he had accidentally gone AWOL once when his ship left port without him, though he still received an honorable discharge (16 May 1943). A tribute to the merchant marine seamen who delivered Lend-Lease supplies to Britain and the Soviet Union at great peril from German U-boats, the movie was a stoic portrait of men doing dangerous work and a showcase for Warner Bros.' highly regarded special effects department. From crewmen bobbing on a raft in a sea of flaming oil and debris after their ship is torpedoed to excellent miniatures and matte work, it may be the biggest-scale movie of Bogart's career, justified not only by momentous times but his new clout. The film had "all the ingredients of a smash action hit," opined *Box Office Digest*, "plus the money certainty that there is now in Humphrey Bogart's name hot on the heels of 'Casablanca'" (28 May 1943).

Made with the star on loan to Columbia, *Sahara* has Sergeant Joe Gunn's tank crew picking up Allied stragglers and mounting a tenacious last stand against a much larger German force. The ragtag unit includes several British, a South African, and a tough French trooper. The allegory of a democratic United Nations struggle against fascism, just the kind the federal Office of War Information (OWI) worked to encourage in Hollywood movies, is complete when Bogie rescues a smart Sudanese colonial soldier played by African American actor Rex Ingram and his humble Italian prisoner, then captures an arrogant Nazi pilot. Typical of wartime idealism, Sergeant Major Tambul (Ingram) and Waco Hoyt (Bruce Bennett) compare backgrounds and decide that even though one is black, Moslem, and African, the other white, Christian, and Texan, they are really mostly alike. From its Hollywood Boulevard office, OWI's Bureau of Motion Pictures, which sought to consult with the studios over war content, often with mixed results, hailed *Sahara* as "an outstanding contribution to the Government's War Information program." They especially liked the period's obligatory speech in which Bogart rallies the men to hold on: "The global character of the war and the heroism of ordinary people everywhere are brought home by Sergeant Gunn's speech when he says they will make a stand in order to delay the enemy, just as the people of London and Madrid and Chungking fought on in the face of overwhelming odds."[4]

Democracy's soldier: As Sgt. Joe Gunn, Bogart takes command of Allied stragglers and a Nazi prisoner in *Sahara* (1943). Copyright 1943, Columbia Pictures, Inc.

What the government analysts ignored in their enthusiasm for the preachy lines was how well they were put over by Bogart's skillful underplaying. Perhaps more effectively, the scene in which Sergeant Gunn confronts the smug pilot visually contrasts Nazi elitism with its antithesis. Even after bailing out over the desert and peeling off heavy flight coveralls, the German stands rigid and immaculate in a clean uniform, wearing medals and a sneer. He insults the group that has just downed him, directing racist slurs at Tambul. Alternating close-ups frame Bogart as democracy's soldier—slouching, sweating, unshaven, smoking, totally unimpressed, and in control: "Wipe that smile off your puss or I'll knock your teeth through the top of your head, *verstehes*?" In the war where American G.I.'s proudly called themselves "dog faces," who better than Humphrey Bogart to embody that common man ideal?

In November 1943, Bogart embarked on a morale-building USO tour, spending ten weeks visiting American troops in North Africa and Italy. The studios did their bit for the war but wanted full credit, too. Warner Bros. photographers took publicity shots of Bogart and Mayo Methot on the set of *Passage to Marseille* getting inoculations for their trip to the front lines.

They also planted amusing news items that played on Bogart's still potent association as a mobster, reporting that an "Arab street urchin" called him "you blankety-blank gangster!," a French waiter insulted Mayo over a linguistic misunderstanding, and the army misplaced their luggage. "'I need the entire mob to straighten all this out,' Bogart snarled, 'and I didn't even bring my gun, figuring it would be like bringing coals to Newcastle'" (*Los Angeles Evening Herald Express*, 20 December 1943).

Yet upon their return *Movie Star Parade* chronicled the trip in a 1944 article "Tough Guy Goes Tender," carefully acknowledging the human misery Bogart and Methot observed in the year American casualties would be the highest, and quietly stressing how welcome the Hollywood entertainers were for the diverting movie fantasies they provoked. The story opens with Bogart and Methot aboard an armored vehicle in Italy when an MP recognizes him and effortlessly falls into gangster shtick with the star: "'What's with Bugsy?' / 'He'll never beat the rap' . . . 'How about Mike?' / 'He hasn't been seen lately,' observed Bogart giving the inquirer a gimlet stare; 'And how's it going with McGurk?' muttered the sergeant playing the scene to the hilt. / 'He'll burn'" (June 1944, 25–26). Later, they visit wounded men in hospitals and see sobbing battle fatigue cases and a young soldier who had been their driver, now missing a leg. "Stubbed my toe," the kid says with a smile, in an episode shaped to convey indomitable courage while still preparing civilians for an awful reality.

In truth, the tour had been a moving experience, prompting the "Battling Bogarts" to call a semi-truce in their own hellish domestic war (Sperber and Lax 227–33). The piece ends with a final lesson for the home front: while driving in Hollywood, the couple "passed a loaded garbage truck. They observed with new clarity that the lettuce leaves were wilted, but green; that there were cauliflower greens piled high, and the shells of half-used oranges. 'In Italy,' [Mayo] said softly, 'that truck would be stripped of every particle before going a block.' 'Watch it,' growled the tough guy, 'or we'll both be singing *God Bless America*'"—still giving the "real" Bogart an in-character crack worthy of Sam Spade. Notably, the writer claims this incident occurred while the couple was en route to the studio where he was about to start filming *To Have and Have Not* (57).

★★★★★ Knowing How to Whistle

Born Betty Joan Perske in Brooklyn in 1924, Lauren Bacall's rise to stardom is well known. The lithe, lovely nineteen-year-old with arresting hazel eyes and air of precocious sophistication yearned to act and had worked as a fashion model before Nancy Raye "Slim" Gross, also a model and wife of director Howard Hawks, spotted her photo in *Harper's Bazaar* and told her husband this girl would be great in one of his movies. He agreed and placed Perske, now working as Betty Bacall, under personal contract. Soon after Hawks changed her name to Lauren Bacall, he introduced her to Bogart, producing "no clap of thunder," she says (Bacall 90). Hawks had an independent production deal with Warner Bros. and was planning to cast Bogart in *To Have and Have Not*, a free adaptation of a minor Hemingway novel. A shrewd judge of character, Bacall recognized that the acclaimed director of *Bringing Up Baby* (1938), *Sergeant York* (1941), and many other good films had much to teach her. Though wary of Hawks's attempts to manipulate her in assorted ways, she readily agreed with his idea that she work to lower her voice to give it a more unusual and confident, if sexually insinuating tone. Shortly before production, Bogart had seen her screen test and was now impressed. "We'll have a lot of fun together," he told her when they met again (Bacall 93).

To Have and Have Not can be grouped with Bogart's war films, but as it played the war was shoved into the background. Hemingway's novel was set in Cuba and involved a populist revolt against the right-wing Batista regime (Mast 246–51), but the film, in part a reworking of *Casablanca*, was set before Pearl Harbor in a Vichy-controlled colony, the French island of Martinique, a quick solution once the script was already started to avoid export trouble due to the government's "Good Neighbor Policy." Bogart is Harry Morgan, captain of a fishing boat who looks after a drunken pal, Eddie (Walter Brennan), and refuses to get involved when he is offered money to transport a French resistance fighter and his wife. Along the way he encounters Bacall's Marie Browning, a stranded American singing in a bar with piano player "Cricket" (Hoagy Carmichael). More like a sophisticated *All Through the Night* than another *Casablanca*, the loosely plotted story features clever dialogue, some great songs, some action, and the sizzling interplay of Bogart and Bacall.

Again, numerous hands (including William Faulkner's) worked on the script, producing Eddie's trademark challenge, "Wuz you ever bit by a dead bee?" to decide if someone is quick or lively enough to be a pal; the couple ruefully calling each other "Steve" and "Slim"; or Bacall's feigned jealousy of the French patriot's wife. When Slim emerges in a clingy black dress to sing, Harry notices but must leave to check on the wounded fighter hidden downstairs. "Give her my love," Bacall taunts. "I'd give her my own if she had *that* on," he retorts. But what came to be called "the whistle scene" made Bacall and the movie. She admits that her inexperience and nervousness

In love onscreen and off. A delighted Bogart and enraptured Bacall in a publicity shot for her screen debut in *To Have and Have Not* (1944). Copyright 1944, Warner Bros. Pictures, Inc.

contributed to what the studio soon promoted as "The Look"—the only way she could keep her jaw from trembling was to drop her chin and her voice even lower when she spoke. Marie and Harry have been sizing each other up, their barbs increasingly laden with sexual tension until she sits in his lap and kisses him. On the way out—not the first or last star launched by a great exit line—Bacall turns, long blond hair falling around her face and magnetic eyes. "You know, you don't have to act with me, Steve. You don't have to say anything and you don't have to do anything. . . . Oh, maybe just whistle. You know how to whistle, don't you, Steve? You just put your lips together and blow." Bogie contemplates this a moment, then lets out a long, low whistle followed by his familiar dry laugh, this time with a certain brightness in his eyes. The unforgettable scene became integral to the movie's promotion and reception.

Studio publicists routinely touted "bright new stars" and "discoveries," but here Einfeld and associates knew they had an authentic sensation. "Warner Bros. daringly teams a great star and a brilliant discovery," shouted the press book, with photos of a rapturous Bacall in the arms of Bogart, who can't quite manage passion for the smile on his lips. Ads and publicity items emphasize the whistle scene. In cut shots, Bacall leans in a doorframe with a cigarette, actually the pose from the pair's first meeting, with Bogart seated in the foreground as in the whistle scene. Others show Bacall lighting a cigarette and the line, "If you want anything just whistle." In tones admiring or near-prurient, most every review noted the scene, which was hot enough to be removed in Ohio, to the disdain of the *Cleveland Plain Dealer's* reviewer who saw it in New York: "I guess that by now you must know the Ohio censors have again saved our fair state from the sinful influence of Hollywood by lopping a little footage out of *To Have and Have Not*." "If crime or delinquency has increased in New York because of carelessness of that state's censors," the reviewer huffed, "no one . . . has said anything about it. But we're still pure" (2 February 1945). Even so, a Los Angeles columnist affirmed that Bacall's talent as an actress and not a fashion model had ensured her success: "Lauren Bacall . . . is a far better argument for stage training than cover girl glamour," noting that "it has been her knowing way with screenwriters' lines rather than those which nature endowed her that has made her a star of the first magnitude" (*Los Angeles Evening Herald Express*, 14 July 1945).

Press coverage of "the Battling Bogarts" had often used the term affectionately, implying a comically bickering couple that always make up, with the "hot-tempered" Irish wife whom Bogart nicknamed "Sluggy" a fitting mate for a tough guy. In truth, Bogart and Mayo frequently engaged in physical as well as savagely emotional combat fueled by alcohol, jealousy, and rage, and often in public. The marriage was crumbling well before he and Bacall fell in love. Still, after Bogart publicly announced he was leaving Mayo, he went back to her twice, the puzzled press reporting and resilient studio publicists selling each reversal. Yet even columnist Hedda Hopper, not a Bogart partisan, took a measured tone, noting "the marriage has weathered a number of storms" while quoting a weeping Mayo saying, "I don't want a big settlement . . . I don't want to do anything to hurt him" (*Los Angeles Times*, 4 December 1944). The young, sultry Bacall might have been painted as a gold-digger despite the studio's vigilant responses to the ongoing drama; Mayo was also an actress and could have played the offended victim to the end, though she soon bowed to the inevitable. Bogart's candor in the mainstream press probably helped. "I'm not the easiest guy in the world to live with," he admitted in an article announcing his engagement. "But I can't say . . . fighting is an extra, added attraction in any marriage. I don't want to end my life punch-drunk and walking on my heels." Of Bacall, he also spoke directly: "My engagement to Baby has nothing to do with this divorce" (*Los Angeles Examiner*, 31 January 1945). Perhaps most important, Bacall's vibrant debut in conjunction with Bogart's obvious delight with her onscreen and off fostered the public's embrace of their pairing.

In February 1945, with Bogie and Baby a sensation, Charles Einfeld arranged a publicity appearance for Bacall at a Washington Press Club luncheon. In attendance was Vice President Harry S. Truman, who gave one of his folksy piano recitals. Seeing gold, Einfeld had Bacall recline atop the upright piano, long legs sprawling and "The Look" at full intensity as Truman played. The photo ran across the country and drew some critical press for such a seemingly frivolous, even scandalous image associated with the vice president in wartime. Truman's beaming face suggests he really didn't mind (Sperber and Lax 299–300). The episode was familiar enough that Bogart could reference it at the start of *Dead Reckoning*. As a soldier accompanying a troubled buddy home to receive a medal at the White House, Bogart says of now President Truman, "Maybe he'll even let you sit on his piano," a self-conscious joke that would not come off as precious or arrogant given the couple's popularity.

Confidential Agent (1945), Bacall's sole forties effort without Bogart, inadvertently became her second movie after Warner Bros. purchased her contract from Hawks and held up release of *The Big Sleep*. It drew mixed reviews, the most negative unfairly directed at Bacall, who actually has a secondary part (Sperber and Lax 320–322). Charles Boyer plays a Spanish Republican agent sent to Britain in 1937 to buy coal to keep it from the hands of the fascist side. Bacall, the blasé daughter of an English capitalist, befriends him.

The studio wanted to keep Bacall, now Mrs. Bogart after their May 1945 wedding, before the public, yet the plot and tone of *Confidential Agent* were not conducive to romance between Boyer and Bacall. (The film ends with the couple half-heartedly together, but audiences knew they were returning to a war-torn Spain where the fascists would soon triumph anyway.) More or less blatant misrepresentation became the solution: "Watch her lips answer the call when Charles Boyer whistles for Lauren Bacall!" The press book accompanies a shot of the osculating couple with images of a woman whispering in the ear of another who looks shocked: "Confidentially, all you have to tell 'em is that Boyer loves Bacall in *Confidential Agent* but here's an all out campaign that tells 'em everything!," playfully implying that Bacall is already cheating on Bogart and tacitly urging exhibitors to sell a romance the movie cannot really deliver. A similar ad acknowledged the heavy press and fan magazine reporting devoted to the Bogarts' recent nuptials: "Confidential: Be on the lookout for a dangerous man who answers to the name of Charles Boyer . . . when last observed he was in the arms of (get *this*, folks) Lauren Bacall." The movie quickly disappeared, leaving Bacall angry and embarrassed (Bacall 147–48).

Reviewing Raymond Chandler's first novel, *The Big Sleep*, in 1939, the *Los Angeles Times* offered a prescient suggestion: "Humphrey Bogart's first starring vehicle is here, readymade, if his sponsors have sense enough to grab it" (19 February 1939, 3:6).[5] Howard Hawks began shooting in October 1944. In mid-1945, military audiences in the Pacific previewed a first cut of *The Big Sleep*, giving it a lukewarm reception. By that point, everyone knew how to whistle, Bogie and Baby had wed, and the studio considered this version promising but still unfinished, particularly after the poor performance of *Confidential Agent*. Now intent on boosting Bacall and repeating the excitement of the couple's first pairing, Hawks and his cast went back to the studio in January 1946 and shot several new scenes between the stars and reshot a few others. Eighteen minutes of footage was scrapped and replaced with sixteen minutes of new or redone material (Thomson 54–59). The final version was released to strong reviews in August 1946. *The Big Sleep* is less tightly constructed than *The Maltese Falcon* though each scene sparkles individually, Bacall making Bogart's Marlowe more relaxed and sympathetic than Sam Spade. The script took much of the terse, ironic dialogue from the novel, with Phillip Epstein's new scenes echoing Chandler's verve while giving the stars some tart exchanges, particularly when Marlowe and Bacall's Vivian Sternwood speculate on each other's sexual prowess amid a seeming discussion of horse racing.

The necessity of strengthening Bacall's role was even more pressing with several charismatic women in supporting parts, each of whom holds her own with Bogart. Hawks cast and directed actors superbly, nowhere more evident than with Martha Vickers as sexy Carmen Sternwood, Dorothy Malone's smart and aggressively available bookstore clerk, and Sonia Darrin's brassy Agnes, impatiently brighter and tougher than her

Detective Phillip Marlowe and Vivian Sternwood amuse themselves bantering with a confused policeman in a new scene added to *The Big Sleep* in early 1946. Copyright 1946, Warner Bros. Pictures, Inc.

wise-guy boyfriend. Transposed into the crime genre, the major shifts in gender roles the war required and abetted produced strong, scheming women and weaker men neurotic often to the point of sexual and romantic obsession. Film noir thrived on such gender disruptions. Though *The Maltese Falcon* and *The Big Sleep* are often grouped in this retrospectively identified genre, neither is a particularly good example, not only because they lack the form's baroque visual style, but because of Bogart's unwavering moral authority. The world is corrupt, but neither of his ironic, self-assured detectives, variations of his winning star persona, ever is. In fact, Hawks removed Chandler's dark ending in which Marlowe, remaining aloof from Vivian, helps cover up Carmen's drug-addled murder of her sister's husband and declares, "I was part of the nastiness now." Hawks's couple is typically provisional—"I guess I'm in love with you," they say to each other on either end of a scene near the climax, the sentiments tossed off between expository lines—but it's Bogie and Bacall so we believe them.

Helping promote release of *The Big Sleep*, the unfettered ids of Warner Bros.' fabled animation department produced the cartoon salute *Bacall to Arms* (1946), in which a horny wolf goes to the movies to see "Bogie Gocart" and "Laurie Bee Cool" in a picture slyly titled "To Have, To Have, To Have—." The images are black and white, yet when slinky Laurie crosses the floor, red and yellow flames trail behind her. The parody again conflates the duo's first encounter with the whistle scene. "Anybody got a light?" Laurie says inclined in the doorframe as taciturn Bogie hurls a huge blowtorch at her, which she easily catches to spark her cigarette. And when the animated Bee Cool asks if Bogie (cleaning a .45, not the fishing reel of the movie) knows how to whistle, the enraptured wolf nearly blows down the screen from his seat. It was a fitting as well as funny tribute to one of the genuinely hottest stars and debuts of the 1940s.

★★★★★ Noir Postwar

Among many off-kilter moments now in *All Through the Night* is Bogart reading enemy documents and asking the female lead, playing an anti-Nazi German, "Where's this place, d-a-c-h-a-u?" Fittingly, the star was a paratrooper returning home at the start of the crime thriller *Dead Reckoning*, but now the country and the world were different. One risk of making political art is that artists may suffer if the political climate changes, which indeed happened swiftly after the official *E pluribus unum* high of the war years. Accomplished screenwriters denounced as "anti-American" in 1947, like Communist Party member John Howard Lawson, who wrote *Action in the North Atlantic* and *Sahara*, had in fact scripted some of the most stirring, blood-and-thunder combat films of the war. In the former, after Bogart's ship fights off German seaplanes, they finally approach Murmansk. The roar of engines overhead again startles them until a seaman calls out, "I think they're on our side! No, they're ours alright!" and we see Cyrillic lettering and a dark star on the fuselage of a Soviet fighter. The Russian plane, with its smiling pilot flashing a V-sign, was indeed "ours," an ally in 1943. But four years later this scene and the last where Soviet dock workers and American seamen exchange happy shouts of "*Tovarich!*" became evidence for some that Hollywood movies were spewing communist propaganda (Cogley 11–13, 211–12).[6] Bogart would be wounded in the political fighting.

Hollywood was already polarized by the House Un-American Activities Committee's investigation of the film industry in October 1947. Livid, John Huston and other liberal industry figures formed the Committee for the First Amendment and went to Washington more to oppose the government's interrogation of individual political beliefs than to support the communist writers and directors who became known as the Hollywood Ten. Members of the group included Danny Kaye, Gene Kelly, and Mr. and Mrs. Humphrey Bogart. In the aftermath of the cynical hearings, the combative conduct of The Ten, and conciliatory or toothless statements of industry leaders, public opinion began to turn against Hollywood's liberal-left as the Cold War's chilliest years began. At the peak of his popularity, Bogart had been prominent in the coverage. An often-published photo showed the Hollywood contingent crossing a Washington street, the Bogarts in the lead (Ceplair and Englund 279–92). The group headed back home, making other public appearances en route as newspapers around the country began to criticize Bogart in particular as either naïve or politically suspect, an advocate of traitors, not free speech.

In late 1946, Bogart had negotiated a new contract that gave him more money, approval of scripts and directors, and freedom to pursue outside projects annually as an independent producer-star (Sperber and Lax 333–34). Accordingly, he was subjected to heavy pressure from Warner Bros. to distance himself from The Ten and finally did so in a public statement in Chicago on 3 December. He had negotiated conditions in which he would not denounce the Committee for the First Amendment or any individuals. He would only admit to having made "a mistake." The statement said in part, "I went to Washington because I thought fellow Americans were being deprived of their constitutional rights, and for that reason alone. That the trip was ill advised, even foolish, I am very ready to admit. . . . I have absolutely no use for communism nor for anyone who serves that philosophy. I am an American. And very likely, like a good many of the rest of you, sometimes a foolish and impetuous American." In full panic, the Hollywood publicity machine required another statement through the fan press. A regretful account of his Washington trip also ran as a by-lined article in the March 1948 issue of *Photoplay*, with a photo of a somber Bogart covered by the title, "I'm No Communist" (Sperber and Lax 387–98).

The Blacklist period was nothing if not maddeningly capricious. Bogart's relatively quick retraction saved his career and Bacall's, but evidently exacted a heavy psychic price, resulting from the double bind that affected everyone touched by the paranoia, baseless accusations, and guilt by association. Smug editorial headlines read, "Actors Are Wilting" and "Tough Guy Waves Flag"; while the *Washington Post*, which had criticized the hearings, said of Bogart, "He had nothing at all to be ashamed of until he began to be ashamed" (Sperber and Lax 398–99). Bogart's statement is hard for the star's admirers to read. It seems impossible that Rick Blaine or Sergeant Joe Gunn would have done this. But the episode draws a quick, painful distinction between an idealized and admirable screen persona and the mere human actor who created it.

The month before the Washington hearings saw the release of *Dark Passage*, the third of four pairings of Bogart and Bacall. Director Delmer Daves adapted the screenplay from a novel about a man wrongly imprisoned for murdering his wife who escapes and undergoes plastic surgery to change his face. Bacall's character, whose father died in prison after a false conviction, helps him. The distorted visuals typical of film noir dominate in the subjective camera used for Bogart's character in the first act, and as the director frames San Francisco locations to create an aura of despair in a sunny, beautiful city—one home to a creepy, back-alley surgeon you wouldn't want near your face with a knife. Bogart and Bacall strike just the right notes of hope and resignation as people keep dying around them. While the tale ends with the couple happily escaped to South America, it feels appropriately unbelievable as everything before has spelled entrapment and doom. The movie drew mixed reviews but did good business, which dropped after the couple's publicized foray into politics.

Before the Washington fiasco, Bogart and Huston had gone to Mexico to shoot *The Treasure of the Sierra Madre*, one of the first of what would become a postwar and post-studio era trend of major stars tackling ambitious roles that undercut or reversed their familiar personae. As Fred C. Dobbs, Bogart is a feckless, greedy coward who teams with two other depleted losers to search for gold in the mountains of Mexico. Now he fascinates by dint of his character's sneaky intensity. Tim Holt and the director's father, Walter Huston, are equally strong, the latter also playing a character far removed from his stern, dignified figures of the past. The movie proves again that for all his star power, Bogart was an exceptionally good ensemble player, at his best when matched by accomplished performers around him. Released in early 1948, Huston's film was a critical and commercial hit nominated for Best Picture, and affirmed that Bogart's "foolishness" was forgiven.

Sierra Madre's gritty location shooting, harsh, ironic conclusion, and risky performances announced a new kind of Hollywood prestige movie, one built around psychologically complex characters in morally ambiguous terrain instead of the reverent treatment of canonized literary works. Still, John Huston directed Bogart and Bacall in *Key Largo*, a film somewhere between the two possibilities, that same year. The adaptation of Maxwell Anderson's play began as Huston's angry rejoinder to the HUAC hearings, though the plot and setting are not unlike *The Petrified Forest*. Edward G. Robinson plays a gangster who holes up in a Florida hotel during a hurricane, making prisoners of returning veteran Bogart, the wife of his dead army buddy (Bacall), and her infirm father-in-law (Lionel Barrymore). Huston wrote Robinson's Johnny Rocco as an implicit domestic fascist, an arrogant cynic eager not only for power but to sadistically dominate and destroy others. Bogie is a weary soldier who must fight one last battle, though he comes to the realization slowly. Bacall's role is limited, with little opportunity for the exchanges with her husband that made her a star. Largely confined to a single location, *Key Largo* could have been tendentious and boring, but the outstanding cast, featuring Claire Trevor's Oscar-winning turn as Rocco's sad, besotted moll, plus Karl Freund's moody cinematography and mobile camera, keeps it engaging. While some reviews accepted the film as another example of the Warner Bros. gangster tradition, it demonstrated Bogart's reach at the peak of his artistic power and box office appeal.

In the decade's final years, Bogart shot his first independent Santana Productions film, *Knock on Any Door* (1949), and his young wife briefly interrupted her career to give birth to the first of their two children. He also started work on Nicholas Ray's *In a Lonely Place* (1950), a movie whose reputation has grown on the strength of his performance. To have begun the decade miscast as a villainous cowboy and ended it playing a tormented screenwriter who may be a misogynistic killer—Sam Spade, Rick Blaine, and Fred C. Dobbs in between—describes a remarkable advance. Bacall never made another film with Bogart but went on to an acclaimed career in movies and theater. Their best moments together on screen were cultural documents of the 1940s, yet neither was defined by them. "Legends" are born of transcendence. Occasionally, the word carries some weight.

NOTES

1. Unless otherwise noted, all clippings of newspaper reviews cited, as well as original press books and other publicity material, were found in the "Publicity" file under the film's title in the Warner Bros. Archives, University of Southern California.

2. Martin Weiser Papers, folder 637, "Bogart, Humphrey" file, Margaret Herrick Library, Academy of Motion Picture Arts and Sciences, Beverly Hills, California.

3. Ironically, director Lewis Milestone had eagerly sought Bogart for George in *Of Mice and Men* but Warner Bros. refused (Sperber and Lax 110–11).

4. "'Sahara' Rough Print Viewed July 7, 1943." "Sahara" file, Office of War Information, Bureau of Motion Pictures division, Film Analysis section. Record Group 208, National Archives.

5. Chandler read the review and agreed. He also liked the movie, noting, "Bogart can be tough without a gun. Also he has a sense of humor that contains that grating undertone of contempt" (Hiney and MacShane 15, 67).

6. *Action in the North Atlantic* was not criticized specifically for alleged "communist" content during the hearings, however. Indeed, whether written by The Ten or not, few movies were discussed besides the wartime films *Mission to Moscow* (1943), *Song of Russia* (1944), and *The North Star* (1945).

5 ✰✰✰✰✰✰✰✰✰✰✰

Claudette Colbert, Ginger Rogers, and Barbara Stanwyck

American Homefront Women

DAVID M. LUGOWSKI

Claudette Colbert portrait, c. 1943; Ginger Rogers portrait, probably for *The Major and the Minor* (1942); Barbara Stanwyck portrait, c. 1941. All photos collection of the author.

Pondering the signature stars of the 1940s, one might not immediately consider Claudette Colbert, Ginger Rogers, and Barbara Stanwyck, who seem so much of the 1930s. Each was, however, a major star who appeared in many hits and contributed excellent performances to fine films. They achieved heights of cultural importance during the forties, and the trajectories of their images, from newfound peaks to postwar declines, are instructive. They had perfected images during the 1930s that still resonated, but the end of the Depression, and the onset of World War II and middle age, revised their personae. Their unique qualities in romantic comedy would shift toward drama; while roles would often be striking—mothers, misjudged outsiders, war wives, historical figures, victims, and villainesses—their overall tone, more dutiful, conservative, and all-American, became inescapably more generic.

Colbert had the greatest box office success. (She carried films by herself, however, the least often.) *Boom Town* was 1940's top grosser, and *So Proudly We Hail* (1943), *Since You Went Away* (1944), and *The Egg and I* (1947) were top films in their years. The latter propelled Colbert to the number nine spot on *Motion Picture Herald*'s list of top ten box office stars, among seven appearances in the top twenty-five from 1943 to 1949. Rogers was RKO's only superstar under exclusive contract from 1939 to 1941, and she accounted for one-third of their top hits (such as *Lucky Partners* [1940], *Tom Dick and Harry* [1941], and *The Major and the Minor* [1942]). Freelancing, she scored two of the highest grossing films of their years (*Lady in the Dark* [1944], *Week-end at the Waldorf* [1945]), and enjoyed hits including *Tender Comrade* (1943) and *I'll Be Seeing You* (1944). Popular wisdom casts Rogers with Fred Astaire, but of these divas, Rogers most often carried a vehicle alone in the forties. Having appeared solo in 1938 among the top twenty-five stars, Rogers returned (unlike Astaire) from 1939 to 1941 and 1944 to 1945.[1]

Polls are quirky, though, for Stanwyck made the top twenty-five in 1947 only. She was not on the list in 1941, oddly, when the popular *The Lady Eve, Meet John Doe, Ball of Fire*, and *You Belong to Me* appeared. Nonetheless, Stanwyck, a pioneering freelancer, made hits for Warner Bros., with *Christmas in Connecticut* (1945) and *My Reputation* (1946) among their biggest. Male stars reversed the female box office dominance of the 1930s, but these three were still top names. In other realms of achievement, Rogers won an Oscar for *Kitty Foyle* (1940), Stanwyck received three nominations (*Ball of Fire, Double Indemnity* [1944], *Sorry, Wrong Number* [1948]), and Colbert one (*Since You Went Away*). Also, they rarely sacrificed top billing: in the all-star *Since You Went Away* and *Week-end at the Waldorf*, Colbert and Rogers, respectively, were billed first. Stanwyck was America's highest-paid woman in 1944, Rogers held that spot in 1945 (and was Hollywood's highest-paid star overall), and Colbert (highest-paid in 1936) netted a large salary too (Vermilye 84; McGilligan 117; Eames 120).

Among other similarities, this trio often worked with the same directors and co-stars, men able to cede ground to these dominant women while shining themselves. Film titles echo each other: Stanwyck's *Remember the Night* (1940) and Colbert's *Remember the Day* (1941); Rogers's *Once Upon a Honeymoon* (1942) and Colbert's *Family Honeymoon* (1948); Stanwyck's *You Belong to Me* and Rogers's *It Had to Be You* (1947). Consistency is germane to each star too. Colbert's *Arise, My Love* (1940) precedes her *Sleep My Love* (1948). Stanwyck's "lady" titles—*The Great Man's Lady* (1942), *The Lady Gambles* (1949)—signal her representative nature, and parallel Rogers's vehicles named for their heroines—*Kitty Foyle, Magnificent Doll* (1946), and her own "lady" (in the dark). And William Wellman directed one raucous comedy about a dancer accused of murder, *Roxie Hart* (1942, with Rogers) followed by another, *Lady of Burlesque* (1943, with Stanwyck)!

Even plot highlights overlap meaningfully, as each star is presented as physically appealing and embodying cultural imperatives. A woman's leg kicks out a door at the start of both *Roxie Hart* and *The Palm Beach Story* (1942). In the latter, Colbert's toes curl up when she is kissed, while Rogers hears bells in *Tom Dick and Harry*. Within one year, all play older women: Colbert dons some gray in *Remember the Day*; Rogers looks amazingly like her actual mother (playing her mother!) in *The Major and the Minor* (1942); Stanwyck impressively plays a centenarian in *The Great Man's Lady*. That film and *Magnificent Doll* enact period dramas of women who, tempted by roués, prefer quiet empire builders. *Remember the Night* and *I'll Be Seeing You* are even closer: with Stanwyck convicted of theft in one, and Rogers imprisoned for manslaughter in the other; both give their heroines Christmas furloughs. Indeed, Christmastime, train stations, factories, and homes—all weighted with wartime resonance—frequent their films.

Fan magazines embellish the cultural work their films enact. Apparently, Colbert was a thoughtful Christmas shopper, Stanwyck always remembered birthdays, and "After giving 13 birthday parties to crew members . . . Rogers, at last, had a party given her" (*Silver Screen*, October 1942, 22). Christmas and birthdays matter to publicists, since such events encourage consumption. Indeed, glorifying stars' individualism effaces stardom as commodity: Rogers "doesn't belong to any fixed group . . . no packaged products to testimonialize" (*Hollywood*, August 1940, 26). Yet advertising shows Colbert peddling soap and Stanwyck plugging baby products for

Christmas in Connecticut (*Modern Screen*, October 1945, 115). Perhaps most hilariously, Rogers is dressed as Dolley Madison, extolling RC Cola (*Motion Picture Herald*, 23 November 1946, 41).

Representing the extraordinariness of the ordinary woman, all three are praised as athletes. Evidently Stanwyck was an ace horsewoman, Colbert one of the best amateur skiers in America, and in competing with Rogers, "Ginger eventually gets the upper hand and . . . never relinquishes it by so much as the flex of a muscle" (*Hollywood*, August 1940, 26). Magazines captured stars enjoying the nightlife too; since fans identified with this trio, seeing them provided vicarious thrills. Still, these Everywomen could hardly be reckless partiers. Magazines therefore display ritzy nightclubs while offering reverse anchorage—captions declaring that stars hate splurging during wartime or postwar austerity: "When Ginger goes dancing, she turns heads, not only because of her beauty but because she doesn't go out very often" (*Hollywood*, December 1941, 6). Stanwyck and husband Robert Taylor, described as homebodies, go jitterbugging several nights a week. Stars apparently prepared for "unstaged" photos, typically looking wonderful: "It's a rare treat for nightclubbers to glimpse vivacious Claudette Colbert, always beautifully gowned and perfectly groomed when she goes out with husband Dr. Joel Pressman" (*Movie Star Parade*, September 1948, 14).

Female stars were expected to be clotheshorses, and fashion sculpted their images. Characterized as not (threateningly) gorgeous, they still delight under any circumstance: a mud-soaked Colbert "couldn't have looked more attractive" (*Silver Screen*, October 1942, 28). They offer tips: Rogers recommends matched jewelry, while "Colbert says it is a sin to clash your lipstick with your clothes" (*Silver Screen*, January 1944, 8). They even kid their glamour, as Stanwyck hid weights under her furs so Van Heflin could not lift her in rehearsal (*Silver Screen*, February 1948, 68). Yet they can't be fussy: Stanwyck's "casual attitude toward her appearance is a source of amazement to wardrobe women" (*Hollywood*, October 1941, 10).

Costumes, makeup, and photography help make their ordinariness glamorous and sexy. Photographers touched up Rogers's freckles, softened Stanwyck's look, and airbrushed away Colbert's shoulders to create a longer neckline (Bego 214). *Lady in the Dark* stills emphasized Rogers's mink dress, possibly the most expensive designed for film to that time, as she opens her fur to expose its bejeweled underside (Lugowski 105). Captions oxymoronically cope with her hyperbolization of sexual difference: her "lady-like stripping . . . [is a] highlight" (*Silver Screen*, April 1944, 47). In *Tender Comrade*, Rogers proves that "you *can* look desirable with your hair just washed and hanging like a wet rag" (*Silver Screen*, January 1944, 37). Stanwyck models a leopard-skin outfit even though she favors "tailored suits, skirts, jackets, not snug-fitting or décolleté." Preview audiences for *Meet John Doe* said Stanwyck's sweater "stole a scene" so "she did a retake, to cover the sweater with a coat." Domestic goddesses can be sexy—in planned doses (*Silver Screen*, June 1941, 74).

Their work, after all, mattered most to them. "Barbara is the kind of gal who'd rather be an actress than look pretty" (*Silver Screen*, July 1941, n.p.). Acclaimed one of Hollywood's best dramatic actresses, she also "sparkles" as a comedienne. "Barbara is the 150th woman [Robert Leonard] has directed. And he claims she's the best yet" (*Silver Screen*, February 1948, 68). Colbert, "one of the screen's most exciting phenomena . . . is versatile. . . . Gifted emotionally, she also knows all the technical tricks" (*Movies*, April 1943, 22, 68). Rogers, meanwhile, took on an "astonishing part" in *Primrose Path* (1940). When one critic complained about her lacking glamour, Rogers retorted, "The character had no relation to the ballroom slickies and society snips I've done in the past. The absence of make-up was no affectation, either; just an honest attempt to approximate the character" (*Hollywood*, August 1940, 50). Stars admired each other, too. Anne Shirley said, "Ginger deserved that Academy Award. . . . I thought she was magnificent. She's my idea of a great actress" (*Silver Screen*, January 1942, 67).

Telling details, however, reveal the falsity of cinematic illusions. After shooting war scenes for *So Proudly We Hail*, Colbert "retreats to her dressing room where awaits her black poodle Lulu Belle!" (*Movies*, April 1943, 22). Clichéd praise inadvertently reveals a flawed performance: "Colbert is delightfully adept in *Sleep My Love*, in which . . . she is being forced into suicide. . . . Claudette plays Alison Courtland . . . entertainingly and with Colbert charm" (*Silver Screen*, January 1948, 58). Rogers was haunted by past associations when *Magnificent Doll* yielded hollow praise: "It's difficult to believe that speeches on democracy and good government could sound so convincing coming from Fred Astaire's former dancing partner" (*Variety*, 20 November 1946, n.p.). And Stanwyck's spontaneity apparently benefited from monetary motivation and good direction: "So sure she was of [*Meet John Doe's*] success after she had been schooled ever so subtly in down-to-earth naturalness that she accepted a percentage of box-office receipts in lieu of the usual salary. . . . It proved a wise decision" (*Silver Screen*, January 1942, 77–78).

However achieved, these three embody the 1940s Everywoman, signified by titles connoting identifiability—*My Reputation*, *Practically Yours* (1944), *I'll Be Seeing You*. Essentially modern types, they struggled in period roles yet created variations of American Ordinariness. Rogers is wisecracking and wary but whimsical, Stanwyck is sharp-edged, sassy, yet sentimental, Colbert is warm but wry and sly. Rogers is defensive, Stanwyck plays offense, Colbert counter-punches. Stanwyck juxtaposes emotional registers, realizing her love for Fred MacMurray in *Double Indemnity* only after shooting him. Rogers's duality is more overt, given her talent for masquerade, as she balances childlike dreaming with proletarian pride (Lugowski 106). Colbert's duality is one of tone, bringing lightness to melodrama and tenderness to farce. Colbert and Rogers befriend other women, whereas Stanwyck is often alone or antagonistic. Colbert (b. 1903) played mothers the most; Stanwyck (b. 1907) mothers pre-teens only; Rogers (b. 1911) gives birth onscreen, but loses several babies. And each has a different relationship to race, if a similar trajectory: Colbert seems the whitest, yet her European exoticism undergoes Americanization; Stanwyck's Irishness vanishes; and Rogers's links to jazz diminish after dancing the Black Bottom in *Roxie Hart*, as the country enters war. In what follows, I survey their films, with special consideration of a timely aspect of their images—as wartime wives.

★★★★★ Dizzy Women: The Prewar Films

Before 1942, these stars' most memorable vehicles are in the screwball comedy that flourished during the Depression, combined with melodramas that also echo 1930s mores. Past and future oscillate, however, demonstrated by Colbert's two 1940 films. *Arise, My Love*, with its Billy Wilder–Charles Brackett script stylishly directed by Mitchell Leisen, offered the European sophistication typical of Colbert's 1930s films, while also containing greater topicality. Opening during the Spanish Civil War as her "Gusto" Nash rescues Ray Milland from execution, the film carries their adventures up to World War II without losing an ambivalence about war still possible in 1940. *Boom Town* also looked back by casting her opposite Clark Gable, but was prescient about what the decade portended. Obsessed with oil money won and lost, this bland film becomes increasingly retrograde about gender. Colbert's Elizabeth, who prefers scrubbing husband Big John's shirts, offers, "I'm your girl. You can lick me if it'll help." One magazine noted, "Colbert has a rather thankless job of looking adoringly at Gable while he gets ready to paste [Spencer] Tracy again" (*Hollywood*, October 1940, 20).

Oscillation continued with *Skylark* (1941), a screwball reunion with Milland, and the warm schoolteacher saga *Remember the Day*. *Skylark* references War Relief Teas and the Burma Road but evokes earlier films, as Colbert teasingly humbles her man. An inability to make coffee on a rocky boat shows Colbert's aptitude for slapstick, suggesting future directions for her

Colbert at her most typical (softly curled bangs, Paramount chic, the left side of her face toward the camera) and at her best (bamboozling millionaire Rudy Vallee) in Preston Sturges's *The Palm Beach Story* (1942). Copyright 1942, Paramount Pictures, Inc.

comedy. *Remember* plays into wartime nostalgia; interestingly, the era revisited was pre–World War I. Dialogue about refugee children feels contemporary, while a railway parting and Colbert's line to husband John Payne, "I'm frightened at the thought of being alone. . . . When you go there's nothing left," anticipate *Since You Went Away*.

Colbert's brilliant hurrah to earlier films, *The Palm Beach Story*, followed. Preston Sturges's satire of both the idle rich and the American inventor was the last great prewar screwball, as Colbert abandons struggling Joel McCrea to secure cash for him by charming the Weinie King, the Ale & Quail Club, and a conservative millionaire. Full of innuendo both overt ("Sex didn't enter into it") and contextual ("I rather enjoyed it," as the millionaire's face is stepped on), it echoes Depression mores with its bickering couple eager to be debt-free. Certainly Colbert's line to McCrea, "I've always done what you've wanted and it's always turned out a disaster," was not common in later World War II films. "Nothing is permanent in this world, except Roosevelt," is a rare topical joke, yet the film proved unexpectedly subversive. The Office of War Information (OWI) felt it sidestepped wartime sacrifices, cheapened morals, and ridiculed "ethnic" allies (Koppes and Black 91–93). Tighter censorship resulted, yet the warm but opportunistic heroine, dizzy yet quick-witted, showed superb resourcefulness, in both her character and Colbert's performance.

Sturges was vital to Stanwyck too, beginning with his screenplay for Leisen's unsung gem *Remember the Night*, featuring her as a felon given Christmas leave by a lawyer. Despite noticeable glamour and enjoyably Stanwyckian chances to rant, she gives her tough New Yorker a warm realism. Her persona dominates: the redeemed cynic, loving Fred MacMurray yet resisting him for his own sake because of her past. Exploring such tensions—the crafty con whose feelings for a guileless man become sincere—anchors her peak in *Meet John Doe*, Howard Hawks's *Ball of Fire* (which Rogers had rejected), and Sturges's *The Lady Eve*. Showing her best-ever comic chops in the latter two as, respectively, a stripper and a card sharp, she is the aggressor. Her awkward heroes (Gary Cooper, Henry Fonda) discover her motivations but forgive her; only Sturges does not compromise, continuing her manipulations with the man never the wiser. *Eve* used mirrors to symbolize her duality; this trope recurred frequently with Stanwyck, but seldom as artfully.

Other films lacked the same resonance. *You Belong to Me* teams a wealthy, useless husband with her doctor; spoofing millionaires stalely mimics Sturges, while suggestions arise that Stanwyck leave medicine to become a wife. Redemption, however, as his money and her talent save a hospital, straddles 1930s calls for recovery with a wartime ethic of recycling available talent. *The Great Man's Lady* is similarly disappointing, perhaps more so because of her virtuoso star turn, moving from Philadelphia youth to centenarian, recalling how her sacrifices aided a man's ambitions. A semi-western Stanwyck collage—winning at cards; brandishing guns; tarnishing her reputation to aid others, as in *Stella Dallas* (1937)—the film never justifies why the "great man" merits glorification.

Like Stanwyck, Rogers embodied proletariats more than Colbert, and in *Kitty Foyle*, she too plays a Philadelphian caught between two men. It eliminated the abortion in its source novel, emphasizing its heroine's romantic quandary, discussed with her own mirror reflection, choosing between a struggling doctor and a married millionaire. Censorship dictated the safe choice but Rogers, brunette for the first time since 1931, carried the film poignantly. Marketed to working women, successfully highlighting love scenes Rogers rarely could enact opposite the recalcitrant Astaire, it was a smash. Some, however, felt she deserved her Oscar as Ellie in *Primrose Path*, an uneven but remarkable comedy-drama by the director and writer who understood Rogers best, Gregory LaCava and Allan Scott. Tomboyishness and working-class slang came easily, as did both her defensive and spirited attacking modes, as she played a shantytown prostitute's daughter nudged into the family profession. Ellie's father's concern about "this rotten environment" was central to 1930s Hollywood sociology, but Rogers's amazingly tarty look alongside her first john anticipates noir's prostitutes. Cinderella elements remain but the seedy docksides and suicidal despair evoke French poetic realism and prefigure Italian neorealism.

Rogers never did anything like it again, but her prewar comedies succeeded on their own terms. *Lucky Partners*, a risqué screwball about sweepstakes winners—more Depression culture—felicitously teamed her opposite Ronald Colman, as she alternated ordinariness ("I'm a perfectly conventional, proper person") with feistiness ("I want to be independent") and is lectured the definitive line in Rogers's films: "Young lady, you'd better make up your mind." Her indecision became dizzier in *Tom Dick and Harry*, as switchboard operator Janie accepts three marriage proposals. (Rogers also proved fickle in her segment of Julien Duvivier's anthology *Tales of Manhattan* [1942].) Playing her first airhead, Rogers employs witty clowning quiet enough to anchor a small-town satire. Its dream sequences, as she imagines marriage to each man, and then bigamy, became a recurring Rogers trope. Topicality is limited to Janie hissing Hitler during a newsreel after a movie parodying *Kitty Foyle*, and the small newspaper headline in one dream, "Adolf Hitler Assassinated" alongside the huge "Janie Gets Married! Local Girl Makes Good!" Otherwise Depression screwball predominates, with Janie and Harry dancing to free music at a record store, and his vaguely Popular Front socialism (penned by Paul Jarrico, later blacklisted): "I don't believe in this 'Every man for himself.' I get lonesome." Janie argues, "It's just as natural for a girl to want to make a good marriage as it is for a fella to want to get ahead," but in *Roxie Hart* Rogers confesses to murder to get publicity herself. Freelancing at Fox, she successfully brought her zanier style to a 1920s farce aiming for guffaws rather than nostalgia. Still brunette, Rogers and director Wellman combined show-stopping teaser dances with scathing potshots at media celebrity as Roxie goes on trial. The war years would retain the backward-glancing nostalgia . . . but tone down the satire.

★★★★★ Blurred Tones: The Wartime Films

Colbert's wartime comedies (such as *Guest Wife* [1945], which briefly shows the right profile she despised) benefited from her smooth technique but strained for the gloss less possible during wartime austerities. She turned a corner with *No Time for Love* (1943) as a photojournalist covering sandhogs; facing underground mudslides clearly connoted the dangers of wartime work. Danger—and tears—were foregrounded in *So Proudly We Hail*, a propagandistic hit with Colbert commanding nurses in the Philippines. Production Code wartime allowances included discussion of suicide if the nurses are raped, as well as Veronica Lake's suicide, killing Japanese with a grenade. Speechifying occurs at Christmastime, and female homosociality is undercut by reliance upon men throughout. Colbert breaks regulations by marrying, shows only her left profile even when comatose, and revives when read a preachy letter (OWI-influenced) from her husband.

Colbert's wartime smash, though, was *Since You Went Away*, as America's Mrs. Miniver (and just as phony). Colbert had played lines like "This is the moment I've dreaded, coming back to our home, alone" in *Remember the Day*, but never before as mother to teenagers. An overproduced three-hour epic, "Written by the Producer" David Selznick, of a homefront family with the father away, the film was a comforting (then) but dated (now) time capsule. Aided by stunning cinematography, some scenes—railway partings, canteen dances, a chance to see the father dashed by transportation delays—are effective. Others rely heavily upon archetypes, with nasty Agnes Moorehead demolished by calls to sacrifice, and icy Monty Woolley melted by tragedy. Not every critic was enchanted, but Colbert dutifully embodied each tearful situation. Such nobility—even a player of gay stereotypes, Grady Sutton, portrays a soldier—required Colbert to forfeit any sensuality, but when an immigrant says, "You are what I thought America was," the canonization of Claudette was complete.

Rogers's propaganda hit was *Tender Comrade*, shorter but equally lachrymose. Also featuring railway farewells and husbands' letters, it provided Hollywood's definitive "Rosie the Riveter" image. Jo Jones drives a war plant forklift and cohabits with other women as they discuss patriotism. As in Colbert's films, female bonding occurs, here undercut by their cooking competition for the first soldier to visit. Tailored to Rogers via dreamy flashbacks typical of her vehicles, the film caused postwar regret when her mother Lela, a HUAC "friendly witness," testified that writer Dalton Trumbo and director Edward Dmytryk spouted communism with lines like "Share and share alike!"

Another film linked patriotism with gender, but *The Major and the Minor* had a lighter, subversive touch, and engaged Lela Rogers more pleasantly. Billy Wilder helped, approved by Rogers to direct his first American film. Evoking wartime economies as heroine Susan Applegate poses as a twelve-year-old for half-price train fare, this uproarious screwball has three women deciding the fate of a myopic major (Ray Milland). His fiancée wants him tied to a military academy, while her sister enlists Susan to help him into active service. Showcasing Rogers's mimicry, and her greatest comic performance, the film even requires Susan to imitate her own mother (well played by Lela). Rogers's child act was never funnier, a feminist masquerade that fools men but not other women. Censors, meanwhile, were not fooled but could do little about the pedophilia Susan inspires, since the character *was* an adult.

Wilder's film was Rogers's 1940s apotheosis, even if Leisen's *Lady in the Dark* had similar ambitions. A return to musicals, and her first color film, it offered a summary role: "Boss lady" Liza—indecisive about three men, hurt as a child when she dropped her defenses—dreams, dances, and dresses up. The Broadway hit lost most of its score on film, unsurpassed for kitsch and big hairdos, retaining the era's fashionable psychoanalysis, with Liza's analyst prescribing "some man [to] dominate you." Working-woman-as-threat and an outrageously gay character were more the domain of Depression screwball than a dramatic musical; delays dated this 1942–1943 production quickly upon its release, even if it proved a hit. It made Rogers's image upscale but only ushered in more hollow glamour. In *Week-end at the Waldorf*—an Americanized *Grand Hotel* (1932)—her unhappy star amusingly mistakes Walter Pidgeon for a thief before a hasty wartime marriage. Earlier she might have played the stenographer (Lana Turner), but MGM only gave Hollywood's highest-paid diva endless hairstyle and costume changes. Rogers's best homefront efforts were more modest. Selznick threatened *I'll Be Seeing You* with typical production largesse, but the simple story and sensitive acting prevailed. Christmas scenes, railway partings, and noir voiceovers appear, as Rogers's convict on furlough falls for shell-shocked Joseph Cotten. Lines like "You learn to compromise with your dreams" and a somber finale are more touching than *Since You Went Away*'s closing good-news telegram.

Stanwyck's films address the homefront less, due mostly to delayed releases. Like Rogers, she did an all-star Duvivier anthology and a dark Wellman comedy. Her *Flesh and Fantasy* segment, as a crook redeemed by shipboard romance, revisits *The Lady Eve*, with irony replacing the laughs. *Lady of Burlesque* substitutes *Roxie Hart*'s satire with backstage mystery. A muddle, the film covers Stanwyck tropes from tough romance to mirrors, catfights, and noir-like murders. Stanwyck cannot sing, but her acrobatic jitterbug is delightful and her line, "You Chinese fight too darn well for us to mix with you," reminded audiences of their wartime allies.

Stanwyck then enjoyed her own Wilder landmark. *Double Indemnity* was outright noir, broadening her persona in ways akin to, but more enduring

Rogers's return to blondeness in *Lady in the Dark* (1944), sporting the most expensive dress in films up to that time. During the film, she splits open her mink to expose the bejeweled sequins underneath. Copyright 1944, Paramount Pictures, Inc.

than, Rogers's move into drama or Colbert's into playing mothers. Colbert (*Secret Fury* [1950]) and Rogers (*Storm Warning* [1950], *Tight Spot* [1955]) made interesting noirs, but Stanwyck's ordinariness was more earthy, her seductiveness more overt, her hysteria more common; these fit noir's villainesses and victims alike. If her phony blonde wig dates, it still became iconic enough to signify Stanwyck misbehavior (*The Furies* [1950], *The Violent Men* [1955]). Her comic flair emerged during the famous "speeding car" sex banter, long before her Phyllis lures an insurance salesman into killing her husband. Set in 1938, the film eschews wartime references, but Stanwyck, atypically playing a housewife, plotting crimes in supermarkets, evoked a negative-consumerist (rather than positive-worker) ethic very much of World War II (Spencer 134).

Stanwyck's versatility—and the era's schizophrenia—dictated that her next fake homemaker appear in her mildest comedy, and her biggest wartime hit. Although *Christmas in Connecticut* opens with a destroyer torpedoed, before long sailor Dennis Morgan and publisher Sydney Greenstreet are being hosted by "America's best cook, Elizabeth Lane," a columnist who is actually unskilled domestically. Although the mirror framings, Stanwyck on her typewriter (like *Meet John Doe*), and her comic finesse (tossing away soiled diapers) were familiar, the film anticipates postwar culture foremost. Greenstreet discussing how babies boost circulation references the nascent boom, Stanwyck's architect fiancé faces "prefabricated methods and postwar plastics," and she represents postwar domestication. One of Stanwyck's finest films was also timely, even if it was held up for years because World War II hits enjoyed longer runs; *My Reputation* suggests wartime, with its railway partings, conga lines, and repressed romance. The premise, however, with Stanwyck's unseen husband dying from chronic illness before love with a soldier threatens "her reputation," suited 1946 ideally. Drama about widows' duties rendered the husband's cause of death irrelevant to audiences, and the somber tone, with lines suiting Stanwyck more than Rogers or Colbert ("I seem to be going to pieces!") worked perfectly.

Despite the many genres each star handled, war uncomfortably blurred the tones of certain films. *Meet John Doe* is mostly successful, with professional "dame" Stanwyck maneuvering a boob for her own gain, only to fall for his sincerity. But then the film ventures into noirish political drama about fascistic businessmen, manipulated masses, and the hero's near-suicide. Indeed, Frank Capra and screenwriter Robert Riskin tested five finales until their sacrificial Jesus and penitent Mary Magdalene are saved by populist sentiment. *Practically Yours*, the least interesting genre blur, trav-

A phony blonde wig, a deadpan yet intense stare, and a gun hidden in a seemingly safe domestic space all mark Stanwyck's move into film noir villainy in Billy Wilder's *Double Indemnity* (1944). Copyright 1944, Paramount Pictures, Inc.

els the opposite tonal path, opening grimly as Fred MacMurray kamikaze-dives upon a Japanese battleship. His farewells are radioed to "Piggy," his dog, but everyone mishears it as "Peggy" (Colbert), a co-worker ignorant of his (nonexistent) feelings for her. He survives, naturally, and the film becomes contrived farce, one of Leisen's few visually dull films (wartime austerity again) and Colbert's sad parting from Paramount, as the reunited "couple" maintains appearances until romance sparks. Rogers's auteur was comic sentimentalist Leo McCarey, and *Once Upon a Honeymoon*, the oddest genre blur, fascinates with flippant switches in tone. From engaging banter between a reporter (Cary Grant) and a showgirl who has unknowingly wed a Nazi, the film has its stars mistakenly classified as Jews and sent to a concentration camp, Rogers impersonating the Statue of Liberty, and a comic finale where she kills the Nazi in self-defense. (Interestingly, Rogers also killed in self-defense in *I'll Be Seeing You*; it is played soberly and she is unfairly convicted of manslaughter.) In all three off-kilter films, the heroines' emotions evolve as tyrants, Pacific war, loves won and lost violently, and the Holocaust surround them. Each star shines, but these piecemeal films wobble amid unresolved wartime implications.

A far better film, *The Major and the Minor* has its heroine assume the many wartime roles women might play. As Susan, Rogers physically or vocally masquerades as, or is misread as, a working woman, a prostitute, a virgin, a tease, her unpatriotically isolationist rival, a sister, and a mother. Finally, she contends that men "underestimate" women who only want to be *wives*: "Perhaps all a woman wants is to be a photograph a soldier tacks over his bunk." While she potently defies such relationships, Susan ends up in the role culture taught women to embrace (Gallafent 138). The film's feminism—with three intelligent women outfoxing the men—and its anarchic pedophilia mingle with conservative signals that patriotic women should consent to marry men heading overseas.

Stars also performed offscreen, selling war bonds and navigating tricky discourses as wartime wives. Rogers seemingly fits the part, given that she wed Private Jack Briggs in 1943. Fan magazines read like movie plots: "Nerves in shreds from the ardors of her [bond-selling] swing through the dusty southwest, the jammed trains, unaccustomed encounters with swarms of people who followed her everywhere," Rogers was grateful when a marine "ran interference . . . protecting her against crowds." They dated "just ten times before their marriage, but the first was enough to convince them it was love." During a Christmas furlough (life imitates art!), they wed. One story credits producer Buddy DeSylva ("Any day you want to get married . . . you have off"), whereas another claims she could not concentrate, prompting Leisen's advice ("Get married so we can get back to work"). Their train station meeting is lushly scripted: "Jack's train . . . an hour late. . . . Ginger waited, chewing her nails frantically. Suppose something had gone wrong . . . then, after eons, he was striding toward her and she was lifted in a pair of strong arms and smothered against a khaki shoulder sobbing, 'Oh darling!'" Briggs's Ordinary Marine is worthy of the Ordinary Diva, gender roles intact: "What cooks on this guy who succeeded where smoothie Jean Gabin, handsome George Montgomery and debonair Phil Reed missed out? . . . Yes, he's younger than Ginger, 22 to her 31 . . . but don't let that fool you—he's a real guy. . . . Don't ever call him Mr. Ginger Rogers—one glimpse of them and it's obvious who's head of that family. Ginger, head over heels in love—humble at the glory of it, is very much Mrs. Jack Briggs" (*Movie Star Parade*, April 1943, 30, 64–66).

In 1945, this "average American girl" was preparing for Briggs's return, since "women should try to be now what her man will want her to be" (*Silver Screen*, May 1945, 80). Rogers encountered no flak for not becoming a mother, and mass culture had moved on before their 1948 divorce; the marriage discourse had fulfilled its duty. Colbert's story is less interesting, given that she was married to one man from 1935 to 1968. This did, of course, suit images of wartime fidelity, but is hardly dramatic. Furthermore, given that Colbert was playing mothers, it didn't help that she lacked children. Stills show her dining alone with her husband away, and Louella Parson found her "cleverly hostessing" Bastille Day celebrations with "French tricolor and U.S. flag motifs" despite rationing (*Modern Screen*, October 1945, 78). We also see her celebrating in 1946 with Pressman in "civvies" and considering adoption plans. Most interesting, however, was Pressman's justification of Hollywood in a wartime letter. She asks, "Why should I stand in front of a camera exchanging bright quips . . . when entire villages are being massacred, when a stricken world is crumbling all around us? Who, in heaven's name, wants to see a gold bathing suit?" Pressman's reply emphasizes morale: "Don't ever say your work is not important" (*Silver Screen*, October 1942, 65).

Stanwyck's discourse held the most potential, but it too had problems. Wedded to an enlisted star sounds perfect, and they have a son, Dion, adopted during her previous marriage. Before World War II, however, magazines sensationalized a possible divorce. "Barbara and Bob . . . led the simple, earthy life of home-loving people." But are they on the "verge of a bust-up"? "Barbara might not be aware of how far women will go to get him to notice them." Italics add drama to this non-story: "She might not be able to subdue typically feminine traits and be calm and passive while her husband usurped all the attention. . . . Is this breaking them up? . . . *Neither Bob nor Barbara will affirm or deny it.*" Apparently she became Taylor's acting coach and "retired for a year so he could get the undivided attention and interest of the public." (Another story claimed she took suspension over poor roles. Her output, however, remained fairly steady.) "Ultimately, though, she wasn't ready to become a domesticated housefrau [sic] while her husband basked in the adoration of millions." Gender roles favor him: "Man is merely supposed to . . . offset her beauty and charm . . . diplomat, strategist, psychologist, lover—all in one." Declaring that "marriage to an idol requires the endurance of a superwoman," the article speculates, "Will Barbara and Bob go their separate ways or will they ignore all the gossip and continue to lead their sheltered lives," before closing with "What God has joined let no man put asunder!" (*Hollywood*, April 1941, 23, 58).

Stanwyck and Taylor divorced in 1951, but during World War II, divorce gossip abruptly vanished once he entered the service. Then "Barbara's first abject loneliness was released in tears. And only her pillow was the wiser." Soldiers dub her "the Chin-Up [rather than Pinup] Girl," the same phrase publicizing Rogers in *Tender Comrade* (*Silver Screen*, September 1944, 87–88). One problem, though, came with Dion: "Dion is proud of Bob, but resents Barbara working. . . . She's too tired at night to romp with him" (*Silver Screen*, July 1942, 32). Another problem was that Taylor's last film before serving was *Song of Russia* (1943), a pro-U.S.S.R. film that embarrassed conservatives like Stanwyck and Taylor (another HUAC "friendly witness") after the war. So whether it was the imperfect family, undramatic monogamy, childlessness, postwar divorce, or the shifts of politics, these stars embodied the wartime wife only fitfully.

★★★★★ Diminishing Success: The Postwar Films

Just as these stars' wartime images faded after the war, so too did the actresses struggle to maintain the courses they had traveled or to broaden their ranges. Colbert's postwar films evoked their milieu while fluctuating between older successes and wartime changes. *Without Reservations* (1946) opens with a newsreel ("When war ended last year . . .") before revamping *It Happened One Night* (1934), with John Wayne and Good Neighbor Policy references joining their road trip. Conflict emerges between novelist Christopher Madden, spouting her book's philosophies of worldwide cooperation, and the war veteran she wants for the film version espousing rugged individualism. Originally named for Wayne's catchphrase, "Thanks, God, I'll take it from here," the film supports his desire for a postwar woman "who's helpless and cute. I don't want a woman trying to tell the world what to do. I don't even want a woman to tell *me* what to do."

Colbert was maternal again in *The Secret Heart* (1946), supplicating a teenaged step-daughter fixated on her late father, typical of the female neuroses frequenting postwar melodrama. In *Tomorrow Is Forever* (1946), she mothered an actual teenager (Richard Long). Colbert's World War I husband (Orson Welles), long presumed dead, unaware she was pregnant, returns in disguise as an Austrian chemist, only to discover their son believes his father is her second husband. Colbert never ages during the story (though we glimpse her elusive right profile in long shot), but deep-focus cinematography and moving performances bolster the improbable storyline. Postwar Hollywood revived sympathetic German speakers, and this film bookends *Remember the Day* in using World War I to highlight contemporary conditions.

Colbert, at forty-four, gave birth again in her biggest postwar hit, *The Egg and I*, joining war veteran Fred MacMurray in his dreams to move to a farm and breed madly ("Whatever my husband chooses to do is all right with me"). Long reappears as the son of Ma and Pa Kettle, whose rustic humor accounted for much of the film's popularity and endless sequels. Audiences bonded with the urban flight and speeches about coping with recent tragedies, but the tone stays light. Colbert gamely plays the pratfalls set against her sophisticated image, even struggling with a pig named Cleopatra (Colbert had played the Egyptian queen in 1934). She even mimics *Kitty Foyle* upon giving birth ("This is what really counts . . .") but the antics of her and Marjorie Main (as Ma) suggest the potency of comedic women despite all the gender conservatism.

The derivative *Family Honeymoon* featured "old couple" MacMurray and Colbert taking her children on their honeymoon, evoking the postwar travel boom and contemporary economizing. At one point Colbert imitates maid Hattie McDaniel; a white-bourgeois star, she does a notably poor job of it. Her worst performance of the decade, however, came in *Sleep My Love*, as husband Don Ameche tries to drive her crazy. Despite Douglas Sirk's compelling visual style, and an interesting Chinese-Christian wedding acknowledging postwar liberalism, this Gothic noir simply trots out deadpan vamps and other clichés, and glib Colbert never worries much about possibly being insane. *Bride for Sale* (1949) timidly recalled her 1930s comedies, with tax expert Nora unethically using company files to seek a wealthy husband. A war veteran of the Philippines (*So Proudly We Hail*), from an oilman's family (*Boom Town*), Nora endures a sleazy Arab club, wrestling, and raw fish dumped upon her. Statically shot on threadbare sets, criticizing "unsuitable" working women, the film has only Colbert's wiles to bolster her "farewell to her kind of romantic comedy" (Everson 137).

Rogers also trod familiar ground with diminished success. Paralleling her political conservatism, she became cautious in choosing roles. As cinema's most frequent analysand, she was offered *The Snake Pit* (1948) before

Olivia de Havilland but demurred; de Havilland also benefited from Rogers rejecting a character growing into middle-aged motherhood (*To Each His Own* [1946], for which de Havilland won the Oscar for Best Actress). Rogers found Dreiser's *Sister Carrie* too left-wing and bypassed Max Ophuls's film noir *Caught* (1948). Colbert alternated mothers with seasoned workers, but Rogers kept husband-hunting and shed her proletarian image; even her destitute Parisian waif in *Heartbeat* (1946) moves quickly, as a trained pick-pocket, into high society. Rogers was as unconvincing playing eighteen at thirty-five as Colbert at forty-four having the first of ten children, or Stanwyck at forty-two as an unwed pregnancy (*No Man of Her Own* [1949]) or as Gale Sondergaard's daughter (*East Side, West Side* [1949]). Rogers admittedly looks younger when made up to look un-made-up, and her busy acting settles and becomes densely intertextual once Cinderella angles develop. *Heartbeat* has modest interest with its imported co-star (Jean-Pierre Aumont), its railway partings, and scenes at a thievery school and a cinema. Hardly innovative, it was, like postwar films by Stanwyck and Colbert, a studio-distributed independent effort. So too was *Magnificent Doll*, a one-shot return (for historical accuracy?) to the "natural" brunette hair she had sported from 1940 to 1942, with Dolley Madison in a love triangle with Aaron Burr and James Madison. Its best scenes come early, as Dolley's religious zealot father returns from war and forces her into marriage. Its finale, with Burr stirring "fear and hate," seems timely given Cold War politics. Not a hit, the film has well-acted moments withering amid stunningly stilted writing ("He's a bachelor, but the father of the Constitution"). Its gender politics emerge during Dolley's constant kissing scenes, with "If I were a man I'd love politics" and Rogers's milliner receiving prominent screen credit and indexing the star's decorative marginalization.

Whereas *Doll* seems an aberration, *It Had to Be You*, Rogers's weakest film of the decade, puts the "tread" in retread. Photocopying *Tom Dick and Harry*, it opens amusingly, with Rogers aborting three weddings. Neither her mugging, nor coyly lightening her voice, nor the dream or train sequences, however, succeed. She is more powerless than ever, told by Cornel Wilde—like Wayne to Colbert—"I want to take a girl to dinner. I ask her, she doesn't ask me." The question of who's in charge also focuses *The Barkleys of Broadway* (1949). Handsomely shot in color, it shows "Astaireandrogers" reunited after a decade, clearly at ease together. Dinah Barkley's squabbles with Josh, and her teasing him near the finale, are genuinely funny, and Rogers's "You've been taking me for granted" speech is her finest acting since *I'll Be Seeing You*. As dancers they had aged, a romantic number relying heavily upon nostalgia, but the splashy opening and a wonderful tap duet recapture their magic. Planned for Judy Garland, the film never intentionally drama-tized Ginger and Fred's split, but Dinah's dramatic aspirations added *roman à clef* angles unfortunate for Rogers. In the film, Josh's coaching enables Dinah's solo dramatic success; in life, this hit restored an image—"Astaire's partner"—that Rogers had brilliantly shaken.

The period was mixed for Stanwyck too, mixing vivid films with her weakest. Her noirs were freshest, summoning the era's sensuality and angst. Material that aped noir or other genres flopped, none more so than what sadly was, thirty more credits notwithstanding, her last comedy, *The Bride Wore Boots* (1946). Drawing upon Stanwyck's equestrian hobbies, it presents her mothering children, displaying her legs as in her 1941 tri-umphs, and doing her worst comedy work ever. The strained situations defeat her, Robert Cummings, and Diana Lynn (wonderful in *The Major and the Minor*), as they overplay forced gaiety and cutesy petulance. Its lone connection to postwar progressivism comes from Willie Best, finally playing an *intelligent* black servant. Equally derivative was her first color film, *Cali-fornia* (1946). Postwar liberalism cameos when a narrator states that one redwood could build "a Presbyterian church, a synagogue and a Baptist mission." Even a Bible reading, "the children of Israel . . . heading for the Promised Land," anticipates Israel's founding in 1948. A card cheat again, Stanwyck joins a wagon train headed by Ray Milland, horribly miscast in a western. She too is uneasy—in frequent long shots—"singing" dubbed saloon tunes.

California unfortunately inaugurated increased physical brutality toward Stanwyck's characters. Her victimization reached its nadir in a Gothic noir worse than Colbert's, *The Two Mrs. Carrolls* (1947, released two years after completion). She was better than co-star Humphrey Bogart—killing wives after painting them, he makes one grumpy vampire—but was only required to enact hysteria. Luckily, juicier psychosis sparked a riveting performance in the engrossingly lurid *The Strange Love of Martha Ivers* (1946). Expertly playing mixed emotions, she accosts Van Heflin with a burning log and then, after he wrests it away, cries out her love. She would not enjoy such a brew of childhood murder, male impotence, and suicide again.

Male insanity climaxed *Cry Wolf* (1947), a mystery masquerading as noir. Her Sandra's motives seem duplicitous when she appears at Errol Flynn's estate: She declares, "I am not a placid girl" and is dubbed "one of the most cold-blooded, scheming women I've ever met." But this promise goes unfulfilled, as her "overage Nancy Drew" seeks her missing husband (Vermilye 93). Two years older than badly aging carouser Flynn, Stanwyck is unconvincingly cast as his nephew's wife; thus, in a film lacking romance, the stars walking off together feels perfunctory. Similarly unlikely was *The Other Love* (1947), with tubercular pianist Stanwyck at a sanitarium (where doctors light her cigarettes!), rejecting her grim prognosis. Alongside *Cry Wolf*'s athletic detective, Stanwyck seems too healthy for this Camille. Hollywood's classical music vogue is evident, while gender mores are tweaked ("I can't face an unknown future with an unpowdered nose") but accepted too ("So good for my morale—to have a man show interest in me").

Stanwyck's onscreen illness anticipated *Sorry, Wrong Number*, while her pursuit of men continued in *B.F.'s Daughter* (1948). As a tycoon's spoiled progeny, she thrusts liberal husband Van Heflin into political power. Ambitious for her men (*The Great Man's Lady*), Stanwyck survives tears, fury, more mirror shots, and dull direction. Individualism and capitalism are defended better than corresponding leftist philosophies, but Stanwyck's trajectory is solely emotional, from "I can make Tom a great man" to "Oh, Tom, I need you." She pressed Warner Bros. to buy *The Fountainhead*, but King Vidor rejected her as too old and insufficiently sexy. She was cast, though, in *Sorry, Wrong Number*. Critics sniped at this radio short's expansion into a feature, with flashbacks within flashbacks, but Stanwyck earned raves as a psychosomatically handicapped woman overhearing her own murder plotted on the phone. Anatole Litvak filmed her scenes in sequence, using mirrors better than other directors to reflect both sympathy and disdain for this unpleasant woman's plight. And yet the entire film is a build-up to punish her for the economic power she wields over her husband. The postwar physical victimization of Stanwyck continued with *The Lady Gambles*. Addiction was popular in postwar film, and Stanwyck's fiercest scenes show her pleading with pawnbrokers for cash. Like Colbert, she plans on ten children with her feckless spouse, but flashbacks, blonde wigs, vicious beatings, and near-suicide counterpoise Stanwyck's performative power with her character's gendered weakness.

★★★★★   **Conclusion: Trajectories of the American Woman as Star**

Although Colbert's image shed the spicier, gossamer aspects of her prewar comedies, innuendoes remained in fan discourses, albeit more graceless ones: "Claudette spills the secrets of a candid camera career girl. . . . She flashes her bulbs at Whataman MacMurray . . . [as things] develop in her darkroom" (*Silver Screen*, February 1944, 7). Meshing with a "gracious-living" bourgeois ideal, she was cast more often than Rogers or

Stanwyck as "classy" types and never as "dames." In *Tomorrow Is Forever*, she inhabits a "resplendent environment, surrounded by all of the beautiful settings into which Miss Colbert fits so well" (*Modern Screen*, April 1946, 8). As in her films, publicity attempts to humble her, catching her near a muddy, shirtless MacMurray or highlighting slapstick in *Skylark*. Magazines render her more ordinary, as when her brother mailed her awkward childhood photos, inscribed, "Every time you think you're a Glamour Girl, look at this" (*Movies*, February 1943, 27).

Colbert had alternated Continental and all-American roles during the Depression but not after, and her wartime image was set by the time one magazine wrote, "Claudette is genuine—straight-shooting. . . . She speaks in rapid colloquial English and in some respects is as American as apple pie. Yet she is French-born, and has an exotic charm." The growing conservatism of her image (such as ads asking, "To which man do I belong?") is supported by interviews: "With me, home and husband come first. The woman who gives up her husband for a career is very foolish. . . . I wish I were a glamour girl. . . . Offscreen, I'm just a wife. I look like somebody who lives next door." Glamour is characterized as innate to her marriage: "It isn't mere glamour that has kept her at the top, though she has it—the real kind, not the orchid-dripping variety. . . . You envy the man who wins her in the fadeout. You know she'll make him happy, and keep him interested in her forever" (*Movies*, April 1943, 22, 68).

Presenting glamour as essence rather than construction promotes Stanwyck too: "Why she can't be a movie star. She looks too natural." Her "soap-washed" glamour is linked with her sentimentality, humor, and, ironically, given glamour's nature, her "intolerance of phonies" (*Silver Screen*, July 1942, 32, 67). Wealthy but ordinary, "Mrs. Robert Taylor" reports that "when they've had servant problems, he pitches in with housework till she hires new ones" (*Silver Screen*, November 1947, 28–29). This "old hoss-breeder herself needs no cajoling to take up simple life on the rancho." The Brooklyn-born orphan describes Capra's "sublimated typecasting": "I could pass for a rough-&-tumble newspaper dame, which is all right with me." Stanwyck's glamour, more outdoorsy than Colbert's, apparently resides in a phrase used about Colbert, "her honesty as actress and woman" (*Hollywood*, December 1940, 46–47). Her heterosexuality also has similarities; ads for *The Great Man's Lady* say, "There's a woman like me in every great man's life . . . living in the shadows, taking my romance when the world isn't looking" (*Silver Screen*, June 1942, 7).

If Colbert's Parisian sophistication was Americanized and then maternalized, Stanwyck's grittier ordinariness shifted as noir elements reflected cultural changes. Ads for *The Gay Sisters* (1942) ("To meet them is to love them—but to love them is dangerous!") have noir tinges (*Movies*, September 1942, 5). Ads for *My Reputation* combine self-reliance ("I'm going to live life my way") and romantic longing ("A woman isn't meant to be lonely, she's meant to be loved") alongside a seductively noir pose of Stanwyck not in the film, and the misleading caption, "Nobody needs to know anything . . . they'd never suspect *you*" (*Modern Screen*, March 1946, 11). Nonetheless, Stanwyck also relates to escapism, even with hard-boiled noir; a review of *Double Indemnity* notes "there's not one mention of war in it" (*Silver Screen*, July 1944, 10).

Rogers's persona appears to perform the most escapist cultural work of the three. Although she made only two musicals during the 1940s, the genre stayed with her image. Astaire, at low ebb in 1940–1941, said he was looking forward to making more films with Rogers, whom he dubbed "an instrument always capable of virtuoso performance" (*Hollywood*, August 1940, 50). She acted in more comedies than Stanwyck, and often as types giddier than sensible Colbert. While Colbert was made maternal through an advice column she wrote, and Stanwyck softened by stories about volunteer work, Rogers offered magazine readers chances to take personality tests or play "Silly-Dilly." The clearest Cinderella of the three, Rogers received her Oscar at a "floral fairyland" ceremony. A beau (according to magazines if not Rogers's memoirs), George Montgomery, described her à la *Major and the Minor*: "She uses no make-up and wears clothes that make her look like a schoolgirl" (*Silver Screen*, January 1942, 68). Asserting how Rogers took charge of her career from her manager-mother, one article contrasts them as "mellowed experience and the fullgrown kid who won't be stopped" (*Hollywood*, August 1940, 51). Even receiving serious recognition, Rogers remained playfully childlike. *Tom Dick and Harry*'s crew donned tuxedoes because "Miss Rogers snagged the Academy Award last night. We're only paying her the respect that is due her." "How does she feel? 'Respiration normal, pulse normal, ceiling zero,' Miss Rogers said, inviting us to have a popsicle" (*Hollywood*, July 1941, n.p.).

An adult ordinariness exists too, initially more proletariat than Colbert's, with *Kitty Foyle* "the First Great Romance of the White Collar Girl" (*Silver Screen*, January 1941, 11). Rogers also combines difference with sameness: Montgomery claimed, "Ginger's different than any other girl I've ever met" yet "she seems entirely unimpressed by her own importance. . . . Ginger's the best little cook you ever saw. And she's handy at washing dishes" (*Silver Screen*, January 1942, 68). Despite the "difficult glamour demands of her work," she wore ensembles "as sensible and normal as the

American College girl's outfit of sweater and skirt" (*Silver Screen*, May 1945, 39). One profile charts her teen vaudevillian days, "no startling beauty, but with plenty of that newly-coined word, sex-appeal . . . captivat[ing] audiences with dancing, singing and baby talk." Pseudo-Freudian analysis appears once she is in Hollywood: "She couldn't compete with exotic glamour. . . . Hollywood actresses were beautiful. She wasn't." She developed an "inferiority complex . . . gaiety and wise-cracking were a defense mechanism. Off guard, she had a sad, wistful gaze." But then magically, with no mention of Astaire, "Six years passed. Ginger became a great star, RKO's greatest box office attraction," and Jean Gabin completed her deification: "Ginger was the only star he wanted to meet when he came to Hollywood from Paris. . . . America, he felt, had produced a wondrous race of women, and Ginger was its most enchanting composite type" (*Movies*, May 1943, 20, 52).

When, in 1942, Rogers made her third *Life* cover (the first person besides FDR to do so), a profile emphasized qualities ("as American as apple pie") fitting all three: "She could easily be the girl who lives across the street. She is not uncomfortably beautiful. She is just beautiful enough. She is not an affront to other women. She gives them hope that they can be like her. She can wise-crack from the side of her mouth, but is clearly an idealist. Her green eyes [actually blue] shine with self-reliance. She believes in God and love and a hard day's work. She is a living affirmation of the holiest American legend: the success story" (*Life*, 2 March 1942, 60). All three embodied this myth for 1940s culture, especially early in the decade and during World War II. As Elizabeth Kendall aptly notes, Colbert's mother roles led to semi-retirement from films the earliest, while Rogers's "dizzy dames" would be "set straight" and Stanwyck's "dragon ladies" punished for their ambitions (180). Such summaries oversimplify slightly, as all three did TV, stage, and film work for decades more, but the age biases of American culture and the need for new icons of Extraordinary Ordinariness asserted themselves. Even as some of their films or roles became retreads, however, their professionalism, talent, and places in our cultural memory remained secure.

NOTE

1. *Motion Picture Herald* annual lists of the top twenty-five stars (28 December 1940, 27 December 1941, 28 December 1946, 3 January 1948, 1 January 1949, 31 December 1949, etc.).

6 ★★★★★★★★★★★

Judy Garland and Mickey Rooney
Babes and Beyond

SEAN GRIFFIN

Early in the musical *Strike Up the Band* (1940), Jimmy (Mickey Rooney) and Mary (Judy Garland) envision their futures as the leader and lead singer in a big band. Jimmy sees these aspirations to popular music as artistically honorable: "Look at George Gershwin. His music's as good as Beethoven or Bach. And best of all, he's American." Audiences in the 1940s seemed to regard Rooney and Garland in the same way: popular and good and American. At the time *Strike Up the Band* was released, Rooney was enjoying the second of a three-year run as the top box-office star in the United States, and Garland would enter the top ten for the first time (second only to Bette Davis as the most popular female performer of

Judy Garland portrait, c. 1942; Mickey Rooney portrait, c. 1942. Both photos collection of the author.

1940). Rooney and Garland at the zenith of their popularity—whether together or on their own—personified a youthful energy and promise that seemed to embody America and its future. For a country emerging out of a Depression and facing another World War, such an optimistic image resonated with moviegoers. Once the United States entered the war, their image of homespun can-do ability helped bolster confidence in American superiority and victory.

By appearing largely in musicals and light comedies (albeit with a dash of sentimentality often included), Rooney and Garland also helped audiences escape from the harsher aspects of the real world. During the early 1940s, Rooney's popularity was strongly tied to a series of films about the fictional Hardy family with Rooney as teenage son Andy, such as *Andy Hardy Meets Debutante* (1940), *Andy Hardy's Private Secretary* (1941), *Life Begins for Andy Hardy* (1941), *The Courtship of Andy Hardy* (1942), *Andy Hardy's Double Life* (1943), and *Andy Hardy's Blonde Trouble* (1944). Garland's career was overseen largely by MGM producer Arthur Freed (and his associate Roger Edens) in a series of polished musicals—*Little Nellie Kelly* (1940), *For Me and My Gal* (1942), *Meet Me in St. Louis* (1944). During this period, both stars were regularly paired together, with Rooney joining Garland in a number of flashy backstage song-and-dance extravaganzas produced by Freed (*Babes in Arms* [1939], *Strike Up the Band, Babes on Broadway* [1942], *Girl Crazy* [1943]), and Garland appearing occasionally in the Hardy films as Andy's friend Betsy Booth (*Love Finds Andy Hardy* [1938], *Andy Hardy Meets Debutante, Life Begins for Andy Hardy*).

In the second half of the decade, the careers of both performers went through major changes. In part, such changes involved their move through adolescence to adulthood. Rooney's popularity diminished significantly in the late forties, as the press and audiences began to regard him as irresponsible and egotistical—claims were made that teenage stardom had "stunted" his emotional growth. Garland remained a major box-office draw, but with a growing public concern about her emotional and physical stability. Instead of optimistic youth, Rooney and Garland—each in their own way— were increasingly regarded as cautionary tales about growing up within the classical Hollywood studio system.

Beyond the problems of transitioning to adulthood, the optimistic Americana that Rooney and Garland had symbolized during the first part of the 1940s no longer seemed to match popular attitudes. The prized innocence of their youth was increasingly anachronistic in the wake of such sobering events as the Holocaust and the onset of the atomic age. Cold War paranoia actually cautioned against American naivety. Although their postwar films do show connections to the first half of the decade, reviewers and columnists began sensing cracks in the façades. Perhaps in an unwitting parallel to the rise of the shadowy distrust of film noir, the postwar images of Garland and Rooney came to represent the dark shadows lurking behind the American Dream.

★★★★★ Born in a Trunk

Both Rooney and Garland entered "the business that is show" at extremely early ages. Rooney, born Joe Yule Jr., had parents who performed in burlesque, and he supposedly began his stage career by the time he was three. Judy Garland, born Frances Gumm, joined her two older siblings in their singing act also at the age of three. Both also headed west to California, each with a mother hoping to forward her child's career.

Rooney got some initial notice playing (and being billed as) Mickey McGuire in a series of comedy shorts based on the *Toonerville Trolley* comic strip (1926–1932). When the series ended, cartoonist Fontaine Fox won an injunction against the young man using the character's name as his own. Thus, when he won a small part in a Universal programmer, he was rechristened Mickey Rooney. With a new name, and with the dark hair color required for the McGuire role having grown out, he managed to draw the interest of producer David O. Selznick. Selznick convinced MGM, where he was working at the time, to put Rooney under contract. A loan-out to play Puck in a stage production of *A Midsummer Night's Dream* (and a film version made at Warner Bros. in 1934) garnered Rooney attention from critics and audiences, which led to larger and larger parts in MGM pictures. During roughly the same period (the early 1930s), the Gumm Sisters bounced around the vaudeville circuit and appeared in a few short subjects with varying degrees of anonymity. Altering their stage names to the Garland Sisters (and Frances to Judy) did not seem to change matters much. Eventually, the older sisters ended their performing careers, and Judy continued on solo, winning an MGM contract in 1936.

Both Rooney and Garland were thus on the lot by 1936—but two among a sea of juveniles. Rooney had to compete with Jackie Cooper and Freddie Bartholomew, both of whom were bigger marquee names in the mid-thirties. Similarly, Garland had to compete with the classically trained Deanna Durbin, as studio executives felt a need for only one adolescent female singer. (While Durbin was the one dropped, rumors have persisted that this was the result of a mix-up, and that the studio had intended to let go of Garland.) Each was also considered problematic to groom for stardom. Rooney was already considered short for his age, and his face was regarded as "snub-nosed and unhandsome" (Thomas Faye, "Turnabout for Mickey").[1] Volumes have been written on how executives considered Garland to have a pubescent "pudgy" body and a lack of potential glamour (see McLean "Feeling").

While MGM may have worried about their visual appeal, various people also recognized the enormous talent both possessed. Selznick specifically enlarged a part in *Manhattan Melodrama* (1934) to showcase Rooney, and Rooney managed to steal most of the attention away from both Cooper and Bartholomew when all three were cast in *The Devil Is a Sissy* (1936). Studio music arranger and vocal coach Roger Edens worked assiduously with Garland to polish her already prodigious singing voice. The year 1937 was key for both. Rooney's career took off with the enormous and unexpected success of a modestly budgeted programmer entitled *A Family Affair*, about the day-to-day lives of a middle-class American family called the Hardys; Garland garnered her first major break, singing a fan letter to Clark Gable, in *Broadway Melody of 1938*. The success of *A Family Affair* was followed by a stunningly popular string of films about the Hardys, increasingly focusing on Rooney's character, the teenage son Andy. In early 1939, Rooney would be presented with an honorary "juvenile performer" Academy Award. Garland's success in her solo spot led to bigger and bigger parts in studio musicals, eventually playing the lead role of Dorothy in the prestige production of *The Wizard of Oz* (1939), which marked her arrival as a full-fledged star. As 1940 began, their ascent was commemorated at the annual Oscar ceremony: Rooney was nominated for Best Actor in *Babes in Arms*, and he also presented that year's honorary juvenile award to Garland.

★★★★★ Gee!

By 1940, MGM had fashioned compatible star images for the two. Rather than working to somehow overcome their perceived lack of conventional star quality (leading-man good looks for him, feminine glamour for her), the studio framed Rooney and Garland as average American teenagers, thus glorifying "ordinariness." Their roles emphasized this sense: Dorothy Gale hailed from a Kansas farm, Andy Hardy and his family lived smack in the heart of Idaho. Rather than erudite, sophisticated dialogue, their characters were consistently prone to phrases like "Gee!" "Swell!" and "Jiminy Crickets!"

Richard Dyer's reading of Garland's star image foregrounds this emphasis on ordinariness: their films together "were clearly packaged and understood as hymns to ordinariness, and promotion material on Garland and

Mickey Rooney and Judy Garland as typical American high-schoolers in the gym after band practice in *Strike Up the Band* (1940). Copyright 1940, Loew's, Inc.

Rooney amplified this, showing them for instance at soda fountains (the innocent meeting place of small-town kids), playing tennis (the small-town game) and singing at a simple upright piano with the Stars and Stripes on it" ("Judy Garland" 152). In the fan magazines, articles almost obsessively reiterated how they were average kids. Rooney is described as "the typical American kid" ("Top Kid Star") or a "genuine, average American" (Ruth Waterbury, "How Andy Hardy Reformed Mickey Rooney," *Photoplay*, January 1940, 9). Letters from fans consider him "Everyman as a boy" (*Photoplay*, March 1941, 18), and "the very fact that he can run, throw, walk and just plain be like a regular boy distinguishes him from most of the other Hollywood boys" (*Photoplay*, July 1940, 13). Similarly, Hedda Hopper described Garland as an "All-American Kid" ("Personality Feature," 29 July 1938).[2] Supposed comments from Garland in an article for *Motion Picture* magazine in May 1940 follow a similar track, as she asserts that she is not "any less normal than anybody else." Interviewer James Reid supports that claim by describing how, "in a commissary full of Pretty Young Things, some of them playing schoolgirls in a new picture, Judy was the only one who looked more like a schoolgirl than a movie actress."

Rooney and Garland were also obviously *extra*-ordinary due to their talent. Garland was the "little girl with the big voice," the "child who sang like an adult." Dyer describes a key component of Garland's image as an excess of "emotional intensity" that is most evident when she sings ("Judy Garland" 158). Rooney was often depicted in the press as a pint-size modern-day Renaissance man, adept at almost anything that struck his fancy: actor, comedian, singer, dancer, musician, composer, athlete, and consummate impressionist. Space was made in films to showcase Rooney's vast talents: doing impressions and playing drums in *Strike Up the Band*, for example, or running hurdles in *The Human Comedy* (1943). In early 1941, Ford would sponsor a CBS broadcast of "Melodante," a symphony in three parts composed by Rooney (Frederick C. Othman, "Mickey Awaits Climax to Musical Labor," *Los Angeles Citizen News*, 6 February 1941).

Furthermore, Garland and Rooney's stunning talents seemed wedded to a limitless supply of drive. A *Movie Mirror* article on Garland divulged that "even when she was a tiny tot named Frances Gumm, little Judy Garland had plenty of pep—and knew how to use it" (Mitzi Cummings, "Punch—and Judy," March 1938, 39). Rooney, in particular, was continuously presented as a whirling dervish of energy, described in *Look* magazine as "the nearest thing to jet propulsion in Hollywood" ("Mickey Rooney—Eager Beaver," 13 May 1947, 67). Their film performances supported such claims, particularly in the musicals they made together. Directed by showman Busby Berkeley in *Babes in Arms*, *Strike Up the Band*, *Babes on Broadway*, and in the "I Got Rhythm" finale of *Girl Crazy*, the characters played by Rooney and Garland regularly tear all over the screen in something almost approaching a maniacal frenzy. They conga, they hoe-down, they jitterbug, they scat-sing, they bounce around on the furniture, they (unfortunately, for today's audiences) throw themselves wholeheartedly into blackface minstrelsy. They are smiling constantly, eyes blazing with confidence—and usually sneaking a quick peek at each other to share their zeal and joy.

The problem was reconciling these two aspects, explaining how they could be both ordinary *and* extraordinary simultaneously. For Rooney, part of this reconciliation involved dealing with potential detractors who saw his cheerful confidence as cocky egotism. Articles about Rooney during the height of his popularity actively negotiate this problem, asserting that Rooney "is sensitive about charges Hollywood writers have made that he is a 'smart aleck and a show-off'" ("*Look* Calls on Mickey Rooney," 7 May 1940, 42), and that "despite his cocky appearance and brash manner, there is no better-mannered young man in all Hollywood" (Lon Jones, "Mickey Rooney Grows Up," *Toronto Star Weekly*, 9 August 1947, 11). As Andy Hardy,

Mickey Rooney as Andy Hardy and Lewis Stone as father Judge Hardy in an undated publicity photo. Collection of the author.

Rooney inevitably brags his way into a mess of trouble that requires hum-
bling himself and asking for help, most particularly from his father (Lewis
Stone) in a "man-to-man" talk that became a standard scene in every film.
Rooney's characters were also often taken down a peg in his musicals with
Garland, usually as he realizes that he has overlooked how much help he
has been given in his various plot endeavors from her.

Similar dynamics worked to reconcile Garland's extraordinary ordinariness as well. Whether paired with Rooney or not, her films during this
period tend to present her as someone with lots of potential (intelligence,
humor, talent, etc.) but who subordinates herself to help others. Garland's
characters were routinely given songs that emphasized how Rooney and
others overlooked her. In *Strike Up the Band*, she intones "Everybody's Got
Someone, But Nobody's Got Me." In *Girl Crazy*, she performs the Gershwin
standard "But Not for Me." In *Ziegfeld Girl* (1941), Garland is given the
lugubrious standard "I'm Always Chasing Rainbows." The plot of the film
shows three young women plucked from obscurity to appear in the Ziegfeld
Follies. As was common for Garland at this point in her career, her character is initially relegated to the chorus while the other two (played by Lana

Turner and Hedy Lamarr) are showcased as exemplars of beauty. Similarly, *Little Nellie Kelly* shows Garland (playing both Nellie and, in the first third of the film, her mother) acquiescing to the overbearing desires of Charles Winninger (playing father/grandfather). While Rooney's characters border on conceited, Garland's border on erasure, thus encouraging the audience to root for her to assert her self-worth.

As a number of the above quotes evince, the extraordinary ordinariness of Rooney and Garland also was resolved by being "American." They represented the average Joe and Jane, but showed just how remarkable the average American could be. One commentator stated directly, "Mickey is a symbol; he epitomizes young America, clean, sincere, honest boyhood" (Thomas Faye, "Turnabout for Mickey"). Granted, Rooney and Garland were not alone in being praised and adored as representatives of ordinary Americans at the time. A number of other Hollywood stars also fit that bill, such as James Stewart, Henry Fonda, and Betty Grable. Yet, as youngsters, Rooney and Garland embodied a generation poised to lead the country (and the world) into a new and better tomorrow. Such images resonated strongly with a country on the verge of another global conflict. One Rooney fan laid it out explicitly: "We need him in the world today" (*Photoplay*, March 1941, 18). The final image of *Strike Up the Band* epitomizes the association: while the title tune plays, the Stars and Stripes are hoisted into close-up, with a beaming Rooney and Garland superimposed over the waving banner.

Practically any of their films from the early forties can stand as an example of these various aspects. *Andy Hardy Meets Debutante* will serve as a representative case. In this chapter of the Hardy saga, Andy aims to meet the current girl of his dreams, New York socialite Daphne Fowler (Diana Lewis). While in the city with his family, Andy meets up with old neighbor Betsy (Garland), whose family now lives in Manhattan. Betsy's pining for Andy goes unrequited, but she provides the key to his dilemma: *she* knows Daphne herself, and takes him to the debutante's coming-out party. At the party, Betsy sings—and Andy realizes he has been chasing after the wrong girl. Betsy sings twice in the film, both prime examples of Garland's typical self-abnegating number: "Alone" and, at the ball, "I'm Nobody's Baby."

The plot shows Andy having to swallow his pride repeatedly, to the point that Andy becomes ashamed of his small-town background. One can almost hear the gasp from MGM czar Louis B. Mayer when Andy verges on critiquing class politics, but luckily Judge Hardy is there to shame the boy into line with another patented "man-to-man" talk. The film consistently shows that the metropolis can learn from small town America. (Judge Hardy takes Andy to the NYU Hall of Fame to show him busts of "nobodys who became somebodys." Of course, the judge himself also manages to out-perform some big city lawyers.) The film also stresses how the supposed opposites of city and country are connected: for example, the judge takes the family to New York because their hometown orphanage is suddenly bereft of its trust fund, since the city bankers invested in European bonds that are now worthless due to the outbreak of war. Most significantly, Andy comes to realize the most worthwhile person in the city is Betsy, an urban-ite who loves small town ways. In an apt commingling of urban and rural, Andy and Betsy ride home from the coming-out ball in a horse-drawn car-riage through Central Park. Rooney and Garland play the scene with quiet intimacy, as Andy gives Betsy her first kiss, causing her to cry a bit. By film's end, Rooney and Garland's charm, talent, and energy have idealized Amer-ican youth and created a stronger sense of national pride. As the ad cam-paign proclaimed: "It's What America Needs Right Now!"

Such star images continued to fit well with audience needs after Amer-ica's entrance into World War II. The Academy awarded MGM a special Oscar in 1942, a year into the fight, specifically for producing the Hardy series. As such, it took little to move Rooney and Garland into more explicitly patri-otic fare. *For Me and My Gal* showed Judy doing her part, entertaining the troops (albeit the doughboys in World War I). In *Babes on Broadway*, Rooney and Garland put on a neighborhood benefit to raise war bonds, including "Chin Up, Cheerio, Carry On," a salute to our British Allies (accompanied by a bathetic series of teary-eyed close-ups of British war orphans). Both Rooney and Garland would do bits during the revue section of the wartime musical *Thousands Cheer* (1943). Furthermore, MGM burnished their images of American youth to the point of iconicity in (for him) *The Human Comedy* and (for her) *Meet Me in St. Louis*.

The Human Comedy feels like a prestige A-budget version of an Andy Hardy picture. Rooney is once again a teenage boy (Homer Macaulay) growing up in small-town America (fictional Ithaca, California). The major difference is that this film more overtly deals with the impact of the war on family life than the Hardy series ever did (to be discussed shortly). As the story begins, father has passed away. With oldest brother Marcus (Van Johnson) off in the military, Homer has become the "man of the house-hold," working as a telegram delivery boy while finishing high school. As such, Homer is shown informing families about the deaths of loved ones fighting overseas—including, at the end of the film, his own family about Marcus. While such a description emphasizes death and sadness, the film displays (through the various rituals and events in the Macaulay family life) that, even in the face of death, life goes on. The film begins with baby brother Ulysses ("Butch" Jenkins) fascinated by the passing parade of life (a gopher hole, a bird's nest, hoboes on trains rolling by). Similar picturesque sequences include an overdetermined wealth of ethnic groups celebrating "I'm an American Day," and Ulysses with a group of boys stealing apricots from the yard of "old man Henderson." As Homer returns home with the news of Marcus's death, he is met by his brother's army buddy, Tobey, an orphan who has come to regard Ithaca as his home from all of Marcus's rhapsodies about the place. Instead of bringing loss, then, Homer brings a new family member into the house. As the film concludes, "The ending is only the beginning."

While written originally for the screen, by the time *The Human Comedy* was produced, it had become a critically acclaimed best-selling novel by William Saroyan. (Saroyan would win an Oscar.) The film was also carefully produced to the last detail. Almost every shot is meticulously lit, and the camera is inevitably positioned a bit below eye level to make everyone seem all the more mythic. As the final line indicates, the film strains at poetic greatness. The various names indicate the epic within everyday America: Ithaca, Homer, Marcus, Ulysses reference the *Odyssey* (which also venerates home). Everyone also speaks just a little too beautifully. By the time the camera captures little Ulysses falling asleep by shooting through Mother's harp as she plays, the Hardy series starts to look Neorealist in comparison.

Meet Me in St. Louis has arguably become the American classic that *The Human Comedy* desired to be. (While *The Human Comedy* was a *success d'estime* for MGM, *Meet Me in St. Louis* became the biggest box-office success the studio had produced to that time.) Such regard is perhaps partly due to the even larger budget, and partly to being a nostalgia piece rather than dealing directly with the war. (The original plan was to redecorate the Hardy street; the final decision to create an entire new block of Victorian home fronts cost the production over $200,000 [Fordin 96].) Similar to *The Human Comedy*'s everyday activities of watching trains and apricot-picking, *Meet Me in St. Louis* revels in ketchup-making, family dinners, and holiday traditions—both films dwell on an overall ambience rather than specific narrative goals. Yet the ultimate impression could not be more different. While *The Human Comedy* strains for a somber, mythic tone, underneath is the equivalent of a sentimental marshmallow. On the other hand, *Meet Me in St. Louis* starts out almost literally like a big Technicolor candy box (thanks to the stitched sampler titles that announce the various seasons), but eventually reveals a dark undercurrent. Nothing in *The Human Comedy*, for example, can match the disturbing hysteria of youngest daughter Tootie (Margaret O'Brien) smashing her snow family to pieces. The threat to the

Macauleys is much greater than to the Smiths, but the possibility of leaving St. Louis somehow seems much more dire than any of the telegrams Homer delivers.

Rooney and Garland also bring new shadings to their personae in these two films. Homer Macauley is more serious and thoughtful than Andy Hardy, and Rooney's second Oscar nomination honored his restrained performance. Esther Smith, on the other hand, is a confident ball of energy. Garland does not play her as shy, retiring, or insecure (unless Esther decides to play that role in order to get the boy next door to help her turn out the lights). While Esther is still a bit worried about being provincial compared to big-city socialites, she asserts that she can juggle a number of beaux at the big Christmas ball. While the two films are arguably the culmination of Rooney and Garland as idealized American youth, the shifts in both roles seem to announce that these two are no longer "babes."

★★★★★ Our Love Affairs

The two stars themselves grew increasingly agitated about being locked into an adolescent mold. Rooney started playing high school student Andy Hardy in 1937; in 1943, Rooney's Homer Macauley is still running hurdles for Ithaca High. Garland was so tired of being cast as a teen that she initially tried to get out of being in *Meet Me in St. Louis*.

Most particularly, Rooney and Garland seemed increasingly bothered by MGM's attempts to keep them from having the personal lives of young adults—in other words, having serious romantic relationships. Dates chaperoned by their mothers or intimations of pubescent crushes were allowed and/or concocted by the studio—but nothing more than that (Proctor). Drinking, smoking, night-clubbing until the wee hours were strictly *verboten* (and the constant claims that Rooney was doing all these things were being squelched regularly in the press) (French). While often promoted and regarded as a team, the image of Rooney and Garland's coupledom is quite bereft of sexual chemistry. Rather, the two always felt like great friends who enjoyed performing together—any sense of love was chaste, innocent, "first love." Attempts to consider the two as a romantic couple offscreen never substantially materialized. Such an assessment carried over to their on-screen pairings. While vague possibilities of romantic interest would be raised between Betsy Booth and Andy Hardy, for example, no serious courtship would ever materialize and the two remained simply kindred spirits. The "Babes" musicals are usually more focused on their attempts to find success in show business than *amour*. The completely unromantic rendition of the ballad "Our Love Affair" in *Strike Up the Band* has Rooney and Garland excitedly figuring out how to arrange the song by creating a dining-room table orchestra out of fruit! These films usually end not with a big embrace but with the two smiling broadly at the end of a stage performance, with Rooney perhaps sneaking a quick peck on the cheek of a surprised Garland.

Intriguingly, both began to break out of this innocent teen mold at the same time. In 1941, each of them got married: he to MGM starlet Ava Gardner, she to musician David Rose (who had recently divorced comedienne Martha Raye). Judging from squibs in the fan magazines, the studio was not too pleased with either development, trying to deny for months that anything serious was happening (and thus that Rooney and Garland were possibly no longer virgins!). For example, although only months away from marriage, a planted bit in Cal York's column in the November 1940 *Photoplay* announced that "[MGM] is breathing relief over the termination of the Judy Garland–Dave Rose . . . romance" (63). Later, after both weddings, studio publicists tried to act overjoyed. An article about Rooney and Gardner states quite baldly, "'He's made a swell choice,' is the universal opinion of a studio that only a short time ago vigorously opposed the marriage of two of its youngest stars" (Sara Hamilton, "Mickey Rooney Picks a Wife," *Photoplay*, March 1942, 70). By the end of 1942, though, both stars were facing separation and divorce, and before the war was over each was embarking on a second try at matrimony (Rooney to Betty Jane Rase, an Alabama girl he met during army training, and Garland to director Vincente Minnelli).

MGM definitely tried to keep them pigeonholed in their onscreen images after the marriages. Columnist Sidney Skolsky wrote that "when the honeymoon (of Garland and Rose) was over, she went back to being a kid again: Mickey Rooney's little girl friend in 'Babes on Broadway'" (*Los Angeles Citizen-News*, 9 September 1941). Similarly, the above article on the Rooney-Gardner marriage reported, "'The *Hardy* series will go right on,' the studio assured us. 'Mickey's marriage will in no way affect his role of *Andy*.'"

Still, MGM executives had to know that the two would continue to grow up, and that things would have to change eventually. As the 1930s ended, other studios had faced the difficulty of shifting enormously popular juvenile stars into more grown-up fare. Twentieth Century–Fox failed completely in trying to refashion Shirley Temple, dropping her contract in 1940. Universal fared somewhat better easing Deanna Durbin from pubescence to adulthood in the late thirties and early forties, although the studio never reestablished the enormous popularity of her early career. MGM

A glamour shot of Judy Garland in chic pajamas, circa 1943, displays her with lightened hair and heavier makeup, announcing a conscious transition away from her earlier "average" teenager image. Collection of the author.

executives (Roger Edens in particular) took extra care to develop Garland's potential, evidenced by careful selection of film roles to help the audience feel comfortable in regarding her as an adult. *Little Nellie Kelly* begins with Garland as a young adult woman, marrying and having a child. Her character, though, dies in childbirth—and Garland plays the daughter as teenager for the rest of the film. *Ziegfeld Girl* introduces her as daughter to vaudevillian Charles Winninger, but shows her gradually becoming the toast of the Ziegfeld Follies. *For Me and My Gal* was her first completely adult role, romanced by George Murphy and newcomer Gene Kelly. *Presenting Lily Mars* (1943) seems to announce the end of Garland's onscreen adolescence, with her character Lily asserting, "I know why you treat me like a child—it's because you're afraid to think of me as a woman!" At the same time, Garland was also very noticeably growing more glamorous. From film to film, she shed pounds, changed her hair style and makeup, and appeared in more extravagant wardrobe. The number of stunning shots director Minnelli got of Garland in *Meet Me in St. Louis* made it almost impossible for audiences to think of her as anything but gorgeous.

Concerns that such a transition would not be welcomed were largely unwarranted. Moviegoer Helen Carden wrote to *Photoplay* in July 1941, just before Garland's marriage to Rose: "Am I sick of all these magazine articles as to whether Judy Garland should or should not get married! As a pretty consistent movie-goer (at least twice a week) and a happily married woman I say what if she does marry Dave Rose? . . . As for alienating her fans— what nonsense!" (86). By the end of World War II, the transition for Garland was largely completed and celebrated in movie magazines (Hedda Hopper, "Here's 'Ugly Duckling' Come into Her Own," *Los Angeles Times*, 10 December 1944, 1–2; Louella O. Parsons, "Judy Garland to Wed in Fall," *Los Angeles Examiner*, 10 January 1945; Elsa Maxwell, "My Nine Most Exciting Hollywood Moments," *Photoplay*, March 1945, 101; Adela Rogers St. Johns, "Judy—the girl who became 'the world's best-dressed woman,'" *Photoplay*, November 1945, 30–31, 121–23).

Part of the success of Garland's newer adult image may have been how it managed to hold onto aspects of her earlier persona. In particular, the ordinariness was maintained through a sense that, underneath the glamour, the old Judy was still there—someone who did not take her new sophistication all that seriously. (A number of people have commented on this aspect of her star persona becoming a key part of her popularity as a gay camp icon [Dyer "Judy Garland "; Cohan].) Particular examples of that dynamic would include her unflappable reactions to being placed in the center of the exotic extravaganza "Minnie from Trinidad" in *Ziegfeld Girl*, the scene of her binding herself into a corset in *Meet Me in St. Louis*, and (perhaps most famously) the "Great Lady Has an Interview" portion of *Ziegfeld Follies* (1946)—in which she simultaneously sends up glamour *and* embodies it. Her willingness to be completely unglamorous in the "Be a Clown" finale of *The Pirate* (1948) and "A Couple of Swells" in *Easter Parade* (1948) also adds to this dimension of her adult persona.

On the other hand, the studio spent less time working on Rooney's transition, basically pigeonholing him as Andy Hardy or a variation thereof. While Garland's range slowly expanded during the mid-1940s, Rooney's actually seemed to diminish because he had played a wider range of character types in the late 1930s. As one reporter wrote, "Mickey is closely identified with the childish phase of his career. . . . We just can't think of the fellow at 40 or 50 as Mickey Rooney. The name just doesn't improve with age, it just doesn't go with the acquisition of gray hair at the temples or children on the knees" (Paul Benedict, "When Tomorrow Comes for Mickey"). An apt comment on the increasingly divergent studio strategies toward the two performers came from Cal York in November 1943's *Photoplay*: "Let's hope M-G-M finally catches on after thinking over 'Girl Crazy' that Mickey and Judy have just about run their course as a musical-comedy team. There's something a bit incongruous about a gal who can play a wife and sweetheart to Gene Kelly, Van Heflin, or George Murphy, or even play a divorced wife off-screen, romping around like a twelve-year-old in a hep cat Rooney film" (16).

The onset of war is a possible reason why the studio kept Rooney's image in arrested development at the same time it was carefully guiding Garland to adult stardom. If Rooney and his characters became more mature, then this "of-age" male would be expected to do his duty and enlist. Sending Andy Hardy off to war might have made for stunning propaganda, but would have also hampered the ability to continue making new chapters of the very profitable series. So, *The Courtship of Andy Hardy*, *Andy Hardy's Double Life*, and *Andy Hardy's Blonde Trouble* continue to show Andy dealing with girl troubles and getting ready to go to college. (The only major acknowledgment of the war would be the repeated anxious looks by various citizens at the new Asian doctor [Keye Luke] in *Andy Hardy's Blonde Trouble*.)

Further, as one of their top box-office earners, MGM was loathe to lose Rooney himself to the armed services (particularly when so many of the studio's leading men had already gone off to war—including James Stewart, Clark Gable, and Robert Montgomery). While one can recognize why the studio would have worked to keep Rooney (and Hardy) out of the service, such plans ultimately backfired. With young men throughout the country putting their lives on the line, many looked suspiciously at Hollywood stars who somehow had managed to keep out of the military, regarding them as over-privileged and unmasculine. Rumors swirled about a number of male stars—but the only concrete example of an attempted deferment was Rooney. In February 1943, MGM appealed Rooney's 1-A classification, "contending that a certain number of stars are necessary to keep the volume of film production up to normal and that motion pictures are needed to build and maintain morale" ("Actor Mickey Rooney Inducted into U.S. Army," *Los Angeles Times*, 15 June 1944, A12; see also Marx 119–20). The resulting negative publicity was so severe that MGM later rescinded the request. Eventually, in May 1944, Rooney would join the army (Marx 121, 131, 141; Schatz 208).

Rooney tried to put a positive spin on the entire debacle, telling reporters, "This is the biggest thing in my life. . . . It makes me happy to know that they've accepted me" ("Actor Mickey Rooney Inducted into U.S. Army"). The gambit seemed to work. At the conclusion of the war, having risen to technical sergeant and getting the Bronze Star, *Photoplay*'s Cal York intoned his opinion that Rooney had done a "wonderful job overseas" (April 1946, 12). Yet while everyone was raving over Garland's triumph as a romantic leading lady in *Meet Me in St. Louis*, Rooney's popularity seemed to be ebbing.

★★★★★ Treat Me Rough

America in 1946 was in many ways a vastly different place than America in 1940. A sobered viewpoint replaced the determined optimism of the early 1940s. Veterans dealing with physical or psychological injuries returned home to families who could not fully understand what they had been through. Awareness of the Holocaust and the dropping of the atomic bomb revealed the extent of destruction humankind could wreak upon one another. On theater screens, wartime propaganda was supplanted increasingly by film noir and social problem dramas. In their films and in their public image, Rooney and Garland reflected these changes.

The reception of Rooney's postwar films in particular show this shift. Audiences no longer wanted Rooney the teenager, but they did not warm to Rooney the adult. His first picture upon returning from the service was business as usual: *Love Laughs at Andy Hardy* (1946). Customers turned away, though, and it ended the entire series.[3] *Summer Holiday* (1948), a musical adaptation of Eugene O'Neill's *Ah, Wilderness!*, also kept Rooney in adolescence. The film sat on the shelf a year after its completion and ended up losing almost $1.5 million (Fordin 203). *Killer McCoy* (1947) finally moved him into adulthood, with Rooney playing a brooding prize fighter mixed up with gangsters. The film verges on noir, now suggesting Rooney's energy and bravado as a cover hiding darker demons. Four years earlier, in the opening number of *Girl Crazy*, "Treat Me Rough," the brashness was

Mickey Rooney (with Frank Morgan) still playing a teenager in *Summer Holiday* (1948). Note the similarities to the photo of Rooney with Lewis Stone. The project was one of producer Arthur Freed's biggest box-office failures. Copyright 1948, Loew's, Inc.

punished jocularly, with chorus girls mussing his hair and pinching his cheek. By the end of *Killer McCoy*, though, Rooney's character is redeemed by being pummeled to within an inch of his life. *Words and Music* (1948), a highly fictional biography of songwriters Rodgers and Hart, is similarly somber, climaxing with Rooney as the tragic Hart collapsing dead and alone on a rainy city sidewalk.

Killer McCoy did reasonably well (largely due to a tight budget), and *Words and Music* was a big hit. Yet neither seemed to bolster Rooney's standing, and audiences may have been uncomfortable seeing Rooney as now a complicated, moody figure. Most people, for example, thought the success of *Words and Music* was due to the number of guest star musical performances (among them Gene Kelly, Lena Horne, June Allyson, and Garland— including her last big screen duet with Rooney, "I Wish I Were in Love Again"). Rooney's performance, on the other hand, was considered one of the weakest aspects (Bosley Crowther, *New York Times*, 10 December 1948). (Granted, the inability of the film—due to the Production Code—to acknowledge Hart's homosexuality hampered the chances for him to create a coherent character.)

While Rooney's characters grew increasingly dark, his relationship with MGM also became less rosy. In early 1944, with encouragement from attorney Morton Briskin, Rooney became the first star on the lot to incorporate himself (thus sheltering his salary from new tax laws) (Marx 130). Over the next few years, Rooney, Inc. regularly asserted itself in negotiations with MGM over salary increases, over greater ability to work independently from the studio, and over not being paid while serving in the military (*Hollywood Reporter*, 28 August 1944, 1; Marx 143–44). Reportedly, Rooney was "the first major star that Metro has ever permitted to negotiate his own outside deals" ("Rooney Given New Pact; Permitted to Do Outside Pix," *Variety*, 2 August 1948, 8).

Playing hardball may not have been ultimately the wisest plan. Rooney felt slighted and insulted by people at MGM when he returned to work. According to accounts the filming of *Summer Holiday* was often tense, possibly due to producer Arthur Freed's lack of personal involvement during the production. Rooney felt ill at ease working with director Rouben Mamoulian, and he reportedly despised working with co-star Gloria de Haven (Fordin 185–203). Similarly, in a 1997 interview with Robert Osborne for Turner Classic Movies, Rooney angrily claimed that Roy Rowland, director of *Killer McCoy*, loudly accused the actor of being self-centered and unprofessional in front of the cast and crew. Although Rooney was by any definition playing the lead part in *Words and Music*, the film listed all the stars alphabetically, thus placing him next to last (before Ann Sothern).

Interviews during the postwar period show his growing testiness, feeling that he was being passed over for properties that would have been right for him. "They gypped me on the billing on 'Words and Music,'" he complained in a 1949 interview, and "they gave 'Merton of the Movies' to Red Skelton. They should have given me 'Battleground,' and they didn't" ("Complaint," *New York Times*, 3 July 1949; see also Stanley Frank, "Hollywood's Fabulous Brat," *Saturday Evening Post*, 6 December 1947, 138). Such interviews were plainly attempts by Rooney to bring his case to the public, but most of these articles tend to paint him in somewhat unflattering terms. Studio PR staff now seemed disinclined to squelch the recurrent accusations that Rooney was brash and cocky. "Whether Rooney is irritating or irresistible seems to depend on the degree of exposure to his personality," wrote Stanley Frank for the *Saturday Evening Post* (143). In late 1948, Rooney had had enough: he renegotiated his contract, agreeing to finish his commitment to the studio by making only five more films at a lower salary, but giving him the ability to do pictures elsewhere in the interim (Marx 159). Rooney's freedom came as his drawing power had been heavily diminished, and the only deal he managed to put together was at United Artists, where he made *Quicksand* (1949) and *The Big Wheel* (1950), two low-budget programmers.

Rooney's personal life was also falling apart as the 1940s ended. He owed a sizable amount of back taxes and had lost a lot of cash gambling on horses. Furthermore, his second marriage had ended in divorce, resulting in both alimony and child support payments for his two children with Betty Jane ("Order Rooney to Pay $5750 Pending Trial of Wife's Suit," *Los Angeles Herald-Express*, 13 June 1947, A9). A third marriage (to actress Martha Vickers) was already on the rocks. To complete the decimation, Rooney came to realize the less than scrupulous dealings of partner Briskin. Moves to dissolve Rooney, Inc. began in early 1949. Rooney's career appeared at its nadir as the decade ended.

On a certain level, Garland's postwar career was the opposite of Rooney's. Rather than performing in low-budget films, she was appearing in high-end Technicolor pictures (*The Harvey Girls* [1946], *The Pirate*, *Easter Parade*, *In the Good Old Summertime* [1949], and guest appearances in *Till the Clouds Roll By* [1946] and *Words and Music*). Other than *The Pirate*, all these films were major successes, and she remained one of the most valuable stars on the lot. These musicals suggest the antithesis of noir and social problem dramas. Her only non-musical (and her only black-and-white film) during this period, *The Clock* (1945), has its dramatic elements, but is generally a light romance of two lovers in New York City.

Yet, in looking more closely, connections between Garland's films and the postwar zeitgeist become more apparent. Musicals were venturing into more dramatic territory (largely spurred by the move toward integrated musicals penned by Rodgers and Hammerstein). Dramatizing Lorenz Hart's death in *Words and Music* is a good example of such evolution, as is the increased use of Freudian dream sequences in musicals like *The Pirate*. The spectacle and comedic mayhem common to film musicals in the 1930s and early 1940s was being replaced by stronger plot lines and deeper character development. Also, one can argue that Garland's performances are pitched differently than during the first half of the decade. The "emotional intensity" associated with her persona definitely remains, but it starts to approach a manic depressive hysteria. The joy and merriment seems strained at points, and the heartbroken moments seem much deeper than, say, her singing "Nobody's Got Me" in *Strike Up the Band*. For example, Garland's performance of "Mack the Black" in *The Pirate* happens when her character is under hypnosis, technically justifying the sense of repressed urges unleashed—but the intensity borders on fanatical. The tremolo in her voice when singing ballads had been slight as the decade started (for example, "Over the Rainbow" in *The Wizard of Oz*); by decade's end, the tremolo had increased into almost (*almost!*) falling out of key (for example, "Love of My Life" in *The Pirate*). While each of these films inevitably ends happily for Garland's character, a precariousness to the proceedings becomes more and more pronounced. If anything, the appeal of watching Garland in projects made after World War II is how far out on the edge she dares to go without falling into the metaphorical abyss.[4]

Of course, today's audiences, having heard a mountain of anecdotes about Garland's insecurities, her drug dependency, and her own claims of exploitation and overwork, cannot help but read those factors into her later performances (and possibly even into the manic wide-eyed energy of the earlier *Babes* films) (Deans and Pinchot; DiOrio; Edwards *Judy Garland*; Finch; Fordin; Frank; Watson and Chapman; Fricke; Shipman; Clarke). Dyer claims that reading Garland as a tragic figure with a "special relationship to suffering" did not begin until the 1950s ("Judy Garland" 138). Yet evidence supports the contention that filmgoers were already reconsidering her image by the mid-1940s. Rather than commenting on her "pep," the press began regularly mentioning her "frailty." As early as June 1942, some were expressing concern over Garland's weight loss. "Judy Garland is now down to ninety-eight pounds and has her studio frantic with concern over her health," wrote columnist Cal York (*Photoplay*, 8). An article in the same magazine in November 1942 informed readers that "Judy Garland is an intense, emotional girl who feels deeply and keenly. The [wartime] blackouts fill her with terror" (Sally Reid, "The Private Life of Judy Garland Rose," 93). By 1944, Louella Parsons was already having to assert that "Judy is *not* dying!" ("The Mystery of Judy Garland," *Photoplay*, July 1944, 29; italics in original).

As the comment from Parsons exemplifies, plenty of articles during this period assert that everything is fine with Garland—just a little nerves, just recovering from an illness, just a bout of insomnia requiring some sleeping pills (Elaine St. Johns, "The Truth about Judy Garland's Health," *Photoplay*, November 1947, 46–47, 85; Hedda Hopper, "Judy Garland—Flesh and Blood"; Hedda Hopper, "Money Need Spurs Judy Garland On," *Los Angeles Times*, 26 June 1949, 1, 3; Carl Johnson, "Why Can't Judy Garland Find Happiness?" *Screen and TV Guide*, August 1949, 36–37, 75–76.). Yet even these articles emphasize how often questions of her emotional stability were being raised. Writers joyously proclaiming that marriage to Minnelli—and then motherhood to Liza—would finally give Garland "the happiness and

fulfillment personally she knows professionally" indirectly suggest a perceived lack of fulfillment (Roberta Ormiston, "Halfway to Heaven," *Photoplay*, October 1945, 34, 107–09; Adela Rogers St. Johns, "Million Dollar
Lullaby," *Photoplay*, November 1946, 61, 161–62; Elsa Maxwell, "Liza, Liza,
Smile at Me," *Photoplay*, May 1947, 40–43, 80–81). Consequently, while a
number of people (friends, MGM employees, industry columnists) tried to
protect Garland's "all-American" image, stories of this troubling side were
nonetheless emerging (Jimmie Tarantino, "Miss G on Probation," *Hollywood
Nite Life*, 13 August 1948, 2). By the end of 1949, even the mainstream
press was referring to Garland's drug use—*Time* somewhat nonchalantly
mentioning how "she had worked herself to a frazzle, complicated by
insomnia and jitters for which she had long been trying to doctor herself"
("Working Girl," 14 November 1949, 103).

Lurking alongside the growing image of Garland as a frail, damaged
creature, though, one could find a young actress trying to assert herself. She
battled over directors (refusing to work with Berkeley, for example, or
attempting to work only with Minnelli from 1944 to 1947) (Fordin 83–84,
140, 146–47, 155, 177). She complained about overwork as well. In contrast to the stories about her absences and breakdowns on the set, Garland
was often able to get a perfect vocal recording in one take (Fordin 102,
155). Furthermore, the picture where Garland seems most relaxed on
screen during this period is *Easter Parade*—after she finally got a substantial
break between projects. So, an image of Garland as a determined performer
struggling for control (much as Rooney was doing at the same time) also
emerges.

But Garland's volatility, whatever the cause, hampered more and more
projects—she eventually was taken off *The Barkleys of Broadway* (1949),
Annie Get Your Gun (1950), and *Royal Wedding* (1951). When this last production was interrupted by chronic absences in June 1950, studio brass had
had enough and informed her that she was being let go. The next day,
headlines in newspapers informed the public that "Judy Garland Slashes
Throat in Death Try" (*Los Angeles Herald Express*, 20 June 1950, 1). As the
1950s began, it seemed as if the earlier images of both Rooney and Garland
had been stripped away to reveal the heavy cost it took to present such
energetic can-do optimism.

⭐⭐⭐⭐⭐ **Conclusion: I Wish I Were in Love Again**

Of course, neither performer's career ended at this point.
Garland spent the rest of her life moving from comeback to comeback (her

concerts at the Palace and at Carnegie Hall, *A Star Is Born* [1954], *Judgment at Nuremberg* [1961], her 1963–64 TV show) until her sudden (but perhaps expected) death from an overdose in 1969. Rooney also managed to turn things around, reemerging in the mid-1950s as a character actor, earning Oscar nominations for supporting actor (*The Bold and the Brave* [1956], *The Black Stallion* [1979]), and continuing to work into the new millennium. While nostalgia still exists among fans for the happy talented personae of their youth, such fondness is necessarily overlaid with the awareness of what followed. After 1950, Garland's signature song, "Over the Rainbow," was no longer a simple paean to happier times ahead. Increasingly, it spoke of grim determination to slog through the worst that life can throw at you. If Rooney and Garland somehow represented what America stood for in the early 1940s, then their subsequent careers and lives might also mirror (this time, uncomfortably) the pressures and tensions structured into American society.

NOTES

1. Some of the popular sources cited in this article are from scrapbooks and folders on Mickey Rooney and on Judy Garland (as well as folders on individual film titles) in the Margaret Herrick Library of the Academy of Motion Picture Arts and Sciences in Beverly Hills. The material in the scrapbooks and folders is not always documented as to source or date, unfortunately, and any textual citation with an incomplete reference is from these holdings.

2. This specific citation is from the Judy Garland files in the Hedda Hopper Collection of papers held in the Margaret Herrick Library of the Academy of Motion Picture Arts and Sciences in Beverly Hills.

3. An attempt to resurrect the Hardys in 1958, with *Andy Hardy Comes Home*, went nowhere.

4. According to Fordin, the filming of "Voodoo," a number cut from *The Pirate*, was an instance where Garland was not able to pull herself back from the edge, becoming hysterical when she was ushered onto the set filled with torches, "screaming 'I'm going to burn to death! They want me to burn to death!' In vain Minnelli tried to calm her. . . . Sobbing, laughing, crying, completely out of control, she was led off the set" (208–09).

7 ★★★★★★★★★★★

Greer Garson
Gallant Ladies and British Wartime Femininity

HANNAH HAMAD

During the first half of the 1940s, Greer Garson was a star with extraordinarily high visibility, appeal, and timely cultural resonance. Audiences responded enthusiastically to her persona and its dominant characteristics, which seemed to embody homefront fortitude and resilience, striking such a resonant chord during wartime that Garson, and the iconic character she played in *Mrs. Miniver* (1942), came to epitomize England and womanhood to enormous success on both sides of the Atlantic. Garson's persona was so of its time and context that it both rose and fell in line with the start and end of World War II.

Greer Garson portrait, c. 1942. Collection of the author.

There are a handful of words and phrases that crop up time and again in the innumerable discussions of Greer Garson and her stardom that have appeared in print since her small but star-making turn as Katherine Chipping in her inaugural screen role in *Goodbye, Mr. Chips* (1939). Through latter-day retrospectives and the myriad obituaries that followed her death in 1996, Garson continues to be described as gracious, poised, dignified, gallant, self-sacrificing, a great lady, the perfect wife and mother, and lovely. In fact, Bosley Crowther, the *New York Times* film critic throughout the 1940s, described her as "lovely" in his reviews of her films on six consecutive occasions from *Pride and Prejudice* (1940) on, up to and including *Random Harvest* (1942) (15 December 1939, 33; 9 August 1940, 19; 27 June 1941, 14; 5 September 1941, 19; 18 December 1942, 23; 8 October 1942, 36).

In 1955, the findings of an audience study that had been undertaken by the sociology department at McGill University into the uses and gratifications that audiences derive from their engagement with and consumption of Hollywood stars were published. A selection of high-profile stars from the 1940s and early 1950s were chosen as representative of Hollywood's roster of bankable stars, and Greer Garson was among those selected.[1] One participating audience member was quoted thus:

> Greer Garson plays in serious pictures. She looks her age and doesn't try to act young or light-hearted. She tries to help people out. She gets what she wants and would tell people off when they needed to be told. She'd be quiet and dignified until pushed too far. But then watch out! She's a temperamental and quick-tempered person. She's not very finicky about her clothes, she's too independent a woman to worry what other people think about that.
>
> (Elkin 101–02)

This response to Garson, which contains no direct references to any individual films that she starred in, serves as a useful and illuminating microcosm of Garson's persona itself, and of audience understanding and recognition of its defining traits and recurring characteristics.[2] Her pictures were "serious" in that they tended to be prestige pictures and melodramas with various literary, historical, or contemporary origins, including literary adaptations such as *Goodbye, Mr. Chips*, *Pride and Prejudice*, *Mrs. Miniver*, *Random Harvest*, and *That Forsyte Woman* (1949),[3] and biopics like *Blossoms in the Dust* (1941), based on the life of a Texan benefactress to orphaned children, and *Madame Curie* (1943), based on the life of the revered scientist. Her personification of womanhood was both mature and often matronly, prompting one journalist from the *New Yorker* to remark that Garson "really deserves the compliment of being called a woman, too; most Hollywood actresses are girls, and remain girls to the bitter end" (Troyan 109).[4] This emphasis on her maturity and womanliness over and above the more commonly prized youth and recent girlhood of most female Hollywood stars speaks to the virtuous maternalism that her dominant persona was imbued with, following the success of what would become her signature role as the eponymous *Mrs. Miniver*. This saw her play an idealization of middle-class motherhood and stoic homefront bravery during wartime, in a romanticized version of England that existed nowhere but on celluloid.

Garson's screen attempts to "help people out" often required a great sacrifice on the part of her characters, and suffering on her part in order to benefit the greater good, whether a single individual or vast swathes of humanity (highly apposite thematic recurrences for a wartime audience). For example, *Random Harvest* sees Garson suffer silently for years, on the advice of a doctor, as the secretary to her beloved amnesiac husband, and later as his nominal wife in a loveless marriage while she waits patiently, stoically, gallantly, for his memory of her to return naturally, with no guarantee that it ever will (it does). The "quick temper" referred to, while seemingly an unlikely aspect of a persona characterized by graciousness, dignity, poise, and gallantry, was factored into her stardom as a corollary to her redheadedness, a physical characteristic itself presented as an upshot of her Celtic background, and seized upon by her studio, MGM, in its publicity buildup of the star. As her career progressed, Celtic ethnic inflections to her persona would function to counterbalance the potential for a staid and sober personification of womanhood that the matronliness of her dominant persona might develop into, by adding various sexualized, exoticized, or unruly dimensions to her image, of which the aforementioned quickness of temper was one.

While the costuming of Garson's characters was an important and meaningful addendum to her performance on a number of her occasions— Mrs. Miniver's excited purchase of a new hat, Paula Ridgeway's dressing-room transformation into a "highland lassie" in *Random Harvest*—it was nevertheless a part of her persona that she was not finicky about clothes. As Jeanine Basinger confirms, "Garson was never a clotheshorse" (Basinger 43). One fan magazine of the time stated bluntly that "Greer is not interested in clothes except for necessary decorative effect" and "she prefers them simple" ("Cameo of Greer Garson," *Picturegoer*, 1 November 1941, 6). The quoted subject of the audience study puts this indifference down to her "independence," and this is indeed something she is required, often in trying circumstances, to demonstrate. Time and again, her wifely characters are depicted bravely continuing their lives for the benefit of others following the absence and frequently the death of their husbands, children, or both. Edna Gladney in *Blossoms in the Dust* in fact withstands the deaths of first her adopted sister, then her son, and then her husband, but continues her effort alone, working tirelessly on behalf of the parentless children of Texas, whom she has made it her life's work to place in homes.[5] Paraphrasing from the responses of various other participants, the author of the findings of the study summarizes the most commonly identified facets of Garson's persona thus: "She represents the moral respected housewife and mother who voluntarily makes sacrifices to help other people" (Elkin 102).

With the regard to the way that her stardom was visually constructed, commentators have often referred to Garson's onscreen "luminosity." This came from the high-key lighting that was used to light Garson's face, usually in such a way that emphasized both her high-cheeked bone structure and the right side of her face, and often by her frequent collaborator, cinematographer Joseph Ruttenberg, who recalled that "Greer had one good side, and I recognized what it was. . . . Metro even built sets to favor her right side" (Davis 236–37). Gregory Peck, who starred with Garson in *The Valley of Decision* (1944), also recalled that "every time I was in a scene with her, her face was a lovely luminous moon floating in the center of the screen and I was the rather dim figure beside her in semi-shadow" (Freedland 66; McDowall 172). Similarly, in MGM's makeup department, William Tuttle was responsible for designing Garson's look, and, in collaboration with the star, decided that "it was the angular lines of her face that we wanted to emphasize" (Troyan 74). This combination of lighting and makeup thus led to Garson's signature look onscreen that highlighted her "fabulous cheekbones" to optimum effect (Basinger 43). So effective was the creation and repeated utilization of Garson's signature facial look that the angularity of her seemingly sculpted high cheekbones was exaggerated in a cartoon caricature depicting Garson and Colman in *Random Harvest* as part of an advertisement for the film in the 26 December 1942 edition of the *Motion Picture Herald* (23). In this way, the luminosity cited as characteristic of Garson's lighting is a visualization of her dominant persona. The halo of light produced around her within the frame was indicative of the saintliness that her characters were frequently imbued with in their personifications of ideal womanhood.

Garson played a succession of heroines characterized by their nobility (of character if not heredity), indomitability, altruism, and stoicism. In due course, the unique context of World War II, and the attendant alliance of the United States and Great Britain, led to a period of extraordinary success; and for a time, in the aftermath of the twofold success in 1942 of the box office giants *Mrs. Miniver* and *Random Harvest*, the prestige of Garson's star status was unparalleled in Hollywood. The scale of her exalted position in Hollywood's star hierarchy in the first half of the 1940s seems surprising from a retrospective viewpoint, given that it is little remembered today. Her stardom is seldom held up as an iconic personification of its period in the manner of Bette Davis, Katharine Hepburn, or Joan Crawford. However, the fact remains that Garson was dubbed MGM's "queen of the lot" with ample reason, recognized by her peers, her fans, the critics, and of course the studio's bottom line.

Garson was nominated for the Academy Award for Best Actress six times in a seven-year span from 1939 to 1945, winning for *Mrs. Miniver*.[6] In 1942, *Mrs. Miniver* and *Random Harvest* were, respectively, the highest and third-highest grossing films in the United States, and each year thereafter at least one of her films featured among the top ten highest grosses of the year (Schatz 466–77).[7] The *Motion Picture Herald*'s annual poll of film exhibitors on the top moneymaking stars of the year placed Garson among the top ten every year from 1942 to 1946; she rose as high as third in 1945, which also, and for the first time, placed her above Betty Grable, her only serious female competition for a high place on this list (26 December 1942, 13; 25 December 1943, 13; 30 December 1944, 12; 29 December 1945; see also Schatz 470).[8] An annual readers' poll conducted by the British fan magazine *Picturegoer* saw Garson voted the favorite actress for an unprecedented three consecutive years from 1942 to 1944 ("Our Gold Medal Winners," 8 July 1944, 11), something that no actress achieved again. Gallup polls twice found her "the most popular star in the United States" in 1942 and 1943 (Troyan 183), and *Film Daily*, which polled critics and reporters, found her to be their favorite actress of the year in 1942, 1943, and 1945 (*New York Times*, 22 December 1942, 31; 22 December 1943, 26; 9 January 1946, 21). Notwithstanding the global turmoil effected by World War II, Garson achieved widespread popularity on as much of a worldwide scale as was possible given the circumstances, similarly topping 1944 polls in Canada, India, Mexico, Sweden, France, Portugal, Belgium, Africa, Australia, Argentina, and Palestine (Troyan 183).

★★★★★ Metro's Glorified Mrs.

Greer Garson was contracted to MGM for the duration of the 1940s, and her tenure at the studio saw her complete two full seven-year contracts, after her transatlantic move from the London stage of the 1930s to the Hollywood studio most highly reputed for its stable of stars. This move followed an offer made by studio chief Louis B. Mayer. Upon seeing one of Garson's theatrical performances in 1937 while visiting Britain to inspect MGM's British studios in Denham, north of London, Mayer promptly offered Garson a contract, which she accepted. Garson set sail for the United States on 16 November 1937, eventually arriving in Los Angeles on 4 December. There she joined a thriving community of British thespians who now made their living acting in Hollywood films, which included Ronald Colman, Cary Grant, Ray Milland, Leslie Howard, and later Vivien Leigh, Laurence Olivier, and Deborah Kerr, to name only some. Garson's initial experience in Hollywood was disappointingly anticlimactic. When she arrived at MGM, they had no parts for her for the first year of her contract. Eventually, she was sent to England for a shoot in 1938, after reluctantly agreeing to accept the small role of Robert Donat's wife in *Goodbye, Mr. Chips*. Garson was so disillusioned that she intended not to return to America on its completion. However, fortunately for her career she was persuaded to return, *Goodbye, Mr. Chips* was a success, she was widely praised for her performance, and she received her first Academy Award nomination for Best Actress. After a successful turn as Elizabeth Bennett in *Pride and Prejudice* (and a less successful turn in *Remember?* [1939]), Garson's star was in the ascent.

So successful were Garson's film releases in 1942 that it was later dubbed the "year of Greer" (Troyan 163), and her persona became so fixed and identifiable from her characters in *Mrs. Miniver* and *Random Harvest* that she was nicknamed "Metro's Glorified Mrs." (Theodore Strauss, "I Wasn't Born with a Bustle," *New York Times*, 19 July 1942, SM14). Her characterization of Kay Miniver, a wife and mother who steadfastly provides emotional support to her family during the early years of the war, led to her canonization as "Cinema's blitz heroine" (Catherine Pepinster, "Cinema's Blitz Heroine Greer Garson Dies at 92," *The Independent*, 7 April 1996). Mrs. Miniver watches her husband (Walter Pidgeon) go to Dunkirk, her son join the RAF, her daughter-in-law die in a bombing raid, all the while reassuring the smallest of her children, "It's all right, darling," while she clutches him to her bosom in the family's makeshift bomb shelter. She also calmly deals with an inconvenient intrusion from a German pilot on her way to collect the milk for her morning tea. *Mrs. Miniver*'s interpretation of small-town life in middle England during the war was fantastically popular (if not very realistic). Released on 4 June 1942, on the second anniversary of Churchill's famous "We shall never surrender" speech to the House of Commons (Troyan 147–48), the film was a clear message from Hollywood to its audiences as to where its allegiance lay. In this regard, Garson's Kay Miniver was a persuasive figurehead to garner sympathy toward the

Representing stoic homefront bravery in the family's makeshift bomb shelter, the Minivers continue to convey their quintessential Englishness as Kay (Garson) knits and Clem (Walter Pidgeon) drinks tea. Copyright 1942, Loew's, Inc.

British. As Siegfried Kracauer has noted in his discussion of Hollywood's treatment of Britain in its wartime output:

> Once the war was on, national exigencies encroached on the tendency toward objectivity. American public opinion endorsed the war effort, and Britain was now an Ally. For these reasons Hollywood could no longer afford to approach the English in that spirit of impartiality which is indispensable for an understanding of others. Rather it was faced with the task of endearing everything British to the American masses. The task was not simply to represent the English, but to make them seem acceptable even to those sections of the population whose pro-British feelings were doubtful.   (Kracauer 64–65)

Garson herself was, in her words, "very worried about the anti-British feeling in America" (Troyan 107), but she need not have been. She and Mrs. Miniver became Hollywood's poster girl (or rather its poster "lady") for this change in the increasing number of cinematic treatments of the British. (Garson's image was even able to produce representations of various ethnic identities within Britain, and dissipate some of the tensions between them, as the subsequent section explores.) The enormity of the film's success and the popularity of Garson for the duration of the United States' direct involvement in the war is testament to this. As Alison Light has noted, "If the name now conjured up anything, then it is probably as a byword for Britishness during the war that Mrs. Miniver stays in popular memory. Greer Garson gamely seeing her family through the bombing and her husband off to play his part at Dunkirk was for cinema audiences around the world the epitome of the wartime spirit of England" (Light 113).

Also testament to Garson's box office power during the war is that two other of her vehicles, *Random Harvest* and *The Valley of Decision*, "were the only films of the war years to achieve grosses of more than $8 million and profits of more than $3 million," while *Madame Curie*, *Mrs. Parkington* (1944), and *Adventure* (1945) were all among the top ten grossing films of their respective years (Gomery 107–08). Of course it is true that the Hollywood film industry profited enormously from the economic boom that occurred in the United States during World War II, and average box office grosses were thus higher than they had been previously throughout the industry (Schatz 1–6). Notwithstanding this corollary of the war, Douglas Gomery helpfully contextualizes the extent of *Mrs. Miniver*'s phenomenal success: "Top grosses were usually in the range of $3.5 million to $4 million in the early 1940s, but *Mrs. Miniver* earned the best gross ($8,878,000), and the best profit ($4,831,000) of any MGM film to this time" (Gomery 107). Its run at the prestigious Radio City Music Hall in New York "broke all previous box-office records, running an unprecedented ten weeks, drawing 1,499,891 theatergoers and grossing $1,031,500" (Troyan 148). It did not sustain this record for very long, because the film was overtaken later that year by Garson's next vehicle, *Random Harvest*. Garson's stardom literally surpassed itself in this instance as the film played at Radio City for eleven straight weeks to $1.55 million in just one single venue (Troyan 155).

Madame Curie also found its way to strike a resonant chord with the wartime context. It was marketed on the reteaming of Garson and Walter Pidgeon,[9] on the marquee value of their now iconic characters from their previous vehicle, with the tagline "Mr. & Mrs. Miniver . . . together again!" Furthermore, the film was set in France (then occupied by Nazi Germany) and told the story of a Polish heroine (Poland was also then occupied by Nazi Germany), a revered historical figure, and of course featured Garson, a British star (Britain was under constant threat of invasion by and was fighting against Nazi Germany) who had by now come to epitomize Hollywood's overly romanticized and idealized imaginings of British femininity. *Madame Curie* was thus, as Christopher Frayling has argued, "a hands-across-the-seas tribute to America's European allies" (157). Further, characterization of the film's eponymous heroine was another continuity of Garson's stock character type that had been developed from one vehicle to the next since *Goodbye, Mr. Chips*, and it prompted one journalist to quip that her Marie Sklodowska Curie was "'Mrs. Miniver' in a French gown" (W. H. Mooring, "Greer in the Grip of Greatness," *Picturegoer*, 22 July 1944, 8).

Contemporaneous with her onscreen efforts and wartime morale boosting, Garson, along with a gamut of other Hollywood stars, took part in various fund-raising war bond drives. In 1942, she went on a "morale boosting junket" for the "'Victory Loan campaign' raising $58,500,000 in one day alone" (*New York Times*, 15 March 1942, X3) and later that year on "an extensive tour selling Victory Bonds as a representative of the United States Treasury Department" ("'MGM's Glorified Mrs.': Concluding the Life Story of Greer Garson," *Picturegoer*, 11 December 1943, 8). She appeared in a six-week run at Hollywood's El Capitan Theater in Noel Coward's *Tonight at Eight Thirty* as part of a fund-raising effort to make money for the British War Relief. The production raised over $25,000 (Elsa Maxwell, "Gold Medal Lady," *Photoplay*, May 1945, 27).

★★★★★ Ethnic Inflections

Garson's dominant persona painted a picture of her as quintessentially English, and it made frequent use of archetypally English motifs such as tea and roses in both visual and discursive contexts. Michael Troyan cites a journalist from the *San Francisco Examiner* who reported from the set of *Remember?*: "Come what may the English must have their tea. . . . Miss Garson has ordered it at the usual time of four o'clock, and when a kettle has to boil it boils regardless of movie scenes or what have you" (Troyan 100). He later goes on to describe a tea party at her Los Angeles home, with "china teacups, saucers, cream, sugar, and a platter of sliced cucumber and cress sandwiches, with cream cheese, Banbury tarts, [and] marmalade rolls. . . . Greer prepared her own tea ('two bags, the cream goes in first')" (Troyan 173). Ysenda Maxtone Graham also adds that while having "tea, by the poolside . . . Greer Garson loved to chat about her favourite poet, John Donne" (Maxtone Graham 187). Similarly, one *Picturegoer* journalist, interviewing Garson in 1944, was comfortably accommodated by her attendance to this archetypal English social ritual and attests, "Like two English people, hostess and guest, we had a cup of tea and talked" (W. H. Mooring, "Greer in the Grip of Greatness," *Picturegoer*, 22 July 1944, 6).

Roses featured equally prominently in the construction of Garson's image as an English lady, predominantly due to the famous scene that introduces audiences to the "Miniver rose" in *Mrs. Miniver*. On having the village

Henry Travers presents "the Miniver Rose" to Garson, further enshrining her as an icon of English wartime femininity. Copyright 1942, Loew's, Inc.

station master James Ballard's personally cultivated rose named after her, Mrs. Miniver quite literally becomes an "English Rose," that archetype of feminine Englishness, invoked to suggest the natural beauty and whole-someness of the recipient of this label, "beauty and sweetness," as Ballard describes his rose in the scene. The rose motif would follow Garson throughout the rest of her career, continuing to invoke notions of idealized English femininity. In fact, MGM was quick to pick up on the potential iconicity and obvious symbolism of the rose motif, and at the *Mrs. Miniver* premiere at Radio City Music Hall in New York "the centrepiece of the Music Hall lobby display was a 'Mrs. Miniver Rose.' Dr Eugene Boerner, an American botanist, had produced the rose for MGM publicity purposes. In many of the major cities in which the movie would premiere, such roses were presented to women on the home front who had made significant contributions to the war effort" (Troyan 148).

Also part of the *Mrs. Miniver* publicity drive was a personal appearance by Garson at the headquarters of the Volunteer Army Canteen service on Sunset Boulevard, where she posed for photographers with a shovel as she planted the first registered "Miniver Rose Bush" (Troyan 178–79). It was reported in profiles that she would entertain guests over tea in her rose garden on the grounds of her home, in which "the Greer Garson and Mrs. Miniver roses grew" (Troyan 173).

Despite the emphasis on Englishness, Garson's stardom demonstrated the ability to successfully traverse boundaries of British and Irish regional identities, allowing her to perform (and her stardom to epitomize) such female ethnic/national archetypes as the Scottish "lassie" in *Random Harvest*, the Irish "colleen" in *The Valley of Decision*, and the English "rose" in *Mrs. Miniver*. The aforementioned ambivalence in the United States for supporting the British could in part explain the success of Garson's all-encompassing British ethnic markers, in that Irishness would have provided a site of identification to counter this ambivalence toward the Englishness of her dominant persona. She was thus able to personify a composite of the beleaguered nations of the Allies in such a way that solicited identification and offset ambivalence from U.S. audiences.

However, she is denied the opportunity to extend this mobility of ethnic and/or national performativity outside of these roles, so synonymous is her star persona with Britain and Ireland. This phenomenon is exemplified by the fact that she remains English-accented when playing Americans such as Edna Gladney in *Blossoms in the Dust* and the Polish Marie Sklodowska in *Madame Curie*. Garson's appearance on a 1950s edition of the television show "What's My Line" while publicizing her then-current film *Julius Caesar* (1953) demonstrated that she was not incapable of adopting non-British accents when she affected a high-pitched nasal New Yorker's voice to disguise her own deep and well-spoken Queen's English from the blindfolded contestants. Furthermore, Garson had earlier described herself as having "always been good at dialects" as part of an anecdote she told *Picturegoer* in 1943. Claiming to have performed with an American accent as part of her role in the London stage production of *Golden Arrow* in 1935 to such convincing effect, she goes on to assert that she was mistaken for an actual American in press write-ups of the show ("The Life Story of Greer Garson," *Picturegoer*, 27 November 1943, 8).

Garson's Celticness, both Irish and Scottish, was frequently emphasized in publicity, though somewhat disingenuously. While it never superseded her dominant persona, her origins were modified to accentuate her Celtic roots rather more pointedly than fact would have allowed. Such disingenuousness about stars' origins was by no means an atypical occurrence in the classical Hollywood star system of the studio era. On the contrary, it was fairly standard practice: "A fake biography would be created, working as much from a basis of truth as could be logically saleable" (Basinger 47).

Throughout her career and right up until her death, Garson claimed to have been born in County Down in Northern Ireland, and the publicity department at MGM as well as innumerable popular press profiles of the star, in fan magazines, newspapers, trade papers, and the like, all corroborated this falsehood. Garson was in fact born in London, the truth of which emerged only after her death in 1996.[10] Garson had family links to Scotland and Northern Ireland through her grandparents on both sides, but all claims that she was "Irish by birth," whether from MGM, various print sources, or Garson herself (Alyce Canfield, "X-Ray of Greer Garson," *Screen Stars*, October 1946, 70), are erroneous.[11] It is not clear whether MGM was aware of Garson's actual birthplace, but its archives confirm that Howard Strickling, the studio's head of publicity, acted upon information that Garson was only nominally Irish while formulating and honing her persona. As Michael Troyan documents, Strickling sent his research department "on a search for interesting Irish trivia" that could potentially be used in Garson's introduction to the press and fan magazines, and came up with the fact that "the earliest native word for Ireland is Eriu. It means 'the most beautiful woman in the world!'" (Troyan 74).

The fallaciously overstated Celtic side to Garson's persona was constructed and disseminated both onscreen and off, appearing across a variety of primary and ancillary platforms, in various guises that included genealogical, physical, nostalgic, discursive, and performative, and in terms of Garson's personality, palate, appearance, and birthplace. Her Celtic genealogy was frequently discussed in terms of what was claimed to be her familial link to the Scottish folk hero Rob Roy MacGregor. One popular press profile printed in the *New York Times* at the time of the release of *Mrs. Miniver* referred to the star as "an Irish-born descendant of Rob Roy MacGregor" (Theodore Strauss, "Veni, Vidi, Vici!" *New York Times*, 15 March 1942, X3).[12]

Ruth Barton has pointed out that Irishness in Hollywood frequently played out as a narrative of diaspora, and that rather than treating the homeland as a "site of an old trauma," classical Hollywood's imaginings of Ireland are often nostalgic and romantic, treating the "originating identity as the ideal" (Barton 7). This is also the case for Garson's stardom and the way her memories of Ireland are posited as nostalgic in ancillary texts. As part of a 1941 *Photoplay* interview, Garson herself is quoted speaking about her childhood in London, during which she "longed for the summer months when we escaped back to Ireland for heavenly long visits to my grandparents' home in the sweet green countryside" (Troyan 13), while one obituary in an Irish newspaper quotes her as saying: "I remember playing under blue skies in County Down and even today, when I hear Irish music, tears well in my eyes" (Troyan 15). This nostalgia also comes across in Garson's evident partiality for Irish and Scottish cuisine, given that "her favorite foods [are] potatoes, Irish stew, and haggis," and according to Troyan, "she still enjoyed a bowl of stewed fruit, which reminded her of her childhood on the farm in County Down" following her emigration to the United States (Troyan 173–74). She is similarly described as enjoying "a truckdriver's helping of Irish stew" following a long day at the studio ("Ideal Woman," *Time*, 12 December 1943), and serving "Scotch scones" with her tea (Troyan 173).

It has been established that fashion did not play a major part in Garson's stardom, but when it came to "the wearing of the green," she made sure to emphasize her fondness for attiring herself in Ireland's signature color: "Her favorite colour [is] green," and she fondly mentions her "green silk dressing gown" as the favorite item in her wardrobe ("Cameo of Greer Garson," *Picturegoer*, 1 November 1941, 6). The homeliness of her choice thus corresponds to her dominant persona, while the color maintains its ethnic inflections. Responding to an interviewer's question about what color clothes she prefers, she is so enthusiastic for the ethnic signifier that she names it twice: "Green, orchid, black, white, grey, yellow, blue—and GREEN!" (Alyce Canfield, "X-Ray of Greer Garson," *Screen Stars*, October 1946, 70).

It was Garson's physical attributes characteristic of Celticness, and frequently incorporated in stereotypical constructions of it, that were most frequently cited in constructions of the Celtic inflections to her persona, namely her green eyes, pale skin, and red hair. Barely a press profile of Garson seems to exist that does not describe her in such terms, as "flame-haired Greer Garson" (Fontaine 148), a "titian haired beauty" (Harvey 18), or a "green-eyed young woman [with] a thatch of bright red hair" ("Cinderella Is a Red Head: The Life Story of Greer Garson," *Picturegoer*, 13 November 1943, 11). Fellow Hollywood actor Roddy McDowall has described Garson's "translucently beautiful Irish complexion" (Troyan vii); a fan magazine profile that appeared around the time of the release of *Adventure* called her "the green-eyed, Scotch-Irish star, whose hair is the color of leaping flames" (Charles Samuels, "Greer Garson—The Duchess," *Motion Picture Magazine*, 1945, 123). More direct publicity for individual Garson vehicles similarly foreground her redheadedness. One of the original posters for *Pride and Prejudice* is largely monochromatic but includes one noticeable splash of color to highlight Garson's red hair. The cinematography in *Pride and Prejudice* is of course black and white, but Garson's first Technicolor screen outing, *Blossoms in the Dust*, and its marketing took full advantage of the opportunity to show off its star's red hair. One original advertisement for the film incorporated a quotation from the *New York Herald Tribune*'s review that described her as a "ravishing redhead" in large and prominent typeface. Similarly, although the black-and-white cinematography prevents the audience from seeing it for themselves, the screenplay of *Random Harvest* reminds them when Garson's character Margaret Hanson's hair is described as "bright red in the sunshine."

Red hair, itself an archetype of Celtic identities, has similarly been stereotypically associated with quickness of temper or a "fiery" temperament, and this association was also used in constructions of her persona that described "the mercurial Garson temperament" (Troyan 174–75). One of the original posters for *Pride and Prejudice* marketed the film with the tagline "Greer Garson is lovely to look at . . . lovelier to love, but what a temper!" Garson's fury that the press was speculating she was pregnant led her reaction to be described by one reporter as "red-headed mad" (Mary C. McCall, cited in Troyan 167). In 1941, Garson described herself to Gladys Hall of *Silver Screen* as "Celtic by birth and temperament" (Troyan 14). This temperament of which she speaks presumably refers again to shortness of temper and rebelliousness, in another reductive association with feminine redheadedness, to which she herself alludes when trying to recall what made her "rebel" against her family's wishes for her to enter the teaching profession: "Maybe it was my red hair" ("The Life Story of Greer Garson," *Picturegoer*, 27 November 1943, 7). Like her redheadedness, her "fiery" temperament again features in her onscreen persona as well as in publicity discourses, when in *Madame Curie*, during one scene that takes place at the Curie family home, Garson's Marie Sklodowska is described by her future mother-in-law as "Fiery. Flame-like. Something like a flame." In this way, the apparent contradiction of Garson's short temper with her "great lady" persona speaks to the growth of greater independence for women during the war as contained within an overall sense of being ladylike.

Michael Troyan highlights audience responses to the Technicolor spectacle of Garson's pale skin, red hair, and green eyes by quoting from the 19 December 1939 issue of *Screenbook*, reporting the screening of a publicity preview for *Blossoms in the Dust*: "Greer should be filmed in Technicolor to do her justice. Black and white gives no hint of the burnished copper tones of her mass of fine and fluffy hair, or the whiteness of her skin which portrays a natural red head or the oval depths of her eyes which . . . are green" (Troyan 113). Similarly, *Picturegoer* stated in 1941 that "Greer's red hair is her crowning glory, a Technicolor symphony with her green eyes and white skin" ("Cameo of Greer Garson," 1 November 1941, 6). A publicity puff piece about Garson's love life in *Photoplay* even went so far as to insinuate that it was these archetypally Celtic physical characteristics that first attracted the romantic attention of the man who would later become her second husband, actor Richard Ney, who played her eldest son Vin in *Mrs. Miniver*:[13] "What he saw was a *pale*, humorous face framed in an incredible nimbus of *red gold hair*. His startled blue eyes flashed to her slender ankles, even as Greer's startled *green eyes* took heed of the width of his shoulders; and then their delighted glances met again, met and locked and held" (Troyan 128, my emphasis).

As Diane Negra states, "female redheadedness has come to signify a largely benign Irish-inflected whiteness" (Negra 11), and this certainly seems to be the case in the way that Celticness was negotiated through Garson's persona. This placed high visibility on the discursively prominent ethnic signifier of her red hair, often in tandem with her green eyes and/or pale skin. In Garson's case, these physical characteristics allowed her to traverse boundaries from Irish to Scottish as will or necessity dictated, in line with her personal biography that places her in both these Celtic contexts. However, in the context of Hollywood and of the United States at large, with its large and increasing number of Irish Americans,[14] audiences would more readily associate these physical characteristics with Ireland, unless Scottishness were heavily foregrounded or spectacularized, to the extent that it is by Garson's stage performance in *Random Harvest*. As Amanda Third has pointed out in her discussion of the way that redheadness functions as an ethnic signifier in women, "In English-speaking cultures, redheadedness is broadly associated with Celticness but in particular with Irishness. Indeed, the two are often conflated in the current era of high-profile Irishness, to the degree that Irishness has colonized the meanings of Celticness, including identity signifier of red hair" (Third 229).

That said, while Irishness does tend to dominate in secondary publicity materials about Garson, notwithstanding her "Scotch scones" and the "Scottish crests on the doors" of her Los Angeles home (Maxtone Graham 187), Scottishness did on one occasion feature quite heavily in a performative context, in *Random Harvest*. Heretofore, Garson had been introduced to the viewing public wearing a Scottish-style Tam o' Shanter hat in her inaugural scene in *Goodbye, Mr. Chips*, but it is the music hall sequence in *Random Harvest* that really foregrounds Scottishness as part of her screen persona, as she gives an accented and kilted caricature of a performance in the persona of a Scottish showgirl for the number "She's Ma Daisy."[15]

Garson plays stage performer Paula Ridgeway, who performs the lead role in a music hall act called "The Highland Lassies," dressed in a costume

Garson performs Scottishness as an ethnic spectacle in *Random Harvest* (1942). This image was heavily used in marketing the film, and thus promised the novelty of a sexualized Greer with her legs uncharacteristically on display. Copyright 1942, Loew's, Inc.

that incorporates traditional Scottish garb including a modified version of a tartan kilt and a sporran. Throughout the performance, she speaks and sings in an affected and exaggerated Scottish accent and in Scottish vernacular. Promoting *Random Harvest* prior to its release, Garson told *Silver Screen* of her delight in being afforded the opportunity to perform the Scottish number: "I love to dance. . . . The Scotch and Irish are always dancing and their natural sense of rhythm was born in me" (Troyan 141). Garson thus publicly demonstrated and willingly shared a somewhat essentialist approach to her perception of her own Celtic ethnicity rather oxymoronically, given the highly performative nature of this particular ethnic spectacle. Also indicative of her desire to draw on her Celticness to nuance the dominant Englishness of her screen persona is the fact that it was reportedly Garson herself who proposed performing "She's Ma Daisy" for this scene, and to do so dressed in a kilt (Troyan 141). This scene also aligns ethnicity with sexuality: *Random Harvest* was marketed around its promise to reveal Garson's legs, most often with a picture of her in her Scottish garb including a version of the traditional kilt, so short that today it would likely be termed a micro-skirt. Sexuality was not usually something foregrounded in Garson's persona. On the contrary, her dominant "great lady" and "self-sacrificing" wife and mother persona was in many ways antithetical to the sort typified by stars like Betty Grable and Rita Hayworth, for whose personae sexuality was a defining characteristic. Thus ethnicity (and hence sexuality) in *Random Harvest* is a costume, to be discarded in order to allow the dominant persona to ultimately take control of the narrative. Performative Scottishness has, however, served its purpose as a marketing hook for the film, and to keep the sideshow of Garson's ethnicity functioning as a visible enough presence to remain salable as an inflection and nuance but without threatening the dominance of the "lady," for whom these could have potentially troubling implications. Furthermore, the ideological function of ethnic performativity had implications specific to shifting gender roles during World War II, as Sean Griffin highlights: "Considering identity as a role you can take up but then discard could also work as a hegemonic negotiation of gender roles in ultimate support of patriarchy: suggesting to all those Rosie the Riveters in the audience that their new 'masculine' behaviour was just a temporary persona that should be taken off once the war was over" (Griffin, "Wearing" 78).

In a similar way, Garson's character in *Random Harvest* sheds her carnivalesque, sexualized, and ethnic role as independent and autonomous showgirl Paula Ridgeway, lead performer of the "Highland Lassies," and dutifully assumes the roles of Mrs. Smith (wife and mother), then Lady Rainier, constant long-suffering companion to the "industrial prince of England," then back to Mrs. Smith again. Similarly, Mrs. Miniver is relieved to absolve herself of the responsibility of having to disarm rogue German pilots in her kitchen (as she famously does in one scene) upon her husband Clem's safe return from Dunkirk. Also comparable is Garson's own willingness to massively streamline her acting career (although the sharp decline of her stardom after the war probably contributed to this decision) in order to sequester herself in the Southwest to play the real-life role of Mrs. Buddy Fogelson on her oil baron husband's Forked Lightning Ranch in New Mexico. Garson's stock character was hence well known for being a wife, fiercely loyal to her husband and his wishes, even in his absence or in the event of his death, a character that was of high cultural resonance in a wartime context. Shifting gender roles resulted from the dramatic change in the gendered makeup of the workforce at this time, but she seemed to contain the potentially troubling effects of these shifts (for the long-term status quo).

Garson's "independence" was contained within a character type that was impossibly reverential toward a model of femininity that prized spousal loyalty and virtuous maternalism above all else, to the point that self-sacrifice was the norm for her characters. For example, Edna Gladney of *Blossoms in the Dust* and the eponymous *Madame Curie* devote their lives to a cause (the placing of children in adoptive homes and the discovery of radium respectively) for the benefit of both individuals and humanity. Edna takes on the law and changes it, and Marie defies conventions of gender behavior in her pursuit of science, but they are both portrayed as doing so at the behest of their encouraging husbands, who both subsequently die, leaving Garson's heroines to gallantly continue their personal crusades alone as obedient tributes to their deceased husbands. The end of the war meant that Garson's persona had served its ideological purpose to contain female independence within the aforementioned boundaries by presenting her qualities as admirable and righteous in the extreme. From a contemporary standpoint, the saintliness of the self-sacrificing Mrs. Chips, Miniver, Rainier, Curie, and Parkington seems utterly anachronistic in its conceptualization of ideal femininity as wholeheartedly altruistic. Thus, set pieces of spectacular ethnicity like the one in *Random Harvest*, as well as wider public discourses surrounding Garson's ethnicity that attempted to align her Celticness with her independence of spirit, served the larger ideological purpose of allowing ethnicity and its attendant suggestions of female independence, autonomy, and sexuality to be sidelined.

Garson overtly performs Irishness onscreen for the first time in *The Valley of Decision*, and is to some extent playing against type as Mary Rafferty in that the character is working class (a maid). However, in casting her as a newly arrived Irish immigrant, the film capitalizes upon the Celtic inflections of her persona that heretofore had been largely confined to extrafilmic discourses. Previously, there had been only the occasional nod toward the Celtic angle in her screen roles (as described above), which preferred to figure her as epitomic of middle-class English femininity, and of course did so to extraordinary success. This also took place within the by-then familiar narrative-of-immigration context widely used in Hollywood in its treatment of ethnically inflected subject matter. Garson's performance incorporates an Irish accent throughout, but it is difficult to read this as a mark of authenticity (see Barton) given that her roots were widely known to be in Northern Ireland and nary a Northern inflection can be heard in her cartoonish brogue, which incorporates well-known colloquial speech ("darlin'" and "sure it is"). Thus, the performance of ethnicity is in this case another example of the temporary adoption of a very particular form of Irish identity. This comes across in both her performance and the film itself, which sees Mary mischievously play up to mythical preconceptions about Ireland, when she jokingly relates her transatlantic voyage to her new employer: "Oh, I didn't come steerage, sir. I'll tell you how I got here. Would you believe it—one night in Ireland I was strollin' and stepped into a Fairy-ring, unbeknownst. All at once I'm surrounded by the little people, the mischievous ones, and suddenly, in the midst of it all, the leprechauns raise me up and whisk me away over the clouds and out across the ocean— and here I am in the castle of my dreams!" Latterly, both Ireland and Scotland have continued to treat and honor Garson as one of their respective native daughters. This can be seen by the University of Ulster's decision to award her an honorary doctorate in 1977, and the American Scottish Foundation's presentation to Garson of its Wallace Award, which it describes as "a singular opportunity to recognize the extraordinary diversity of contribution that Scots have made to the world."[16]

★★★★★ Mrs. Miniver Is Dead

Garson's first vehicle to be released following the end of World War II, *Adventure* (1945), paired her with returning veteran Clark Gable, who prior to his enlistment had been MGM's most significant male star. For Garson's character, the film was a transformation narrative that saw her develop from prim and proper to playful and vivacious. This narrative scenario was actually quite indicative of the transformation that Garson hoped to effect to her own persona, tired as she was of being "Metro's Glorified Mrs." She hoped to move further into the realms of farcical comedy and slapstick, the antithesis to the sorts of film her stardom had thus far been confined. Schatz describes her predominant genre as the "wartime woman's picture," and as he goes on to point out, for the duration of the war she worked "almost exclusively in that genre" (Schatz 229). Garson was right to want to develop her persona, given that the one that had typ-ified her stardom had lost its resonance outside the wartime context that gave rise to it. However, despite her efforts in films like *Adventure* and her subsequent comedy *Julia Misbehaves* (1948), neither audiences nor critics responded well, and her stardom dissipated almost as dramatically as it had ascended. At the time of *Adventure*'s release she was still riding high on the prestige status of her wartime pictures, and, in pairing her with Gable the returning hero, the film had a lot going for it in terms of marquee value. *Adventure* ended up doing solid business, grossing $4.3 million, which placed it among the top ten highest grosses of the year (Schatz 468). How-ever, the film received horrible reviews, and Garson's subsequent output would continue to suffer the same fate at the hands of the critics but with-out the high grosses to make up for it. After 1945, she never made a top grossing film or featured in the "top money-making stars" list ever again. Louis B. Mayer still believed in her stardom enough to give her a new seven-year contract, which she worked through the rest of the decade and on into the 1950s (Troyan 206). He also granted her wish to do comedy, but to less than stellar results. The response of *New York Times* critic Bosley Crowther was indicative: "It is hard to conceive of [Garson] attempting anything more impulsive or crude. . . . When the dignified lady starts scrambling about on the heads of a troupe of acrobatic tumblers as Lou Costello might do; when she goes down gurgling into a lake in a leaky row-boat and then ends up wrapped in a tablecloth, she's out of her element" (*New York Times*, 8 October 1948, 30).

Nothing drew a clearer line under the irrevocability of Garson's A-list status than the disastrous commercial performance and popular and critical reception of *The Miniver Story* (1950), an ill-begotten sequel to her most iconic film that catches up with the Minivers in the postwar years. It lost $2.3 million for MGM (Troyan 238; Maxtone Graham 255) and killed off the beloved character that Garson's performance had made so famous. Bosley Crowther broke the news: "We bring you sad tidings this morning. Mrs. Miniver is dead. That is to say, the English housewife whose gracious-ness and bravery during the war were so warmly and effectively manifested in the film, 'Mrs. Miniver,' eight years ago, finally succumbs to cancer and painful inadequacies of her script in Metro's postwar sequel" (*New York Times*, 27 October 1950, 24).

Given the production and representational trends in postwar Holly-wood, it is not a great surprise that *The Miniver Story* failed to find a recep-tive audience. In 1949, Siegfried Kracauer noticed what he refers to as "Hollywood's neglect of postwar Britons" (70). This followed a sustained period of time contemporaneous with the duration of the war when Britain was an ally of the United States, and during which "Hollywood loved Britain" (Glancy 1). The astronomical rise and subsequent postwar decline of Greer Garson's stardom were a part of this phenomenon.[17] As Kracauer states, "The war over, one might have expected Hollywood to resume its relatively objective approach to contemporary Britons, yet it preferred, and still prefers, to ignore their existence" (64). A year later, Hollywood acknowledged their existence (and the dearth of Hollywood films that depicted postwar Britain) with the release of *The Miniver Story*, to disastrous effect for both MGM's investment and any hope of a return to form for Garson's star status.

Greer Garson's stardom thus sharply declined contemporaneously with the arrival of peacetime and the postwar era in the United States. Her megastar status proved to be historically and culturally specific to such an extent that it was confined to America's World War II era, and the national feeling and appetite for her embodiment of femininity that went with it.[18] Her type chimed with a mood born of its World War II context that idealized her particular model of femininity, exactly at the time it was under threat from both invading antagonists and from shifting gender roles that changes in the gendered makeup of the workforce prompted. Thus, the "gracious lady" and "long-suffering wife" roles found extraordinary success—popular, critical, and commercial—while obvious breaks from type (which increased in number as the postwar era made the self-sacrificing wife redundant and her cultural resonance irrelevant) failed to achieve anything extraordinary on all the aforementioned counts. The spectacle of Greer Garson imitating hens and cockerels, flirting in bars, and breaking crockery over Clark Gable's head in *Adventure*; naked in a bubble bath, performing a striptease for a roomful of drunken sailors, and impersonating a sea lion (using both vocal and physical gestures) in *Julia Misbehaves*; and as the ethereal and unwitting temptress of *That Forsyte Woman* were all anathema to the "great ladies" who characterized Garson's heyday. Furthermore, these breaks from type, along with the coming of peace that altered the viewing context of the consumption of Garson's stardom, worked together to remove her from the privileged position that had typified her career and her place in the Hollywood star hierarchy for the first half of the decade. Just as Garson herself had occupied and then individualized the space made available at MGM by the decline and departure of Norma Shearer and Greta Garbo, so Deborah Kerr arrived at the studio to take up aspects of the Garson persona that she had either grown tired of or no longer had the marquee value to sustain. In fact, as a 1947 profile in *Time* magazine characterized her, Kerr was "really a kind of converted Greer Garson, womanly enough to show up nicely in those womanly roles which have always proved so soothing to Metro audiences" ("A Star Is Born," 10 February 1947). These were roles heretofore the domain of Garson, upon which her stardom was built in the earlier part of the decade to huge profit and prestige for studio and star alike. Garson would continue to find regular work and sometimes moderate success in leading and supporting roles throughout the 1950s (at the turn of the decade she still had four years on her second seven-year contract at MGM) and beyond, even receiving yet another Academy Award nomination for another "great lady" role as Eleanor Roosevelt in *Sunrise at Campobello* (1960).

The career of Greer Garson has not been retrospectively canonized, culturally venerated, or nostalgically and fondly remembered by latter-day audiences to remotely the extent of so many of her contemporaries. Stars like Katharine Hepburn, Judy Garland, Greta Garbo, and Bette Davis are only a few female stars of Garson's era whose popular public identities and images have all achieved a level of iconicity that has eluded Garson. Conversely, she has been omitted from the collective cultural memory of the film stardom of classical Hollywood, a memory that instead recalls, if anything, only "Mrs. Miniver." From a present day standpoint, it is easy to dismiss her stardom as trite, overly contrived, patronizingly propagandist at times, and inaccessibly dated; not to mention tainted by the widely disseminated anecdote that she is the all-time favorite actress of George H. W. Bush. However, the magnitude of her popularity with audiences, the real commercial gains for MGM that resulted from the marquee value of her name, the critical acclaim heaped upon her, and the cultural resonance of her persona in the context of the times that saw her stardom rise and peak cannot be overstated. Garson's dominant persona followed her throughout her career, in the years after it had peaked and declined, and to the end of her life. It now lives on in her absence, as the inscription on the headstone at her grave exemplifies. It reads: "Greer Garson Fogelson 1904–1996; Dignified Lady of Grace and Beauty" (Melzer 57).

NOTES

1. In addition to Garson, the stars selected as objects for the participating audience members were Betty Grable, Bette Davis, Katharine Hepburn, Rita Hayworth, Lauren Bacall, James Stewart, Clark Gable, Humphrey Bogart, Van Johnson, James Mason, and Errol Flynn.

2. While it is true that Garson was commonly thought of, with some measure of justification, as a star with greater appeal for women than for men, the extent to which the study's participating audience members can be considered a representative sample is limited due to the fact that the published article deals only with responses made by those from a

quite specific demographic: subjects were all "upper lower" and "lower middle" class adult American women, most of whom were wives and mothers themselves, meaning that Garson's wifely and motherly persona would provide numerous sites of identification not necessarily available to audience members with different demographic profiles. Of course, it is also true that audience demographics themselves shifted during her box office heyday, which occurred contemporaneously with U.S. interest in (and then direct involvement with) World War II and that removed a significant number of male audience members from cinemas.

3. Adapted from novels by James Hilton, Jane Austen, Jan Struther, James Hilton, and John Galsworthy, respectively.

4. Such commentators had in fact hit closer to home than they knew: Garson was four years older than her publicized biography stated. Born in 1904, not 1908 as was commonly believed, Garson was already thirty-five years old in the year that her first film, *Goodbye, Mr. Chips*, was released.

5. In addition to *Blossoms in the Dust*, Garson's character loses her husband to death in *Madame Curie* and to traumatic periods of extended absence in *Mrs. Miniver*, *Random Harvest*, and later *The Miniver Story*.

6. For *Goodbye, Mr. Chips*, *Blossoms in the Dust*, *Mrs. Miniver*, *Madame Curie*, *Mrs. Parkington*, and *The Valley of Decision*, respectively.

7. *Madame Curie* in 1943, *Mrs. Parkington* in 1944, and both *The Valley of Decision* and *Adventure* in 1945.

8. This indication of Garson's marquee value is all the more noteworthy given that for the duration of the 1940s, the appearance by female stars on this list never equaled, let alone outnumbered, male stars (Schatz 469–71) despite the fact that some of the most bankable male stars like Clark Gable and Tyrone Power were absent from screens during the war, having joined the armed forces. In fact, for 1942 and 1943, Garson's most successful years, she and Grable were the only female stars to make the list.

9. Greer Garson and Walter Pidgeon were one of Hollywood's most popular screen couples in the 1940s and starred together in *Blossoms in the Dust*, *Mrs. Miniver*, *The Miniver Story*, *Madame Curie*, *Julia Misbehaves*, *That Forsyte Woman*, and *Scandal at Scourie* (1953).

10. According to the British Film Institute, Garson's "birthplace [is] often given as Ireland in sources, but [her] birth certificate at St. Catherine's House, London has been checked" (http://ftvdb.bfi.org.uk/sift/individual/15021).

11. Garson was not the only star to be deliberately Celticized during the 1940s. Australian-born Errol Flynn, known at the time for playing Englishmen in films like *The Adventures of Robin Hood* (1938) and *The Sea Hawk* (1940), was similarly "remade as an Irishman" (Glancy 162). As Flynn attested in his autobiography, "They wanted me to be Flynn of Ireland" (Flynn 165). Another tangible manifestation of the Celtic vogue in Hollywood in the 1940s was the cycle of Irish-themed musicals produced by Twentieth Century–Fox, such as *Sweet Rosie O'Grady* (1943) and *Irish Eyes Are Smiling* (1944) (see Griffin "Wearing").

12. Michael Troyan summarizes the lineage that connects Garson and her mother's family to Rob Roy MacGregor from the early seventeenth century onward, and also traces the migration of her ancestors from Scotland to Northern Ireland, where they remained until her mother moved to London, where Garson was born and where they lived (Troyan 8–10).

13. This was one of many such articles to enthusiastically devote column inches to the story of Garson's relationship with Ney, *after* the release of *Mrs. Miniver*. Garson had agreed to withhold the story from the press due to MGM's concerns that the implication by association of incest would damage the film's box office (Troyan 147). Their marriage was short-lived and dissolved in 1947.

14. Irishness was a point of identification for many American audience members, with likely a significant proportion of Irish Americans among their number. Over 4.5 million people emigrating to the United States from Ireland over the centuries has led to many tens of millions of U.S. citizens who self-identify as Irish American (Hout and Goldstein 64).

15. "She's Ma Daisy" was a well-known song by popular Scottish 1910s music hall entertainer Harry Lauder, who would perform his novelty Scottish songs (other examples include "I Love a Lassie," "Stop Yer Ticklin,' Jock," and "Wee Nellie McKie Frae Skye"), similarly accented and attired in kilt and sporran (Johnston 22).

16. American Scottish Foundation, http://www.americanscottishfoundation.com/tartan Day/wallace.html.

17. Glancy identifies over 150 films made between 1930 and 1945 that demonstrate Hollywood's interest in portraying British-themed subject matter, with several Greer Garson star vehicles among them (1).

18. In this regard, Greer Garson's stardom is comparable to that of Shirley Temple, whose stardom was as ideologically synonymous with its Depression-era context as Garson's was with its World War II context (Eckert; Dyer, *Stars* 25–26; Fuller-Seeley).

8 ✩✩✩✩✩✩✩✩✩✩

Betty Grable and
Rita Hayworth
Pinned Up

ADRIENNE L. McLEAN

In March 1949, *Look* magazine published a cover story entitled "The American Look Is a Proud Thing." Just as "American Marshall Plan money rejuvenates the world's economy," *Look* writes, "the American Look rejuvenates its women, for this look is being copied all over the world today"—indeed, the "lithe and vibrant" beauty of the American woman had

Betty Grable portrait, probably for *Mother Wore Tights* (1947); Rita Hayworth portrait, c. 1946. Both photos collection of the author.

become "the world's beauty standard" (71, 73). The article names as responsible for the international "penetration" of the American Look "GI's, American movies, [and] the well-traveled American woman herself" (73). In the same issue, *Look* features a story about Rita Hayworth, who was about to marry Prince Aly Khan and was retired, at least for the time being, from her job as a movie star. But she was still a pinup: as the lead into Hedda Hopper's article ("Is Rita Hayworth Washed Up in Hollywood?"), *Look* offers a full-page version of what it claims was "the most famous shot ever made" of Hayworth, the star kneeling on a satin-sheeted bed in a negligee with a black lace top in 1942 (26).[1] Hopper's piece, while largely bent on excoriating Hayworth for having "abdicated her throne" as "Queen of Hollywood," also repeats Hayworth's life story, beginning with her birth in Brooklyn, New York, in 1918, as Margarita Carmen Cansino, "daughter of an American mother and a Spanish-dancer father," and continuing through her rise to Hollywood stardom and, now, international celebrity and potential princess (27–33).

For perhaps obvious reasons, it is hard not to link the two *Look* stories. The "American Look" and its circulation by "GI's" and "American movies" point specifically to Hayworth and the earlier pinup photo that *Look* conveniently reprints, with both movie star and pinup the implied source of many of the particular physical and temperamental characteristics that made the American woman as significant a symbol of "Uncle Sam" as "America's Jeeps, Nylons, skyscrapers, Cokes, sweaters with pearls" (71). Although Betty Grable is not mentioned by name, her image is certainly invoked by *Look*'s terminology; Grable's wartime pinup photo, the one in which she poses standing in a white bathing suit, circulated among GI's more than any other (second in popularity was Hayworth's). Grable had in 1948 appeared in a *Time* magazine cover story, called "Living the Daydream," in which the photo is reproduced and Grable's life story is recounted as well, beginning with her birth in Missouri in 1916 and detailing her rise from chorus girl to happily married (to big-band trumpeter Harry James) Fox musical star to "top ten" in "box-office pull" (23 August 1948, 40–44).

Taken together, all these stories certainly suggest that by the end of the 1940s the movie star as pinup had become a defining visual and discursive representation of perfect American womanhood. On the one hand it was a static, still, and highly sexualized but domesticated image, metonymic of an ideal of femininity that appeared at once easily obtainable and impossibly perfect. On the other hand it was a literal as well as figurative freedom of movement: onscreen, both Grable and Hayworth sang and danced and conquered their films' narrative difficulties with ease, bearing in their bodies and performances the "security," in *Look*'s words, to "stride freely and easily forward, meeting challenges in a charming, natural, unaffected way" (71).

But if Hayworth and Grable are alike in becoming popular and world-famous as pinups and as stars known primarily for musicals during the war, their images and their significance in the 1940s are otherwise very different. To be sure, there is a lot to link the two stars superficially not only to each other but to all women stars whose appeal was ostensibly based on their physical pulchritude and glamour. Much of what appears in fan magazines and other mass-market publicity material is depressingly similar in describing the processes of "improvement" such women stars underwent thanks to Hollywood's expert corporeal ministrations to hair, skin, teeth, and weight, and there may be no big female star in classical Hollywood who was not referred to as Cinderella at one point or another. In Grable's and Hayworth's cases, they also share at least one pushy parent—Grable's "stage mother," Hayworth's father—who thrust them into show business at an early age at the expense not only of a "normal" childhood but of any regular formal education (neither Grable nor Hayworth graduated from high school). Grable reportedly was forced to take lessons in "toe-dancing," tapping, piano, ukelele, drums, and the saxophone and to perform locally in St. Louis when her older sister refused to do so; by 1929, her mother had moved her two children to Los Angeles and the thirteen-year-old Betty, advertised by her mother as being older, was signed to a contract at Fox later that year (Fox fired her almost immediately because they suspected she was underage). She was then hired by Sam Goldwyn and appeared as a chorus girl in often unbilled bits or specialties in the early 1930s and in several low-budget "college musicals" in the latter half of the decade (wrote the *Saturday Evening Post* in 1950, "The girl who'd never graduated from any school anywhere was to become—as far as the movies were concerned—the most thoroughly college-educated miss who ever parked on a lonely road for a spot of moonlit smooching" ["The World's Most Popular Blonde," 15 April 1950, 111]). It took success as the second lead (after Ethel Merman) on Broadway in *DuBarry Was a Lady* in 1939 before Grable was signed at Fox again and became a big star by replacing Alice Faye in *Down Argentine Way* the following year.

Hayworth, at the age of twelve, became her father Eduardo Cansino's dancing partner in vaudeville and in nightclub acts, eventually attracting the attention of a Fox Hollywood talent scout who signed her to a studio contract in 1934 after learning that she spoke English instead of Spanish

(Hayworth did not last long at Fox either; her option was dropped in 1935). The sixteen-year-old Rita Cansino, like Grable, also appeared as a specialty in her earliest films and, also like Grable, failed to attract much notice at first (she changed her name to Rita Hayworth in 1937 when she signed a contract with Columbia and began to appear mostly in low-budget programmers). There was no single film that made Hayworth into a star as arguably had been the case with Grable, but after she was loaned out for a number of popular properties, among them *Blood and Sand* and *Strawberry Blonde* in 1941, she returned to Columbia as a headliner whose musicals would become the studio's biggest wartime successes.

Again, beyond these sketchy similarities and but for a certain reliance on "rags to riches" discourse and a continual reiteration of the trajectory of their rise from obscurity to stardom (a conventional feature of all publicity discourse in classical Hollywood), Grable's and Hayworth's stories notably diverge in the 1940s, their individual narratives and their film roles enabling them, like all stars, to serve as palimpsests on which the needs and desires and frustrations of a mass public were written and rewritten over and over across the decade. As this chapter argues, Grable's popularity seemed to rest on a truly hyperbolic ordinariness, marked as such on two levels: by a well-publicized absence of acting, singing, and dancing talent, and on an eroticism, if such it was, that was contained and made comforting by domesticity and a working life presented as being subsidiary to the needs of husband and children. In contrast, although subject to studio manufacture, Hayworth's star image is marked by both a discourse of authenticity—she was truly talented, truly beautiful—and by an increasingly melancholy awareness and understanding that her eroticism, beauty, and even performing talent were powerful but in ways that would keep her forever outside the comforts of domestic life and happiness. The significance of Betty Grable and Rita Hayworth in, and to, the 1940s lies in two spheres: in their identities as energetic and competent working women during the war and later in a postwar environment notably ambivalent about the professional labor of women; and also as wives and mothers whose bodies were socially and culturally, if not legally, subject to the needs of husband and children but whose commodity value also happened to reside in the public representation and specular availability of said body. Grable and Hayworth, then, matter both as representations, as a "look being copied all over the world," and as stars whose labors, domestic and professional, were imbricated in the often intractably conflicted meanings of femininity in wartime and postwar culture in the United States.

★★★★★ Betty Grable: I'm the Kind of a Girl Truck Drivers Like

To those for whom the phrase "blonde movie star" instantly conjures Marilyn Monroe or Jayne Mansfield or even Jean Harlow, the physical ordinariness and comparatively scandal-free existence of Betty Grable in the 1940s may come as a shock. If all stars are already paradoxes because they are ordinary and special at the same time, Grable is a paradox because she is ordinary and, by her own admission, not at all special in any way—to wit, "I don't sing too well. I don't dance too well. I don't act too well. It's on the combination of doing all three just passably that I get by" (*Screen Guide* c. 1946);[2] "If I had to depend on singing alone or dancing alone or acting alone I'd be nowhere. But with the three in combination I've been lucky in my career" (Ruth Waterbury, "They'll Remember Mama," *Photoplay*, January 1948, 90); "Betty Grable herself admits that she's neither a good dancer nor singer, and Harvard students elected her the World's Worst Actress. Yet her box-office success is unapproached by any other female in theatrical history" (*Saturday Evening Post*, 15 April 1950, 26). This last quotation, especially, perfectly encapsulates the particular contradictions of Grable's stardom, that she was a musical star who could not sing or dance well and whose acting was average but whose musicals were the major source of her extraordinarily popularity. And popular she was, the only female studio star ever to remain a top box-office performer for ten consecutive years according to exhibitor polls (her first appearance on the list was in 1942 and she remained there until 1951; she was the most popular star, male or female, in 1943) and the highest-paid woman in the United States. in the latter part of the decade.[3]

By the time Grable was called upon to replace Alice Faye in *Down Argentine Way* she had already appeared in more than fifty films. Grable's twenty 1940s films were of course all star vehicles, but that does not obviate one remarkable fact: that with only a couple of exceptions—and in contrast to Hayworth or indeed virtually any other big female Hollywood star—Grable was a success in one genre and one genre only, the Technicolor musical comedy. Moreover, most of these are of the "backstage" variety in which she plays either someone aspiring to be a musical performer in show business or who sings and dances in the course of hanging out at one or another nightclub, vaudeville theater, dance hall, canteen, or juke joint. Sean Griffin also points out that Grable was rarely the sole attraction of most of her star vehicles, the wartime films especially; *Down Argentine Way* was Carmen Miranda's first Hollywood film (and the start of Fox's cycle of "Good Neighbor musicals"), and Griffin argues that Miranda was as great a box office draw as Grable (Griffin, "Gang's" 32–34). If it is hard to distinguish one 1940s Grable vehicle from another, particularly those made in the first half of the decade, it is because they frequently star the same leads, character actors, and even specialties, take place in similar (or at least similar-looking) locations, and, of course, involve similar plot permutations. Moreover, Grable never changes—she sings similar-sounding songs and performs similar-looking dances, is always blonde, blue-eyed, rosy-cheeked, her costumes and hairstyles of similar cut and variety from film to film.

Despite their similarity, there are three groups into which most Grable films fall. One comprises those that are set in the present, but usually in some exotic location: *Down Argentine Way*, with Miranda, Don Ameche, and Charlotte Greenwood, and Grable as an American girl who falls in love with a wealthy racehorse owner; *Moon Over Miami* (1941), with Ameche, Greenwood, and Carole Landis, and Grable pretending to be an heiress in order to attract a rich husband; *Song of the Islands* (1942), with Victor Mature and Grable as the daughter of a Hawaiian cattle baron; *Springtime in the Rockies* (1942), with John Payne, Cesar Romero, Miranda, and Greenwood, in which Grable leaves the womanizing Payne to take up with former show-business partner Romero. In the second group are musicals of the nostalgic turn-of-the-century or Americana variety, which other studios also made during the war (see *Meet Me in St. Louis* [1944] at MGM): *Tin Pan Alley* (1940, black and white), with Payne and Alice Faye, in which Grable and Faye play sisters romanced by a team of songwriters; *Coney Island* (1943), with Romero and George Montgomery, in which Grable is a singer romanced by both men; *Sweet Rosie O'Grady* (1943), with Robert Young and Adolph Menjou and Grable a former burlesque queen engaged to a British duke who is exposed by newspaperman/songwriter Young; *The Dolly Sisters* (1945), with Payne and June Haver, in which Grable and Haver play Hungarian sisters who seek fame on Broadway; *The Shocking Miss Pilgrim* (1947), with Dick Haymes and music from the Gershwin songbook and with Grable playing a Boston "typewriter" who becomes involved in the women's suffrage movement but ends up marrying boss Haymes; *Mother Wore Tights* (1947), with Grable and Dan Dailey as a vaudeville team who get married and raise a family; *When My Baby Smiles at Me* (1948), with Grable and Dailey as another team of performers, but this time with Dailey an alcoholic whom Grable must rescue.

The third category consists simply of films that do not fit into the first two: *A Yank in the R.A.F.* and *I Wake Up Screaming* (both 1941, both black and white), the former with Tyrone Power as a pilot and Grable as a WREN who, of course, fall in love, the latter a detective film with Grable the sister of murdered Carole Landis who helps Victor Mature to find her killer (neither film contains musical numbers); *Footlight Serenade* (1942), again in black and white with Mature and Payne in a boxing-meets-Broadway musical; *Four Jills in a Jeep* (1944), in which Grable as well as stars ranging from Alice Faye to Martha Raye to Carole Landis to Kay Francis play themselves in a fictionalized U.S.O. story; *Pin Up Girl* (1944), with John Harvey and Martha Raye, in which Grable is a canteen hostess in Missouri who ends up in Washington, D.C., and which is discussed further below; *Billy Rose's Diamond Horseshoe* (1945), with Dick Haymes and filmed partly in the club of the same name; *That Lady in Ermine* (1948), Ernst Lubitsch's final film (it was completed by Otto Preminger), a weird fantasy musical with Douglas Fairbanks Jr. and Cesar Romero in which Grable plays both a nineteenth-century Italian countess and an ancestor who steps out of a portrait to help her deal with some marauding Hungarians; and finally Preston Sturges's *The Beautiful Blonde from Bashful Bend* (1949), with Grable as a jealous six-shooting saloon singer (she performs two numbers) who ends up hiding out in the boonies pretending to be a schoolteacher, and which helped to end Sturges's career in Hollywood (Grable hated making it, too).[4]

The films in the first two categories were Grable's only reliably popular 1940s movies, but they star no outstandingly able male musical lead of the stature of a Fred Astaire or a Gene Kelly, there are few standards among their sound tracks, and they were not directed and choreographed by anyone who has since acquired the reputation of an auteur. Concomitantly, the fact that Grable's musicals are, in Griffin's words, made according to the "Fox formula"—"a standardized plot, broken up by various performers (who often play little or no part in the narrative) coming out and doing numbers" (Griffin, "Gang's" 29)—means that they are not integrated, one of the defining features of which term is not only a cohesion of style in numbers and narrative but some sort of unified aesthetic and stylistic vision imposed by a (virtually always male) director or choreographer-director (Vincente Minnelli or Gene Kelly and Stanley Donen at the Freed Unit at MGM, for example). Thus, Grable's films have likely been denigrated over the years not only because they are similar to one another but because of the status so many filmmakers and scholars have granted to integration as the apotheosis of the classical Hollywood musical. Instead, Grable's films are what I have elsewhere termed "women's musicals," because it is on the performances of women that they were sold and it is largely women's energy, personality, and, yes, talent (Grable was a more than competent singer and dancer) that still make them worth seeing now (see McLean *Being Rita Hay-*

worth; McLean "Putting 'Em Down"). But again, Grable's films are also full of other women and men who perform as specialties with often incredible skill and competence too—Carmen Miranda, Charlotte Greenwood and her wacky physical gyrations, wide-mouthed Martha Raye, choreographer-dancer Hermes Pan, various ballroom teams, the tap-dancing Condos Brothers as well as the Nicholas Brothers, and even a roller-skating troupe and a brigade of precision-marching WACs in *Pin Up Girl*. If Grable made popular films, in other words, it is not always clear that she was the source of that popularity as much as it was a combination of her appeal with the vaudeville tradition and plethora of performing riches that the Fox musical represented (see Griffin, "Gang's" 28–39).[5]

In addition, the promotional material for Grable and her films, which included pinup photographs, played an unusually significant role in her fame and popularity, especially during the war. While many female stars, Hayworth included, made "leg art" as starlets and much of that art ended up pinned to a barracks wall somewhere, a single Grable image, the swimsuit photo, was so extraordinarily famous that a film was made as an homage both to the term "pinup girl" and to the photo itself. The photo was shot by Frank Powolny in 1942—Powolny later claimed that the term pinup was "born" with the photo—during wardrobe tests for *Sweet Rosie O'Grady*; airbrushed out of the image was a garter on her leg (Warren 77–79). It was printed in *Time* magazine's overseas edition and in the G.I. magazine *Yank* (Gabor 151), and more than half a million copies of the photo were sent by the studio in response to servicemen's requests. It was apparently the coyness of the over-the-shoulder smile—"Follow me home, boys, I'm what you're fighting for" (Gabor 135)—and the "gams" that gave the photo its appeal; Grable immediately became known as the "gal with the gorgeous gams," "the girl with the million-dollar legs," or the girl with "the limbs that launched a thousand sighs" (Warren 79–80). The centrality of Grable's gams to her image was cemented, literally, when a cast of her leg and feet was made in the forecourt of Grauman's Chinese Theatre in February 1943. According to the *Hollywood Reporter*, Grable "took off her shoes before stepping into the cement—having shoe rationing in mind" (Warren 79). That same year a single pair of her nylons was exchanged for a $40,000 war donation (Renov 184).

The film *Pin Up Girl* therefore ranks as an obviously significant intertext in relation to Grable's popularity. Certainly the title and the process it signifies seems, more baldly than any other musical one might name, to define "girls" like Grable as passive, still, and inactive objects of the male gaze. Michael Renov, in fact, writes that Grable's stardom "was, in terms of Laura

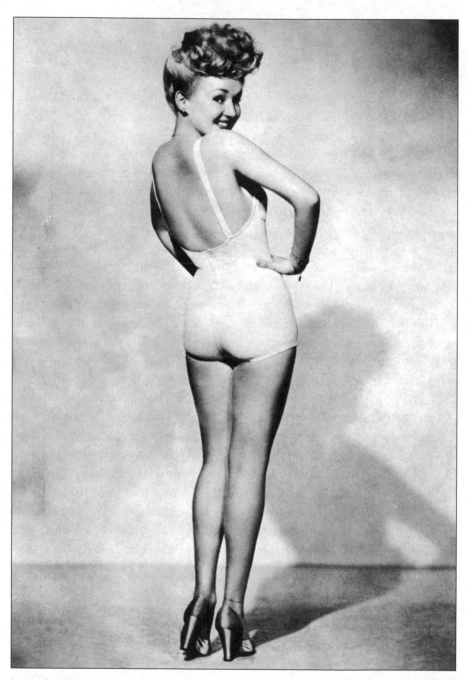

Betty Grable as the most popular pinup of World War II. Photo by Frank Powolny, 1941. Collection of the author.

Mulvey's dichotomous formulation, a product of spectacle rather than narrative" (Renov 184). But Grable was not only a pinup, she was a singer and
a dancer; and many scholars have pointed out that Mulvey's schematic
equation of "showgirls" like Grable with passivity as well as fetishization
ignores the particular functions of singing and, especially, dancing as forms
and mechanisms of communication, self-expression, identification, and
subjectivity (see Thomas 154–61, 165–73; McLean *Being Rita Hayworth*;
McLean "Putting 'Em Down"). Grable was not a virtuosic dancer and singer
but she was able to embody some of the senses of joy, agency, and competence that the musical number represented for men and for women. Yet in
Grable's case (though arguably not Hayworth's, as discussed below) it is also
hard *not* to agree with Mulvey, because of the primacy of discussions of
Grable's body—not only her "million-dollar legs" (which the studio reportedly insured) but her "Modern Venus" proportions (despite an extremely
short neck), her hair, her blue eyes, her smile, etc.—as being the product of
nature rather than of Hollywood's manipulation and manufacture (Betty
Grable "never had a skin treatment or a body massage, does her own finger-
and toe-nails, and squanders four whole dollars a month on cosmetics"
[*Screen Guide* c. 1941]). And the case is also made because of the very lack
of an extraordinary or unusual talent that Grable's performances seem to
represent, particularly in a film that makes so much of a still photograph.

Pin Up Girl is a typical Grable (indeed Fox) musical, in other words, but
stands out for the way in which it uses Grable's extratextual meaning as a
popular wartime pinup both to signify and to undermine her narratively
inscribed ordinariness. The film's first image is an attenuated and much
curvier artist's rendering of the photo itself, which is emblazoned, in color,
on the screen throughout the credit sequence; golden rays of light are
painted all around it. The opening number begins when hordes of enlisted
men arrive at a Missouri canteen where they sing "Won't you be my pinup
girl" and "You're my little pinup girl" to all the women they see. Since
women working in such canteens were not supposed to date the men
whose morale they were meant to boost, the singing women substitute
apples, pie, and hotdogs for their own bodies, which are off-limits. The song
itself, of course, is also about what the pinup means; not only does the
pinup have "the grace of an angel, the face of a movie star" but the men
sing, en masse, "I need to have that smile before me no matter where I
roam"—the smile, face, and grace of the uncredited women who are
singing back to the men, but also the smile, face, and grace of Grable herself, who soon appears and sings the song to all the men solo. Thus is the
pinup linked with American womanhood generally; again, the pinup's

function (or one of them) was to remind the enlisted man what he was fighting for. Indeed, one soldier appears with candy and flowers and announces himself as Grable's fiancé. But he is mistaken; it turns out that Grable has become engaged to hundreds of men already—to every single man she has signed a pinup photo for. And the photos she signs for the adoring soldiers at the end of the scene, before going off to Washington, D.C., with a less glamorous friend (she wears eyeglasses) to do clerical work for the navy, is the famous Grable pinup that existed in the world as the de facto basis for this film, and yet is not sufficiently interesting *in* the film to enable Grable to do anything but get a job taking dictation from Eugene Pallette.

The male lead in *Pin Up Girl*, John Harvey, was not a movie star (this was his second film, after *Four Jills in a Jeep*); he plays a war hero vaguely "from Guadalcanal." Grable and her friend lie their way into an exclusive nightclub in Washington by claiming that they are his guests, not knowing that he is going to be at the club himself. When they are seated at the same table, Grable lies again about what she does and claims to have starred in a Broadway musical that has just closed. When pressed by Martha Raye, as a jealous performer in the club who has her suspicions about Grable, Grable is able to stand up and perform a number with a male chorus with no trouble at all. Grable becomes a singer in Washington but continues working as a secretary by day, disguising herself with her own eyeglasses because her boss, Pallette, assigns her to the war hero himself, who has been told by Raye that Grable is engaged to be married so he has rejected her. He asks the Grable in glasses—he cannot see through her disguise, although her voice, hair, makeup, and clothing are the same—out on a date, finds out who she is and that she is not really engaged, and the film ends with Grable winking at him from behind a rifle in the film's big finale.

The finale in *Pin Up Girl* is not a musical number, however; rather, Grable leads a large drill team of real-life WACs in rifle maneuvers in a giant but amorphously defined space (it is supposed to be a nightclub stage). Grable barks orders and the women's precise marching is spectacular, so spectacular that the film ends when the "number" concludes, allowing the narrative to intrude only to the extent that we witness Grable's wink to her hero seated at a club table, smiling to indicate that everything has ended happily (there is no final romantic clinch). And there are other non-Grable riches in the film, from the Condos Brothers and their extraordinary tap-dancing to a giant roller-skating production number to the antics of Martha Raye to Charlie Spivak's orchestra, with Jane Hutton singing. But Grable's numbers are fine, too—upbeat, nicely choreographed, mostly shot in takes

Betty Grable publicity photo from the martial finale of *Pin Up Girl* (1944). Copyright 1944, Twentieth Century–Fox, Inc.

long enough to convince one that she knows what she is doing, and demonstrating that she is not as "ordinary" a performer as she repeatedly proclaimed herself to be.[6] But she does not have to be great given the revue-style variety that the rest of the film offers. Paradoxically, then, what *Pin Up Girl* suggests is that the pinup itself is insufficient to explain the popularity of Grable or the musicals in which she appears, and also that the pinup is significant because of what it represents, which is the hope and promise of normality at a moment when the fighting was both at its worst and when it seemed as though an end might be in sight (see also Spencer).

Michael Renov claims, in fact, that Grable's stardom "was less identifiable with her wartime roles than as an emblem of healthy American womanhood—well-scrubbed, full-bodied, beyond suspicion"; her eroticism was "undiminished by her chaste image" and the "plumpness of [her] open face and form, the wide-eyed expression betraying neither judgment nor substantive intent, offered an unthreatening version of female sexuality for the fighting man" (Renov 184). But in *Pin Up Girl*, as well as several other films (*Moon Over Miami* and *Footlight Serenade*, to name two), Grable plays women whose "open face and form," as well as their "wide-eyed expressions," only enable them to deceive men more easily. Grable's characters always own up to their deceptions in the end, but they lie—a lot—before they do. Therefore, it was undoubtedly Grable's offscreen life, less so than the narratives of her films, that made her image seem open and unthreatening. Grable was briefly married, from 1937 to 1940, to former child star Jackie Coogan, and early in the decade she was linked in gossip columns with a married man, George Raft, whom she believed would divorce his wife to marry her (the wife, a devout Catholic, would not divorce Raft). Nevertheless, no major scandal ever circulated around Grable's image, and her 1943 marriage to Harry James, and the birth of her first daughter in 1944 (a second was born in 1947), helped to cement Grable's sexuality as a symbol of a deferred domestic contentment—a conclusion supported by her mother's published remark that the soldiers and sailors who sent letters to Grable during the war "never wrote her improper suggestions" (*Saturday Evening Post*, 15 April 1950, 113) as well as a popular parodic song lyric of 1943: "I want a girl just like the girl that married Harry James." In *Time* magazine's assessment at the end of the decade, "To millions of Americans, the pert, sexy, but basically 'nice' girl that Betty plays on the screen is young American womanhood at its best. . . . Betty represents an attainable goal, a daydream that might come true. Grable's own life is a proof of the dream" ("Living the Daydream," 40). Moreover, when Grable had her first baby, "her G.I. admirers promptly wrote their No. 1 pin-up girl to tell her all about their wives and their babies" (42).

However prosaic and repetitive the publicity and promotional material published about Grable during the 1940s seems now, the endless stories about her happy home life—the way she decorated the Hollywood house as well as the ranch she and James acquired in Calabasas, the number of horses they owned, the numerous spreads picturing and in the process eulogizing Grable's skills as a mother to Vicki and Jessica ("Betty has accepted the responsibilities of marriage and motherhood with more real understanding than almost any other glamour girl in Hollywood," wrote Louella Parsons in 1948)—it must all have been inordinately comforting to a fractured wartime and postwar United States. Certainly Grable's offscreen life as "Mrs. James" cannot be discounted in attempting to understand the popularity that continued into the early 1950s. Although the amount of their income was manifestly unusual, as was the fact that Grable was a working movie star, the discourse about her marriage and home life was couched in terms that made both seem utterly conventional—articles never failed to mention that "no career conflicts loom over Betty and Harry James. His income . . . tops Betty's," and she is quoted as saying, "If the career ever interferes with the marriage, I'll drop the career in a minute!" (Robin Coons, "Betty Grable," *Screen Guide* c. 1946–1947). Grable and James were homebodies, owned few books, seldom traveled except to their ranch, and rarely went out; in 1946 one magazine reported that, since her marriage to James, Grable had "gone nightclubbing only once, because Harry wanted to hear the band at Ciro's." Once her children are born, naturally Grable's status as a mother becomes as significant as that of wife: "She has her hairdresser come to her home in the morning, so she can spend more time with the baby. She quits work at six on the dot every night, so she can have dinner with Vicky" (Carl A. Schroeder, "The Shocking Miss Grable," *Screen Guide*, April 1946). And "after working all day at the studio she hops into her Cadillac convertible and does her marketing. 'It is important that my husband and babies have the right food'" (Herb Howe, "Beautiful Blonde from Calabasas Ranch," *Photoplay*, April 1949, 92).

Louella Parsons, after writing about Grable "playing with her youngsters at the beach or romping with them around the swimming pool," quotes the star as saying, "We have never gone to Europe because we can never tear ourselves away from Del Mar [California]. The beach is here, and golf, tennis, racing and everything we want. What more can anyone ask?" Parsons then asks, "You are happy, aren't you, Betty?" To which Grable replies, "'At this moment,' she said, 'I have everything in the world I want. The only cloud appeared when I made "The Beautiful Blonde from Bashful Bend." I didn't want to do it, but I have never interfered with my studio'" (Louella Parsons, "Harry James and Betty Grable," *Los Angeles Examiner*, c. 1949). In a piece called "If You Were the Ranch Guest of Betty Grable," the author eulogizes that Grable and James will go on forever having fun and being admired "so long as they keep on being *people!*" (Dorothy Deere, *Photoplay*, May 1946, 108). Another article claims, as rumors about problems in the

Grable-James marriage began to circulate toward the end of the decade (the couple did not divorce until 1965), "Certainly, no top actress in Hollywood, and Betty is *the* top, with her $208,000 income for 1948 and her place in the Big Ten at the box office for the past six years, has ever sublimated her career to marriage and home any more than Mrs. Harry James." The article even calls her "Betty James—the wife, mother and home-maker," because "Betty, herself, has put career second, marriage first. (That's why we were concerned about that talk of separation.) But she is dead serious about her job, *while she's doing it*, and has the reputation of being about the hardest-working star on the lot"; in fact, it is because "Mrs. James" has done such a wonderful job of balancing marriage and family that hers is "the kind of marriage we would like to see go on and on" (Diane Scott, "Blonde Bonanza," *Photoplay*, September 1949, 98).

What one comes away with from all of this is that Grable was an image, indeed an icon, of Hollywood ordinariness, an ordinariness that, while obviously still invoking "white" as the symbolic "apotheosis of female desirability," in Richard Dyer's words (Dyer 64), also possesses specific class dimensions. There is a slight sneering tone to some of the discourse, although it is astonishing how much of the sneering is made to seem as though it comes from Grable herself: "I'm the kind of a girl truck drivers like," she reportedly claims (Jerry Mason, "I Danced with Grable," *Los Angeles Times This Week*, c. 1942–1943); and in 1950, the *Saturday Evening Post* states that Grable "needs color to make her shine. . . . In black and white she'd be just another good-looking broad from a five-and-dime-store basement" (*Saturday Evening Post*, 15 April 1950, 106). The *Post* also claims that Grable's "appeal lay in the fact that she's a no-highbrow girl, and the arty boys to the contrary, the picture business has got to face the fact that there are more lowbrows in the world than highbrows" and that Grable's "machine-turned torso and her smoothly textured face" were "unburdened with any distracting hint of a Bryn Mawr–Vassar type of intelligence that might give a male beholder a feeling of inferiority" (27, 106). Of course, Grable was an ordinary housewife and mother *in public,* and despite professing that she would give up her career "in a minute" if it interfered with the marriage, in 1950 she was reported as telling "Harry," "You know . . . I've been thinking. What the heck would I do with myself if I ever did quit?" ("Glamour from Nine to Five," *Modern Screen*, c. 1950–1951).

As has become the stuff of legend, Grable passed on her crown as pinup queen of Fox and Hollywood to Marilyn Monroe—who was much less equipped to handle it—in the 1950s when the two starred together in *How to Marry a Millionaire* (1953). And while I still cannot find Grable, despite her popularity, very interesting as a film performer—most of her star vehicles do "come off the sound-stage assembly line as similar as a row of shiny sport convertibles rolling from a Detroit factory" (*Saturday Evening Post*, 15 April 1950, 109)—I can feel the force of her optimism and what all reports express as a contentment about her career and her life. If she seems a bit too complacent about her own mediocrity, that mediocrity, no less than the complacency, was also ours. Hollywood musicals, hers included, began losing money in the 1950s, and Grable abruptly left Fox and the film industry for good; but when she and Harry James put together a Las Vegas nightclub act in 1956, it was Grable who insisted the show begin with a projection of her famous pinup photo, as though to remind audiences about how much she had once meant to them.

★★★★★ Rita Hayworth: California Carmen

When Rita Hayworth died in 1987, many if not most of the obituaries reproduced her famous pinup photo but accompanied it with remarks that signaled how limiting an image it had been for Hayworth as a movie star and as a woman. In contrast to Grable, accounts of Hayworth's life and work link her status as an arguably vastly more erotic pinup during the war to a sense of potential unfulfilled, as an eventually malign identity that she was never allowed to transcend. But the persona of Hayworth during the 1940s is more complicated and generally much less melancholy than the obituaries made it seem; and certainly throughout the war she was one of the hardest-working and best-liked young stars in Hollywood, and her musicals almost as successful as Grable's at the box office. But where Grable seemed to enjoy her status as a pinup and as a musical comedy star whose films made more money when her legs were on view, Hayworth's problem was that she was more ambitious—not to become a bigger star but to improve herself as an actress, to overcome her deficiencies in education, to expand her horizons beyond Hollywood, and to prove that she was more than just a lovely face and body. During the war, of course, Hayworth was perfectly happy to have a "V" for victory painted on her forehead for publicity photos, to become known as "the sweetheart of the A.E.F.," and to pose with servicemen in ads for RC Cola, tour in U.S.O. shows and appear in war-bond drives, and make patriotic and escapist, if not always lighthearted, movie musicals that showed off her legs as well as her substantial dancing prowess.

Hayworth's ambition, however, especially at the beginning of the decade, was portrayed as less her own than that of various male mentors—first her father, then her first husband, a much older and somewhat shady Holly-wood character, Edward Judson, whom she married in 1937 and divorced in 1942. From her Spanish father she inherited both her dancing ability and the ethnic heritage that initially limited Rita Cansino, as she was first known, to all-purpose ethnic, often foreign, film roles. In contrast to Grable, it required a lot of effort to manufacture both Rita Cansino's ethnicity and what would become Rita Hayworth's peaches-and-cream Americanness. Rita Cansino's normally brown hair had to be dyed black, and makeup was needed to darken her fair skin; to become Rita Hayworth in 1937 her hair color was changed to red and her low hairline raised with painful electrol-ysis—and all these processes of transformation and fabrication were carried out in full view of the public. But while, with Judson's publicized help, Hayworth's name and face appeared frequently in magazines and news-papers by the end of the 1930s, her film roles at Columbia remained, with a few notable exceptions like Howard Hawks's *Only Angels Have Wings* in 1939, nondescript. Her first 1940s film was a low-budget musical with Tony Martin in which she did only a little dancing; her next, all in 1940, were *Blondie on a Budget* (playing Dagwood's old girlfriend), *The Lady in Question* (with Glenn Ford), and *Angels Over Broadway* (a dark and depressing, but generally affecting, Ben Hecht film about a suicidal embezzler, with Hay-worth playing a sympathetic call girl). None of these films attracted much attention, although Hayworth's promise and beauty were singled out in reviews. Columbia decided to loan her out to other studios, and at MGM she appeared as a supporting player in a Joan Crawford vehicle *Susan and God* (1940); at Warner Bros. as the "other woman" in the very successful period comedy *Strawberry Blonde*, with James Cagney, and as a newspaper girl in *Affectionately Yours*; and at Twentieth Century–Fox in Rouben Mamoulian's remake of the bullfighting epic *Blood and Sand* as Doña Sol, the temptress who brings down matador Tyrone Power. Although she was not very convincing as a "bad woman," her beauty and her ability to move, in Mamoulian's words, "like a great cat" sent her back to Columbia as a bona fide movie star.

In her transformation from Cansino to Hayworth, much of the public-ity material that circulated about her explained that she was discarding dancing because she "didn't want to be typed as a Spanish dancer" (*Movie Stars Parade*, c. 1940). "I never really cared for dancing, despite the fact it's in my blood," she told an interviewer in 1940; "I want to be an actress" (Franklin Edgars, "She Dances but Prefers Acting," *Movies*, September 1939, 38). But the first tailor-made (though black and white) vehicle in which she appeared after her return to Columbia was one of the first musicals with a wartime setting, *You'll Never Get Rich* (1941), in which her dancing talent, if not her singing of the Cole Porter score (it was public knowledge that her singing voice was dubbed, but no one seemed to care), was fully exploited in a very successful partnership with Fred Astaire. When Hayworth appeared on the cover of *Life* in 1941 with the famous pinup shot on a full page inside, the magazine now called her "a triple-threat song & dance star" (11 August 1941, 33). *Time* magazine put her in a cover story called "California Carmen" (10 November 1941) and named her "the right girl" for Astaire: "Those who saw russet-haired, incandescent Rita Hayworth dance before the movies drafted her knew she was a dancer to partner even the great Astaire. But few of them would have expected her to keep up with his wry, off-beat brand of comedy. She fills both assignments in *You'll Never Get Rich*" (90). More loan-outs, from which Columbia, if not Hayworth, raked in enormous amounts of money, followed in 1942—to Fox for a Grable-like Technicolor period musical biopic, *My Gal Sal*, starring Victor Mature as Paul Dresser, and to play a short part in the *La Ronde*–style film *Tales of Manhattan*, which followed a mink coat around New York as it changed hands.

The box office returns on *You'll Never Get Rich* as well as *My Gal Sal* made another musical seem like a safe bet, and *You Were Never Lovelier* (1942), again with Astaire and with music by Jerome Kern, was even more successful. Kern also wrote the music, and Ira Gershwin the lyrics, of her next film, *Cover Girl* (1944), a huge hit co-starring Gene Kelly (and one of Grable's frequent supporting players, Phil Silvers). The lag between the last two musicals was occasioned not only by the greater preparation time given to what were now being treated by Columbia as A-pictures—*Cover Girl* was Hayworth's first Technicolor film at the studio—but also by Hayworth's divorce from Judson in 1942 and her work for the war effort. Columbia became the villain of the piece when it refused her permission to appear in Orson Welles's Mercury Wonder Show in 1943, a magic and variety act that was free for servicemen and had been endorsed by the Hollywood "Victory Committee." Columbia's ostensible reason for not allowing Hayworth to perform was its investment in *Cover Girl*, but what they were really trying to do was get her away from Orson Welles. Although Hayworth left the Wonder Show (replaced by Marlene Dietrich), she continued to perform in troupe shows for servicemen in Los Angeles and at camps around the country, becoming one of the best-loved as well as most pinned-up of Hollywood's glamour girls. But as Columbia had feared, she did fall in love with and marry Welles in 1943, the same year that Grable married Harry James; Hollywood wags quickly dubbed Hayworth and Welles "Beauty and the Brain." Hayworth's first child, like Grable's a daughter, was also born in 1944.

Rita Hayworth in a publicity photo from the finale of *Cover Girl* (1944). Copyright 1944, Columbia Pictures, Inc.

Hayworth's final wartime film was the women's musical *Tonight and Every Night* (1945), in which she was the main attraction (her co-star was Lee Bowman, who neither sang nor danced). It took place in London and ended with a close-up of Hayworth's tear-stained face as she sang the film's title song about going on and on "tonight and every night" after the death of her best friends in a bomb attack next door. Few musicals, even wartime musicals, were as somber as this one, and *Tonight and Every Night* was not as popular as Hayworth's previous films. Her personal life made more news than her films at this point; Orson Welles had begun to be seen with a succession of other women after the birth of their child, and in 1945 she left him during the filming of her next Columbia film, a non-musical and her second film with Glenn Ford, *Gilda*.

Unlike Betty Grable, Hayworth had always expressed an interest in becoming a serious actor and in doing dramatic parts as well as musicals, and *Gilda* (1946) set the pattern for something approaching a typical "Hayworth vehicle" for the next several years: a drama in which Hayworth plays a seductress of some kind and that also features her, and usually her alone, in a diegetically motivated musical number (*Blood and Sand* had been her first picture in this mold). Equally important, until *Gilda* the Hayworth screen persona had been either vampish, as in *Blood and Sand*, or all-American, as in her musicals. In *Gilda* she combined the all-American forthrightness and spunkiness of her musical roles with the eroticism and exoticism of a Doña Sol, and the effect was stunning. Gilda was both questionable as to her morals in a sexual sense (she was a woman with a past), but also "decent," and a funny and sweet fair player. Her power comes from her sexuality and her ability to take care of herself and to perform for her own pleasure—there are three musical numbers in *Gilda*, with "Put the Blame on Mame" now an ironic standard about the world's propensity to blame women when things go wrong—even though in the end her options are limited by the structures and strictures of patriarchy. The film made millions, and with the success of the studio's biggest grossing musical ever, *The Jolson Story* (with Larry Parks as Jolson), the same year, Columbia had left "poverty row" far behind.

Not surprisingly, the studio decided to pair Hayworth and Parks for her final 1940s musical, *Down to Earth* (1947), which its choreographer Jack Cole called "sort of a *Gilda* in color" (Kobal 601) because it involves gangsters and a shady show-business scheme and an evil but suave foreign gambler (played by George Macready, who had been the villain in *Gilda*) who is killed at the end. But it was also a fantasy involving Hayworth as Terpsichore, the muse of dance. It was perhaps the film's bizarre and complicated conjunction of crime film and musical fantasy that made it less financially successful than *Gilda*, but the role also helped win Hayworth the title of the "American Love Goddess" thanks to a *Life* magazine review and cover story by Winthrop Sargeant (10 November 1947, 81–89). The limiting but resonant sobriquet followed her for the rest of her life, and while Grable might have found the label congenial (Sargeant only mentions Grable once), Hayworth did not.

Rita Hayworth in a pose from "Put the Blame on Mame" in *Gilda* (1946). Copyright 1946, Columbia Pictures, Inc.

Sargeant titles his article "The Cult of the Love Goddess in America," and turns Hayworth into the symbol of a "phenomenon of profound socio-logical significance," namely the "incarnation" of the "age-old sex goddess" (Sargeant uses "sex goddess" and "love goddess" interchangeably). For Sargeant, Hayworth is an "overwhelming, industrialized Molochian idol to which millions of otherwise sane Americans pay daily tribute" (81). Under

"The Power of Passivity," Sargeant defines Hayworth's fundamental "trait" as "simply the desire to please people"; she "causes or inspires action, but she does not act herself except in response to the desire of others. . . . Rita, like Helen [of Troy] is totally lacking in ambition and is mentally incapable of initiating anything on her own" (89). Rita Hayworth has been manufactured by "masculine effort," and "this fact, added to her rather remarkable physical qualifications, goes a long way toward explaining her success." Her reputation as "being, with the possible exception of Bette Davis, the hardest worker in Hollywood" (89), means only that she works hard at doing what others ask her to do; she has no will of her own.

The misogynistic terms with which the twin labors of female stardom and female spectatorship are defined in Sargeant's article once more invoke Laura Mulvey's passive "showgirl" and the paradigms of Hollywood's visual pleasure she describes, and the baldness of Sargeant's presumption in speaking both for "the feminine point of view" and "the real Rita," as two of the article's sections are called, suggests that what we now read as contempt was viewed then as simple reportage rather than a rhetorical strategy designed to undermine women's status and authority. As part of mainstream postwar discourse, however, it is impossible now not to notice its cracks and contradictions, the ways in which a woman's passivity is made to seem generated by her own lacks rather than being the result of a structural oppression in which women's "point of view" is always already that of men *about* women and their actions. Although he does not specifically champion domesticity over Hayworth's hard work as a star, Sargeant does explicitly characterize her as being like a "little girl" appearing in a "school play," only happy if she can "[elicit] an approving smile or a pat on her shaggy head" from a "director or the publicity man or some other factotum in charge" (89). What makes Hayworth an "extraordinary relief" in Hollywood is that she is precisely *not* one of those "ambitious, self-propelled, predatory, sugar-cured, artificially glazed and chromium-plated" women (like Betty Grable) with which the city "crawls" (89). In some senses, then, Sargeant is participating in an attempted postwar realignment of femininity away from the power of women's own efforts and actions and toward a rendering of women's sexualized images as existing, in an "age-old" tradition, by and for the contemplation and inspiration of men. But ironically, he also reinscribes one of the most interesting features of Hayworth's stardom generally, that rather than being "artificial" Hayworth's talent and hard work as well as her eroticism are genuine and "real."

Hayworth's anger, and that of her relatives and friends, at being characterized specifically as passive and inactive, even as she was described as a hard worker, was publicly circulated after the publication of Sargeant's article and helped to negate its worst presumptions. Moreover, in 1947 Hayworth had formed her own production company, the Beckworth Corporation (named for her and her daughter Becky); she was the first woman since the 1920s to do so. In a *Photoplay* article by Louella Parsons called "Ask the Boss" (March 1948), Hayworth is quoted as saying, "The idea all through [Sargeant's article] is that I can't make up my own mind on anything. That I let other people make all my decisions. . . . That's the most unfair, most ridiculous thing that was ever written about me. I'm sure my business associates know I am quite capable of making up my own mind. My producing unit, the Beckworth Company, has just been formed. I sign all the checks—I've got one of the best contracts ever drawn up for an actress in motion pictures" (90). There is only "one statement in that magazine story," Hayworth claims, "that is very true: I want people to like me!" (92). And Parsons concludes her story with the statement that "a far better label than The Goddess of Love for Rita as she is today is 'Miss Independence'" (92).

Hayworth's next film, however, was in some ways the flip side of *Gilda* and went far in further identifying her image as implacably passive and sexual. In an attempt to help Welles make some money so that he could pay child support (she divorced him at the end of 1947), Hayworth agreed to appear in *The Lady from Shanghai* (1948), playing the evil and platinum-blonde seductress Elsa Bannister. In contrast to Gilda, Elsa is a humorless though at times pitiable character (she does sing a song, lying flat on her back and barely moving) who is left dying on the floor at the end, but despite Hayworth's excellent performance the film was one of her few 1940s box office failures. She then made *The Loves of Carmen* (1948), the first movie released by the Beckworth Corporation but her last of the decade, based on the 1845 Prosper Mérimée novel *Carmen*. *Newsweek*'s cover story "Carmen Hayworth" (August 1948) also mentions Beckworth as Hayworth's "own production company" and her contract as "the best contract" that anyone has "ever negotiated with a major-league distributor like Columbia." But the article also writes that Hayworth's "unquenchable wholesomeness" gives her a "hard time" being "as dirty and nasty as the part requires"—despite Carmen being a "natural" role for Hayworth because of her Spanish "antecedents" (79–80).

Exhausted after several years of nonstop work, Hayworth was on a trip to Europe in 1948 when she first met and was wooed by Prince Aly Khan, a well-known European playboy who was still married to the mother of his two sons. As Betty Grable had discovered during her romance with the married George Raft (and as Ingrid Bergman was discovering at about the same time as Hayworth, when the married Bergman began her affair with the still-married Roberto Rossellini), there was little public sympathy in American popular culture for extramarital romance; and Hayworth's peripatetic courtship by Aly Khan met with some strong press disapproval. When their engagement was announced in 1949, however, "Rita and Aly" became the couple of the year, and their wedding in May turned all the negative press positive and positively glowing as they discussed the nuptials and the new "Cinderella Princess." Hayworth was pregnant at the time of the wedding, and her second daughter, a literal princess, was born in December. But almost immediately, the marriage began to falter amid rumors of Aly Khan's further womanizing, and by 1951 Hayworth left Europe for Hollywood again, where she was granted a divorce by default in January 1953 and where she made several more films for Columbia (and would marry again too, twice, but never for more than a couple of years each) before the end of her contract in 1957. She made a few more films in the 1960s and 1970s before succumbing to the Alzheimer's disease that would eventually kill her, and which she helped bring to widespread public attention for the first time.

★★★★★ Rejuvenating Women

In contrast to Grable, then, Hayworth's post-1940s career is a tragic record of how the promise and potential power of "Miss Independence" was derailed and overtaken by a series of domestic scandals, but perhaps Hayworth's very public attempts to reconcile her roles as working woman, wife, and mother also served as useful sites of negotiation for other women facing similar issues in their own lives. When *Look* discussed "the American Look" in 1949, it made specific reference to the appearance of American women as "reflect[ing] American freedom" and enabling them to "carry their heads high" (71), and both Grable's and Hayworth's images in this sense can only be read as part of a much broader mosaic made up of other women stars whose "look" was also "copied all over the world." If Hayworth seems to me to be a much more interesting star than Grable by the end of the decade, I am uncomfortably aware that the elements that make her so interesting are themselves the result of my own training in an academic field that for various reasons has an established canon of significant works, that valorizes the films of particular directors it has deemed auteurs, that until only relatively recently had ignored the musical as a genre altogether, and that still sees originality as more significant than convention and repetition.

And while I do not want to denigrate Grable's image as a happily married working mother—indeed, it is arguably one of the most potent factors in her continued appeal to a wartime *and* postwar audience—I also find Hayworth's insecurity and yet inability to tolerate the philandering and fecklessness of her husbands (she always threw them out, in the end, even Welles and Aly Khan) and her success in raising two daughters as a single working mother very bracing and inspiring, however much her failure to "find love" and a "proper husband" might have represented the unintended consequences of abuse she suffered as a child.[7] Hayworth seems more modern, more relevant, both to the "rejuvenation" *Look* claimed for women and to subsequent developments in feminism. And I admire Hayworth because she worked hard as a dancer and an artist, learning from and improving with every choreographer and teacher she met; she was more intellectually curious, trying always to rectify the lack of education she suffered as a child; she had problems she could not always control, but she struggled to understand them. Grable, on the other hand, while honest about her own deficiencies as a performer, seems to have been happy to be the same from year to year, her satisfaction with the terms and meaning of her own "artificially glazed and chromium-plated" stardom thereby becoming a form of ossification, and her films seeming, even by 1950, again no different from one another than a new model of car might be from a predecessor (something one certainly cannot say of the much more diverse films of Hayworth).

But in the end, for neither Grable nor Hayworth was being pinned up a sign of their passivity and inactivity; and if they were not quite able to achieve the "security" that *Look* pointed to with such confidence at the end of the decade, and if their "stride freely and easily forward" would soon become a hard and often heartbreaking slow trudge, they were still "carrying their heads high."[8] Whether smiling down at us from a barracks wall or a movie screen, Grable and Hayworth contributed mightily to America's ability to keep on going through a world war and its aftermath, embodying and representing sexuality and eroticism but also a sunny cheerfulness, the importance of hard work, and a literal as well as figurative grace under pressure.

NOTES

1. Although *Look* captions the photo as "the most famous shot ever made of Rita Hayworth," it is actually not the one originally published in *Life* on 11 August 1941; it is a slightly different pose from the same session with photographer Bob Landry.

2. Many of the popular sources cited in this article are from the Constance McCormick Collection of star scrapbooks housed at the Cinema-Television Library, University of Southern California; there are five scrapbooks for Grable, seven for Hayworth. Most of the material in the scrapbooks is not always documented as to source or date, unfortunately, and any textual citation with an incomplete reference is from a CMC scrapbook.

3. The polls I refer to were published annually in the *International Motion Picture Almanac* (New York: Quigley Publications) and have been reprinted online at http://reelclassics .com/Articles/General/quigleytop10-article.htm. Bing Crosby remained a top ten star for twelve years, Bob Hope for thirteen; but Grable's record is not approached by any other female star (and Rita Hayworth never appears at all).

4. Grable was very public in her dislike of *The Beautiful Blonde from Bashful Bend*, but only after it had failed at the box office. She claimed that if Zanuck "ever gives me Preston Sturges again, you'll hear Grable's voice. However, I don't think Mr. Zanuck will ever make me do a picture again that I am as much opposed to as I was the Sturges atrocity. In fact, I have the studio's promise that I can do the things that my fans like best, and that is musical comedy" (Warren 117).

5. *The Shocking Miss Pilgrim*, according to *Time* ("Living the Daydream," 23 August 1948, 42), was "an attempt to tinker with the Grable formula" by covering her legs "behind long skirts and a prim Victorian manner"; the film was a "rare Grable picture that lost money" but it is possible that the film's departure from the "Fox formula" and the vaudeville aesthetic, which was also the case with *That Lady in Ermine* and *The Beautiful Blonde from Bashful Bend*, was as much to blame for its box office failure.

6. Choreographer Hermes Pan, who danced with Grable in several films (*Pin Up Girl* included), said that Grable "really was not a great tap dancer. . . . But she could move, and she had beautiful legs, and she had a certain magnetism when she was on screen. Her color was beautiful and she was pleasant to watch" (Kobal 630). Jack Cole, who also worked with Grable, said that while Hayworth "always did it for real," Grable's "problem was that she could do all those pictures forward and backward, which she did. She never looked at a script, she'd just come in, put on her makeup, look at the three pages they were going to do that day and then go, ready. She could do it all in a haze, you know, while thinking about what horse was going to win that day" (Kobal 597).

7. Barbara Leaming, in her biography of Hayworth, claims that Hayworth was sexually abused by her father. While this information was not publicized during Hayworth's career, her father's restrictiveness and abusiveness on other levels were. See McLean *Being Rita Hayworth*, chaps. 1 and 2.

8. Grable never married again, and died of lung cancer in 1973.

9 ☆☆☆☆☆☆☆☆☆☆☆

Cary Grant and Katharine Hepburn
Domesticated Mavericks

CHARLIE KEIL

Katharine Hepburn and Cary Grant are rarely considered an onscreen "star couple" in the conventional sense of the term. Unlike Astaire and Rogers or MacDonald and Eddy, they did not become linked to each other in the public eye through repeated teamings in a series of star vehicles. In fact, the two appeared together just four times, in a period spanning five years. By the time Hepburn had switched from RKO to MGM (a studio that she remained attached to for the entirety of the 1940s), Grant had established himself as a free agent, never staying at one studio for more than a film or two. Their careers would intersect only once during the decade, when Grant was purchased as box office insurance to launch Hepburn's

---

Cary Grant and Katharine Hepburn. Both photos collection of the author.

career at MGM in 1940. Had Hepburn had her choice of leading men, Grant would not have co-starred with her this one final time; instead, it would have been the first film that she made with Spencer Tracy, her future studio stable-mate and the actor with whom she has always been most strongly associated, both on and offscreen. Eventually, Tracy and Hepburn would co-star in six films together over the course of the decade, to be followed by three more before Tracy's death in 1967. So, if Tracy and Hepburn were the star couple formed and solidified during the 1940s, why consider Grant and Hepburn together in the context of this chapter? The answer rests in the complementarity of their star personae, in particular the ways in which their onscreen roles and offscreen lives (as reported by Hollywood) resisted certain orthodoxies concerning sexuality and gender. That shared resistance was evident only briefly, during their three appearances together during the 1930s; the 1940s demands attention for the manner in which each star forsakes the associations established during the prior decade, remolding his/her persona for the purposes of an industry and audience whose needs and desires no longer seemed as tolerant of the transgressive potential these stars held forth for a few years at the close of the 1930s.

★★★★★ Hepburn and Grant in the Late 1930s: A *Holiday* from Conformity

Hepburn and Grant's last appearance together occurs at the outset of the decade, in a film designed to showcase its female star—*The Philadelphia Story* (1940). But the circumstances of their final collaboration demonstrate how much can change in a star's career in a relatively brief time. When they first worked together, in *Sylvia Scarlett* (1936), Hepburn was indisputably the bigger name, with Grant finding himself billed below Brian Aherne and acting in support of the female lead. By the time the two reunited in a pair of films from 1938, *Bringing Up Baby* and *Holiday*, Grant's star was clearly on the ascent, as he had come off the great success of two comedies from the previous year, *Topper* and *The Awful Truth*. The failure of *Baby* and *Holiday* ensured Hepburn's absence from the screen in 1939, while Grant rebounded by triumphing in an entirely different genre that year, proving himself adept at adventure in both *Gunga Din* and *Only Angels Have Wings*. By the time Hepburn returned to films with *The Philadelphia Story*, she required the presence of Grant to ensure audience interest: he commanded the higher salary (as a loan-out) and top billing. *The Philadelphia Story* served as Hepburn's opportunity to reestablish herself as a star; for Grant, it merely confirmed his preeminence.

Having established a reputation as a skilled comedic performer in the late 1930s, Grant saw himself transformed from handsome but bland leading man into a true star: an actor with an identifiable persona to which audiences responded. Hepburn, rare among actors who gained prominence during the early sound era of the 1930s (her first film was *A Bill of Divorcement* in 1932), was recognized and promoted as a star almost immediately. She received an Academy Award for her third film, *Morning Glory* (1933), and her fourth, *Little Women* (1933), reunited her with *Divorcement* director George Cukor (who would collaborate with her on ten occasions in total) and proved a commanding popular hit, as well as garnering her a Best Actress accolade from the Venice Film Festival. Few stars vaulted to such heights as rapidly as Hepburn, and few came to be known for their blue-chip credentials (affluent Connecticut upbringing, Bryn Mawr education) and idiosyncratic behavior (preference for slacks, disdain of the press) to the same degree. Contracted to the smallest of the major studios, RKO, Hepburn was indisputably its biggest star (along with Astaire and Rogers), and arguably her successes and failures were scrutinized more carefully for their influence on the company's bottom line. By the time she came to make *Sylvia Scarlett*, a loosely structured tale of cross-dressing, with Grant (and Cukor) in 1936, Hepburn had weathered more than her share of creaky and poorly received star vehicles; and the film's failure demonstrated with more certainty than any of her prior disappointments that the Hepburn persona was not resonating with mainstream audiences. The third-billed Grant likely benefited from the perception that *Sylvia Scarlett* was a Hepburn film, and the liveliness of his performance as a Cockney con-man demonstrated that he possessed more ability than his roles as a Paramount pretty boy had revealed up to this point.

Grant started his career in films at almost the same time as Hepburn, but his road to star status was far more protracted (if typical) than hers. He labored in numerous films of different types for Paramount, most of them undistinguished and his performances unmemorable. Those few that registered (such as *Blonde Venus* [1932], and *She Done Him Wrong* and *I'm No Angel* [both 1933]) were notable more for their strong female leads (Marlene Dietrich in the first, and Mae West in the latter two) than Grant's negligible contributions. One could say charitably that he proved an agreeable straight man for West and contributed to the elaborate mise-en-scène of the Dietrich venture, directed by Josef von Sternberg. By the time that he was loaned out to RKO to make *Scarlett*, critics had come to expect little from Grant in the way of acting (or even personality), a perception that might surprise those whose familiarity with the actor begins with the series of triumphs that would define his career in the latter part of the decade. If *Scarlett* was the instance where Grant demonstrated that he was capable of being more than window dressing, *The Awful Truth* proved incontrovertible evidence that he was an expert farceur. Many of the attributes we now associate with the Grant persona—sly wit, raffish charm, and an offhanded way of suggesting familiarity and bemusement with the foibles of his female co-star (in the case of *Truth*, the more established and highly regarded Irene Dunne)—emerge convincingly in this film. When Grant reunited with Hepburn for two successive films in 1938, it was as her equal in terms of star power, and her superior as a master of film comedy.

As strange as it might seem now, given its reputation as a screwball classic, *Bringing Up Baby*, the first of these two films, dealt a death blow to the first phase of Hepburn's Hollywood career. Roundly dismissed as out of touch with public taste, it cemented the growing suspicion that Hepburn's star had faded and that she was now a liability to her studio. The nail in the coffin was her prominent appearance on a list of stars that exhibitors proclaimed to be "box office poison," and *Baby* proved a costly confirmation of theater owners' belief that audiences were no longer interested in watching films featuring Katharine Hepburn. That she demonstrated crack comic timing and had found a worthy co-star in Grant seemingly mattered for little. Sensing that her career with RKO was at a close, she bought up the remainder of her contract, made one additional film for Columbia (*Holiday*, with Grant and Cukor), and then departed Hollywood for the uncertainty of the stage. Though less celebrated than *Baby*, *Holiday* is a definitive work for contextualizing the subsequent careers of both Hepburn and Grant. In many ways, it can be seen as lead-up for the better-known *Philadelphia Story*, involving as it does the same two stars, director, and source material (a play by Philip Barry).

It is worth pausing to consider *Holiday* as a key Hepburn-Grant text, for despite its surface likeness to *The Philadelphia Story*, the earlier film emerges as an opposed variation on a similar theme. Though both films are typically described as breezy drawing-room comedies about the idle rich, the characterization fits neither particularly well. Ultimately, the project of *Holiday* is something far more radical, especially for a film made by Hollywood: it questions the devotion to wealth and the subjugation of self required by capitalism. *Holiday* presents capital as a trap that must be consciously resisted, though its apparent attributes (like those of Julia, the more socially outgoing and conventional of the Seton sisters) may make a compelling case for themselves. *Holiday* delivers this message through the conflict of its male protagonist, Johnny Case (Grant), an outsider who has gained access to increased prosperity via his engagement to Julia Seton. Johnny's only interest in making money is the purchase it will provide on freedom: unlike the Seton family, he doesn't wish to amass wealth, but views its (limited) accumulation as a means to an end. The titular holiday represents the life Johnny envisions for himself when freed from his current position in a banking firm: earning a living is his short-term duty, whereas living as he likes will be the benefit that derives from his temporary immersion in the world of commerce.

Were *Holiday*'s aversion to the imperatives of capitalism its only deviation from Hollywood's ideological norms, that would be distinction enough, but it also twists the typical narrative focus on male decision making sufficiently to render the film an examination of how Linda, the other Seton sister, reacts to the presence of the choices Johnny represents. Linda, as played by Hepburn, is immediately pegged as the discordant voice within the Seton household: uncomfortable with the sterile and ostentatious trappings of her family's patrician lifestyle, she holes up in a cozy playroom on an upper floor, a feminine sanctuary defined by the memory of her dead mother, decorated in chintz and dotted with toys and musical instruments. At odds with her father on most issues, she asserts her defiance by isolating herself spatially from his control. Accordingly, Johnny's crisis—should he sacrifice his plans to pursue his long-planned holiday in order to placate his fiancée and her father—offers Linda the opportunity to articulate her support of that opposition on behalf of someone other than herself. *Holiday* thereby succeeds in validating the oppositional values the Hepburn character represents, rather than complicating or recuperating them, as would so often be the case. (In this, it proves an intriguing companion piece to *Bringing Up Baby*, another film that supports the Hepburn figure's unorthodox attitudes, but frames them in such farcical terms that they bear little relationship to recognizable human behavior.) Bound together in their recognition of the salutary effects of a lifelong holiday, Johnny and Linda both choose each other and opting out as mutually inclusive terms of love and devotion. That they must flee the country (and, figuratively, the social constructs of both patriarchy and capitalism) to sustain their relationship suggests the utopianism of their union (to borrow Andrew Britton's term) no less than its radical implications.

✩✩✩✩★ *The Philadelphia Story*: Toppling a Goddess

How different, then, is the situation that Hepburn and Grant, as stars and as the characters Tracy Lord and C. Dexter Haven, find themselves facing in *The Philadelphia Story*. If *Holiday* is the story of *both* Linda and

Johnny, *The Philadelphia Story* focuses emphatically on Tracy; if the former film celebrates its two characters finding a way to forge their own values, the latter works to demolish the singular qualities of its heroine, taking a sledge hammer to the pedestal upon which she has placed herself. Devised to triumphantly announce its star's return to prominence, *The Philadelphia Story* predicates that announcement on the perverse annihilation of the very qualities that initially made her distinctive. If Hepburn herself had not been instrumental in the creation and packaging of the film version of the Barry play, one might be inclined to see it as a singularly sadistic exercise in dismantling a star's standing as an independent female; had the adaptation not proven such a commercially (and critically) successful retooling of the Hepburn persona, the perception would be of a wrong-headed masochism. The story of Hepburn's victorious return to Hollywood via *The Philadelphia Story* has often been told, but deserves a brief rehearsal to properly contextualize the significance of the film's treatment of its heroine. Having bought out her RKO contract in 1938, Hepburn oversaw the writing and mounting of the stage production of *The Philadelphia Story*, which, after a victorious tour, provided her with a Broadway smash in 1939. Assisted by Howard Hughes, she had purchased the rights to the play prior to the tour, and when Hollywood expressed its interest, she negotiated a package that included a hefty price tag for the property, a sizable salary for herself, and input into the selection of co-stars and director. Once the film proved itself to be as popular as its theatrical antecedent, Hepburn secured a contract with MGM and remained at the studio until the early 1950s. Two points about *The Philadelphia Story*'s success deserve underscoring: Hepburn herself engineered it; and Hepburn's previous track record (and, by extension, her established star persona) would prove the largest obstacle to overcome in drawing audiences.

As much as Hepburn stands as the problem *and* solution at the heart of *The Philadelphia Story*, both as text and salable commercial property, Tracy Lord's determination to wed again after failing at marriage the first time finds its counterpart in Katharine Hepburn's attempt to return to prominence as a film star on her own terms. Hence the tempering provided by the film's narrative formula: if Tracy/Hepburn is to be revered for her singularity, any reverence must be accompanied by the acknowledgment that such singularity has invited catastrophe, otherwise Tracy/Hepburn would not be in a position to require the forgiveness of her family/her fans. In this instance, the text deliberately invites the inevitable slippage between the role and the actress: we are encouraged to see Tracy as a version of Hepburn, the chaste goddess whose marked disdain for mere mortals bespeaks a serious character flaw that only the harshest of mirrors will properly reveal. Tracy receives her comeuppance primarily because of the damage her high standards have occasioned, her inability to show proper concern when others have faltered in their moral responsibilities. Held accountable for her father's philandering and her ex-husband's drunkenness, she must come to realize that humanity involves a recognition of human frailty, including her own. Stated in these terms, the message of *The Philadelphia Story* doesn't seem nearly as objectionable as it does via its enactment onscreen. Characters land their body blows to Tracy's flaws with such relish that her toppling comes to resemble blood sport. Moreover, Tracy's behavior registers as particularly damaging because of its adverse effect on the male figures in her life. Here, Tracy's reluctance to offer obeisance to men confirms her limitations as a woman, in striking contrast to the validation Linda Seton's refusal of her father's values receives in *Holiday*.

As a way around the impasse of Hepburn's demonstrated lack of popularity with audiences, the savviness of *The Philadelphia Story*'s approach seems undeniable, and it would be repeated with variations in most of Hepburn's more successful MGM films for the remainder of the decade. To forestall audience members reacting to Hepburn's distinctiveness as proof of their own inferiority, the formula entails coupling the actress's undeniable exceptionality with an attendant deficiency, be it social awkwardness, emotional insensitivity, or a lack of sexual appeal. Hepburn never embodied conventional ideals of dainty femininity with any conviction, nor could she play salt of the earth convincingly. What she was was an iconoclast, rubbing up against the male world with sufficient friction to cause displeasure. Whatever amusement that spectacle might provoke had not previously won over audiences, as *Bringing Up Baby*'s failure demonstrated all too emphatically. The trick, then, was to allow Hepburn her individuality, but at the price of a full accounting of its limitations, preferably administered by a disapproving (if ultimately tolerant) male figure. Spencer Tracy would prove the master of such roles, but in *The Philadelphia Story*, Grant assumes the responsibility, the nastiness of the task compounded by the tacit rejection of Grant's own idiosyncratic 1930s persona. Hepburn's soulmate in the pair of 1938 comedies that brought her to this situation, Grant must now rebuke his former partner in rebellion, as Dexter's chief role is to embody the wreckage Tracy's glacial perfection has wrought. The mutuality of respect for difference exhibited in both *Holiday* and (through a more circuitous and painful route) in *Bringing Up Baby* is abandoned in *The Philadelphia Story*, resulting in a savaging of the Hepburn persona, and a concomitant neutering of Grant's. The two stars' subsequent roles only confirm that *The Philadelphia Story* represents a turning point in their careers.

Hepburn would spend much of the decade sparring with Tracy in a battle of the sexes she was foreordained to lose, before the 1950s saw her embracing spinsterhood as the only way of realizing her uniqueness. Grant followed a more protracted and circuitous path before settling on vehicles that found humorous ways to drain his persona of any threat to normalcy, rendering the irresponsible as merely inconsequential.

☆☆☆☆★ Prewar Grant: Flirting with Seriousness

Grant's most distinctive comedies from the late 1930s provide pleasure stemming from his engagement with the ideal of sexual equality and a shared commitment to fun that releases him from the conventional constraints of masculinity. His vanity in *The Awful Truth*, his clumsiness in *Bringing Up Baby*, his disavowal of the merits of a steady income in *Holiday*, all point toward an image of maleness that, if not always overtly feminized (as it is in *Baby*), is nonetheless liberating in its prospects for unorthodox behavior and redefined male-female relationships. In *The Philadelphia Story*, he stands to one side of the action, engineering events by proxy, but demonstrates less investment in rekindling Tracy's interest than in revealing her shortcomings. In effect, his role in the film is to show how Tracy's prior actions have debilitated him, his lack of narrative agency the surest proof of those actions' deleterious effect. Throughout the 1940s, Grant's roles would often capitalize on one of these two attributes: either the covertly expressed malice, which could manifest itself as misogyny (*Suspicion* [1941], *Notorious* [1946]) or a more generalized misanthropy (*His Girl Friday* [1940], *I Was a Male War Bride* [1949]), or a neutered caricature of maleness, constantly beset by calamity (virtually every comedy from the decade after *Friday*, including *Bride* again). Arguably, the two auteurs with whom Grant worked most consistently throughout his career (and twice each during the 1940s)—Hitchcock and Hawks—recognized the latent malevolence in Grant's persona and worked the most interesting variations on it. Nonetheless, the inherent fallibility that pervaded the majority of his characterizations (consistently working to undercut the pretense of suaveness) doubtless pushed Grant progressively toward comedy as the decade wore on. In this sense, at least, his most famous film from the late 1940s, *Notorious*, is probably also his most uncharacteristic. The barely fettered bitterness of his character in that film finds little leavening via the trademark Grant self-effacing humor (as it will in his collaborations with Hitchcock in the 1950s), but other less felicitous examples of Grant playing it totally straight (as a family man submarine commander in *Destination Tokyo* [1943]

Though he split his choice of vehicles throughout the decade fairly evenly between comedies and dramas, Grant's farces of the late 1940s proved particularly popular. Collection of the author.

or a most improbable Cole Porter in *Night and Day* [1946]) leave one wondering why Grant bothered, so far removed do they seem from the persona's points of reference.

After *Notorious*, Grant's films from the 1940s retreat into a bubble of farcical franticness, recalling superficially the situations if not the emotional dynamics that fueled the heralded comedies from years previous. But the earlier part of the decade saw Grant experimenting with a wider range of generic possibilities, in roles that often blended the lighter and darker sides of his persona. *Suspicion* is one such film, where his charm and magnetism mask a proclivity for lying and recklessness. That the film's ending refrains from labeling him a murderer seems as much a concession to the idea that appearances can be endlessly deceiving as a refusal to sully Grant's reputation. Other films appear more clearly designed to rehabilitate the tendency toward irresponsibility that Grant's carefree attitude suggests: in *Penny Serenade* (1941), his footloose journalist must disavow his allegiance to self-serving independence in order to secure the adoption of a baby; in *Talk of the Town* (1942), flouting convention serves a greater social good, as Grant's character, anarchist Leopold Dilg, harnesses his skepticism regarding social propriety to concern for the common man. Perhaps the film that most adeptly performs this balancing act is 1943's *Mr. Lucky*. The film devotes half its running time to the spectacle of the disreputable side of Grant, playing a gambler and flashy con-man, manipulating the female leaders of a war relief organization before his conversion, where he reveals an emotional vulnerability only to become an eventual defender of American values. An unlikely stew of proto-noir atmospherics and narrative devices (fog-laden piers and a flashback structure) and gentle comedy (Grant offering co-star Laraine Day lessons in Cockney-derived coded slang), *Mr. Lucky* nonetheless marries the screwball antics to wartime moral gravitas in a manner that does full service to Grant's persona. If it fails to reach the comedic heights of his earlier work or to maintain the emotional intensity of the much more fully realized *Notorious*, *Mr. Lucky* still emerges as perhaps the last of Grant's films from the decade to successfully integrate his persona's sinister side into a comic narrative without denying its inherent appeal. As Richard Schickel has convincingly argued of the film, "It is an apt and convenient place to mark the end of an era, an end to the giddy delights of a kind of moviemaking for which we lost the taste for seeing, then the knack for making" (84).

Mr. Lucky, then, was the final instance when Grant would attempt the mix of comedic and dramatic strains, the integration of frivolity and seriousness that suffuses so many of his early efforts from the 1940s. Whatever their merits may be, the four projects that he undertook from late 1943 until mid-1946 are unrelentingly serious and allowed Grant the opportunity to reconsider (and, consequently, recalibrate) his comic persona. Though famed for his astute business sense, which made him one of the most successful freelancers during the studio era, a period when most actors clung to their contracts like life preservers, Grant still expressed periodic doubt about whether to continue working. By the 1940s, when his popularity was unassailable and he had his pick of projects, he developed a work ethic that saw him average two films a year. Even so, in mid-decade, he temporarily halted his career for a year, in reaction to his divorce from Barbara Hutton, but doubtless also chastened by the commercial failure of his two most recent productions, *Once Upon a Time* and *None but the Lonely Heart*, both released in 1944. (*Arsenic and Old Lace* also came out in 1944, though it was shot three years earlier; Warner Bros. had to delay its release until the Broadway source play had finished its run, as contractually mandated.) Grant was accustomed to success—nearly all his films from the 1940s were highly profitable—and this probably explains why he resorted to formula (read comedy) more consistently throughout the latter part of the decade. The failure of *Lonely Heart*, in particular, seemed to have affected him deeply, as the role of the cockney criminal Ernie Mott came closer to Grant's British roots than any role since his breakout con-man Jimmy Monkley in *Sylvia Scarlett*. He often cited it as his favorite part, but the public's rejection of Grant in such downbeat material seemed to push him back to his comfort zone, which, despite the detours of *Night and Day* and *Notorious*, remained within the zone of farcical comedy. Even more to the point, sometime around 1946, Grant's persona seemed to become enshrined in the moviegoing public's mind. He played himself in a cameo in that year's *Without Reservations*, as the ideal choice of a novelist who comes to Hollywood to aid in the casting of the film adaptation of her best seller, and his reputation as the screen's chief romantic star seemed to be confirmed by the enormous box-office receipts of *Notorious*. For Pauline Kael, *Notorious* initiates in earnest his career of playing "the glamorous, worldly figure that 'Cary Grant' had come to mean: he was cast as Cary Grant, and he gave a performance as Cary Grant. It was his one creation, and it had become the only role for him to play—the only role, finally he could play" (25). By 1947, a *Movieland* profile would put it as plainly as this: "But the most intriguing thing about Cary Grant is that he *is* Cary Grant" (Alyce Canfield, "Are You the Girl for Cary Grant?," March 1947).

★★★★★ Hepburn at MGM: Spencer Tracy and the Road to Post-Perfection

The 1940s were a trying time for stars who had become established in the prior decade. The generation of film actors who came to fame in the 1930s could reasonably expect that their stardom might be sustainable for the long haul. This distinguished them from the vast majority of stars who came to prominence in the late 1910s and 1920s, and who saw their careers curtailed by the introduction of sound. Despite unforeseen interruptions (primary among them World War II and the industry shakeup after the Paramount decrees) and competition from new, younger stars introduced throughout the decade, many of the prominent names of the 1930s remained vital forces within the industry during the 1940s. But changing times called for careful revision of preexisting personae, and advancing age meant that roles suitable ten years earlier would no longer be viable as the decade wore on. For the most part, women had a harder time of it than men, if only because female desirability was called into question once actresses neared forty, whereas many male stars could continue to function as romantic leads well past fifty. (Even so, one notes an increasing emphasis on the age of Grant in late-1940s profiles, noting the graying of his temples and even going so far as referring to him as an "old-timer" [Florence Fisher Parry, "I Dare Say," 21 August 1946]).[1] This might explain why Grant's roles in the 1940s often partnered him with a noticeably younger woman as the decade progressed—his two late-decade pairings with Myrna Loy the exceptions that proved the rule—even while Hepburn remained tied to the most part to Tracy, who was seven years her senior. More to the point, Hepburn saw her onscreen persona shift from that of single woman to wife (though rarely mother). In most of her 1940s films, she is either married at the outset of the narrative (*Keeper of the Flame* [1942], *Dragon Seed* [1944], *State of the Union* [1948], *Adam's Rib* [1949]), or finds herself in the role of wife midway through (*Woman of the Year* [1942], *Without Love* [1945], *Undercurrent* [1946]).

Hepburn's image as an "independent" woman underwent modification throughout the decade, and it is instructive to compare her first film with Tracy (*Woman of the Year*) with their third (*Without Love*) in this regard. In *Woman of the Year*, Hepburn's character, Tess Harding, is established at the outset as a dynamic and opinionated voice capable of dissecting affairs of state and the national psyche with equal aplomb. (She is, in fact, presented as only a voice prior to her first physical appearance, introduced via a radio interview where she questions the American fixation on baseball. This gambit presents Tess as a public figure, but also asserts her refusal to adhere to orthodoxy.) Tess's independence of mind seemingly finds its complement in her beauty, which only enhances her attractiveness to sports reporter Sam Craig (Tracy). Sam's first view of her—a shapely set of legs framed to sever Tess at waist level—contributes to the idea that Tess is the sum of her parts. In what functions as a variation on the approach employed in *The Philadelphia Story*, *Woman of the Year* expends considerable effort in its early stages demonstrating Tess's undeniable attributes (the capacity to speak multiple

More than half of the films that Hepburn made during the decade saw her teamed with Spencer Tracy, her partner on and off the screen.

languages, an impressive command of the geopolitical landscape) only to reveal these as inadequate compensation for her failures as a wife and prospective mother, the latter made readily apparent once she and Sam are married. Most critics lament the final reel's extended documentation of Tess's abject failure to perform simple domestic duties (such as the preparation of a cup of coffee) as an almost sadistic rebuttal of her many triumphs on the public stage, but *Woman of the Year* has already done considerable damage to its female protagonist prior to her final undoing in the kitchen. Most egregious is her unfeeling use of a war orphan: unresponsive to his isolation once she has adopted him, Tess fails to understand why Sam returns the boy to the agency. The intimation that Tess has adopted the boy to bolster her public image suggests that she lacks the innate maternal instinct most women possess and verifies her unsuitability for marriage. The film provides numerous signals for Tess to bring her to the realization that her lack of womanly qualities will doom her to loneliness. The eleventh-hour breakfast preparation that closes the film has perhaps proven especially troubling to critics because it confirms that Tess has heard the message and is trying to reform. Her inability to perform standard wifely duties in a competent fashion results in a stalemate only resolved by Sam stating a compromise in terms of his own desires: "I don't want to be married to Tess Harding anymore than I want to be married to Mrs. Sam Craig. Why can't you be Mrs. Tess Harding Craig?"

Some have suggested that the retooled ending of *Woman of the Year* was precipitated by audience reactions at previews, wherein female viewers were beset by feelings of inadequacy when confronted with the overly impressive achievements of Tess Harding. According to this logic, Tess was too much the superwoman for these audience members to feel comfortable with in her winning over Sam unless she were humbled in the process. Given the prior success of *The Philadelphia Story* in proffering a "humanized" Katharine Hepburn, we should not be surprised at the logic of such a response, but the wonder is that any audience watching *Woman of the Year* would have still thought Tess required further comeuppance when the film had so relentlessly conveyed her inadequacies prior to her final humiliation. We can see the one-two punch of *The Philadelphia Story* and *Woman of the Year* as a (commercially) successful attempt to "soften" Hepburn's persona, to temper her reputation as strong-willed and haughty. If these two films brought her down to earth, the question remained of what to do with her once she had settled there. One such answer is put forward by *Without Love*, her third film with Tracy and arguably the first of the 1940s to begin constructing what would become the dominant image for Hepburn in the 1950s: the spirited spinster. While she had already flirted with this aspect of her persona at least once in the 1930s (with *Quality Street*), that was in a period piece, made when she was still (barely) in her twenties. *Without Love* hedges its bets somewhat, making Hepburn's Jamie Rowan a widow, but her own acknowledgment of her social reticence and apparent lack of interest in future romantic entanglements mark her as different in kind from the

Throughout her career, Hepburn rarely played wives, except during the 1940s. This still, featuring her as married lawyer Amanda Bonner in *Adam's Rib* (1949), indicates that the dimension of yearning pathos that would mark her future spinster roles can already be glimpsed in moments of the 1940s work. Copyright 1949, Loew's, Inc.

effortlessly attractive Tracy Lord and Tess Harding. *Without Love*'s narrative development depends upon a central conceit: that Jamie's proposition of a platonic marriage to Pat Jamieson (Tracy) is plausible because she doesn't offer the obvious appeal required for a sexually satisfying union.

Without Love is a decidedly odd vehicle for two actors ostensibly hoping to forge an association as a romantic team in the ticket-buying public's consciousness. But perhaps the "partners rather than lovers" logic underpinning the relationship in *Without Love* did exert some appeal for Tracy and Hepburn: they were forced to keep their own real-life relationship, whatever form it might have assumed, invisible to the public eye in order to avoid the backlash that Tracy's status as a married man would have engendered for them as an offscreen couple. *Without Love* initially deviates from conventions of romantic comedy because the central couple commits to a relationship but does not allow the possibility that love could underpin the union. Eventually, both partners reach the realization that they do love each other, but it is a long time coming and the lead-up involves little in the way of stifled sexual tension, in part because they marry soon after meeting. Significantly, perhaps, Jamie feels the force of attraction first, which invests Hepburn's performance with a quality of longing that will also define many of her prototypical spinster roles of the following decade. It is certainly tempting to see *Without Love* as preparing for the film that follows, *Undercurrent*. In both, Hepburn's character is defined as socially awkward, influenced by a strong male figure with an interest in science, and uncertain how to deal with a spouse who adopts a troubling attitude toward her. But what *Without Love* treats as comedy, *Undercurrent* uses as grist for drama. Generally speaking, critics have found Hepburn unconvincing as a victimized bride (of Robert Taylor, no less), a figure derived from Gothic models and better suited to actresses who could suffuse it with a tremulous frailty. And while Joan Fontaine may have perfected the type in *Rebecca* (1940) and *Suspicion*, one can imagine why Hepburn would have agreed to this property, as it established another avenue for leavening her distinctiveness with vulnerability. The attempt didn't stick, and three of her last four films of the decade were reunions with Tracy, in wifely roles that might have become her fate had it not been for the ironically liberating success of her first full-blown spinster role in *The African Queen* in 1951.

★★★★★ Grant's Late-Decade Comedies: Disgruntled and Degraded

If Cary Grant didn't suffer from the same obvious liabilities as Hepburn in developing a palatable persona to see him through the 1940s, he still never regained the artistic momentum established by the near-miraculous string of enduring films that he made in the late 1930s and into 1940. The unquestioned, and therefore enthralling, frivolousness of screwball, of which Grant had become an acknowledged master, had largely fallen out of favor by the early 1940s, to be replaced by something more hardened, knowing, and frantic: the increasing desperation evident in Grant's purely comic roles of this period (*My Favorite Wife* [1940] and *Arsenic and Old Lace* in particular) emerges as a performative version of flop-sweat. *Wife*, an ill-advised revisiting of the post-marital intrigues that formed the core of *The Awful Truth* (1937), relies on an inherently unfunny premise: Nick Arden (Grant), presuming his wife, Ellen (Irene Dunne), dead after her disappearance seven years earlier in an accident at sea, is shocked when she returns on the day of his marriage to Bianca. Essentially a comic retelling of *Enoch Arden*, *My Favorite Wife* overlooks the tragic pull of the source material and blithely ignores the psychological readjustment required for a family forcibly reassembled after seven years of maternal absence. Instead, it opts for farcical exaggeration, as Nick tries to keep Ellen's return a secret from his new wife while also avoiding consummation of his current marriage. The audience is meant to find the raciness of bigamy hilarious and Grant must sustain several painful scenes of fending off an understandably perturbed Gail Patrick, in the thankless role of Bianca. At one point, the plot contrives to put Nick in front of a mirror, testing out some of Ellen's outfits to see what would best suit her, as a psychiatrist hired by Bianca looks on. The moment invites comparison to the scene in *Bringing Up Baby* when David Huxley is forced to don a negligee. But whereas the former film used cross-dressing as a means to strip David of the last of his socially imposed defenses, in *Wife* the same gesture merely demonstrates that Nick's distraction makes him oblivious to how foolish he appears in the eyes of others.

It is also an intimation of the distressing pattern that will emerge in Grant's later comedies of the decade, all of them box office winners, and all of them of a piece: *The Bachelor and the Bobby-Soxer* (1947), *Mr. Blandings Builds His Dream House* (1948), and *I Was a Male War Bride*. Their overly descriptive, even declarative titles stand in direct contrast to the more playfully allusive quality of *The Awful Truth*, *Bringing Up Baby*, and *His Girl Friday*, thereby confirming the shift in comedic values. Though his roles in the films are quite different, they collectively depend upon Grant's character being subjected to some form of humiliation that will reveal his inadequacies and undercut the suaveness of his earlier persona. Whereas most of Grant's prewar films allowed him to combine lightness and darkness, with a degree of malice always coursing beneath the debonair surface, in these three late-decade comedies the combination no longer comes across as a productive duality. Instead, the films emerge as lightweight contrivances with a frustrated curmudgeon at their center. Grant supplies virtually all

Grant's comic roles in the late 1940s worked to undermine the image of suave control he had cultivated earlier in his career. The nadir of humiliation was probably his drag act in *I Was a Male War Bride* (1949). Copyright 1949, Twentieth Century–Fox, Inc.

the tense energy in these comic concoctions, but his disgruntlement meets its match in degradation: pratfall-laced defeats in folksy county fair competitions like the three-legged race in *Bachelor*, incarceration in a self-locking storage room in *Blandings*, and everything from suspension on a raised railway standard to wearing a horse-hair wig and nylons to impersonate a war bride in the final film. Not only does the duality of Grant's persona experience a forced separation in these films, the sense of mutuality between the male and female leads that was fostered by the earlier comedies has been lost. In much of *Bachelor* and *Blandings*, Myrna Loy stands by as a bemused foil, marveling at her partner's capacity for folly; in *Bride*, Ann Sheridan enjoys herself immensely, but mostly at Grant's expense.

In his earlier comedies, Grant perfected the image of slightly detached confidence, even as the world was spinning out of control around him. Occasionally, as in *Bringing Up Baby*, unflappability would give way to exasperation, but more often Grant remained in control, effortlessly negotiating any comic contrivance. Elegant maneuvering gave way to craven manipulation in Hawks's *His Girl Friday*, a razor-sharp remake of *The Front Page* that pushed Grant into the bully range but also featured a fearlessly charismatic performance that met its match in Rosalind Russell's skilled parrying. Grant's Walter Burns doesn't know how to express love directly, so every act of duplicity can also be read as a signal of affection. This taps directly into Grant's ability to be charmingly despicable/maliciously endearing, and no film has had him poised on the knife's edge between guile and bile more adeptly than this one. But none of his subsequent comedies in the first half of the decade proved up to the task of replicating this feat. (That said, *The Philadelphia Story*'s triumphant, dialogue-free opening comes close: Grant's frustrated C. Dexter Haven, driven to violence by Hepburn's imperious Tracy Lord, plants an open palm against her regal face, forcing her backwards into their home's doorway.) So one is inclined to agree with Richard Schickel, who sees in *The Bachelor and the Bobby-Soxer* a "boldly simplifying, boldly vulgarizing resolution of the identity crisis that plagued [Grant] throughout the 1940s" (93). In Schickel's view, the transformative moment in the film comes when Grant's character, playboy artist Dick Nugent, is envisioned as a knight in shining armor by teenage admirer Susan Turner (played by one-time child star Shirley Temple). By presenting Grant as the literal embodiment of every woman's dreams, the film renders the Grant mystique concrete at the same time that it envelops it in a parodic haze. From this point onward, argues Schickel, it would be difficult to see Cary Grant as anything other than "Cary Grant"—the star image had completely suffused all aspects of his performance. (In this he echoes Kael's earlier assessment, though he selects a different film as the emblematic moment.) And with this establishment of the Grant persona as indelibly self-acknowledging, and, by extension, self-mocking, all subsequent comedies operate primarily as scenarios of reaction. This motivates the string of indignities heaped upon him in *Bachelor* and the remaining comedies of the decade: Grant's feigned superiority invites the upbraiding his characters endure, but his pained air of acceptance (mixed with ongoing annoyance) allows him to retain some measure of equanimity, if not dignity.

★★★★★ Unrealized Projects, Political Skirmishes, Private Lives

Whatever their onscreen profiles might have been during the 1930s, both Hepburn and Grant found themselves associated most profitably with comedy throughout the 1940s: though only half of Hepburn's ten films of the period can be so classified, four of her six pairings with Tracy are comedic in nature and they proved far more popular with the public than did her dramas; thirteen of Grant's twenty films made in the 1940s are comedies, with the final five of the decade falling within that genre. Whether this was a source of frustration to either of the stars is difficult to know, but their correspondence and interviews during the period give some insight into their broader ambitions. Grant had more autonomy in his choice of vehicles, being the superior of Hepburn in terms of box office draw during the decade, so one might be tempted to see his choice of comedy as being more by design than default. Even so, legal documents in his personal files and newspaper reports of the day indicate that Grant never stopped thinking about expanding his repertoire during the decade. He had entered into agreements with both Alexander Korda and Howard Hawks to form co-production ventures; he planned to make a film with British director Carol Reed, in the wake of the latter's critical success with the dark-toned *Odd Man Out* (1947); he contemplated buying the rights to *The Glass Menagerie*, intending to act in a film adaptation opposite Laurette Taylor; and, perhaps most surprisingly, he and Hitchcock were intent on making a modern-day version of *Hamlet*. He was quoted in 1947 as finding his reputation as a light comedian a limitation: "It is sort of monotonous . . . to be typed and not given a chance to play something different. Of course I know it's a standing joke that every comedian wants to play Hamlet and tragedians are always anxious to try their hands at comedy. That's human nature. But variety is the spice of acting, as much as of life" (quoted in S. J. Woolf, "The Philosophical Stilt Walker," *Motion Picture*, February 1947).

Hepburn, for her part, was never completely comfortable at MGM, and certainly relocating to a studio where there were "more stars than there are in the heavens" must have proven something of a major readjustment after ruling the roost at RKO for the better part of seven years. After *Woman of the Year*, she made only three films that weren't vehicles for her and Tracy, suggesting that the studio did not really know what to do with her when he wasn't her onscreen partner. And despite demonstrating considerable business acumen when negotiating contracts for herself and having developed a reputation as headstrong and opinionated on set, one finds little evidence that she pushed hard for roles that might have advanced her career. Perhaps it wasn't worth the fight, if one detailed instance of her attempt to have a dramatic project accepted by MGM is any indication. Writing in 1944, during the filming of *Dragon Seed*, she provides a revealing account of a table-read of O'Neill's *Mourning Becomes Electra*, a property that she was interested in bringing to the screen with herself and Garbo in the leads. As Hepburn recounts it, all the executives gathered round the table bombarded her with arguments about why the play would prove commercially unpalatable: "[One] was saying that people want to laugh after the war—and then I said that I hoped they still might want to think—and Eddie Mannix said—Kate—I think it's a spellbinder but what about the children—And Al Levine—the only sensible one—just said Miss Hepburn—I think it's a bore—and I think it would break your heart at the preview that they would just laugh—." In the letter, Hepburn's awareness of the studio decision makers' aversion to risk—"[They] have never risked anything and just give a lot of easy opinions with no *real* experience"—leads her to dismiss the experience as "hilarious," but she also says that she will "never forget it."[2]

Instead of pushing for challenging parts at MGM, especially in the latter part of the decade, she seemed to devote herself to being Tracy's companion, the two forming a close-knit circle of friends with her director of choice, George Cukor, and a couple who would be screenwriters on two Hepburn-Tracy films, Garson Kanin and Ruth Gordon. The stars' celebrated relationship has been the subject of an insider's best-selling account, Kanin's *Tracy and Hepburn* (published in 1971), and endlessly scrutinized and reevaluated by biographers ever since. Whether theirs was an idealized love affair rivaling that of Bogart and Bacall, as indicated by Kanin, or something far less sustained and passionate, as many others now claim, the relationship occupied much of Hepburn's time and energy in the second half of the 1940s. Though renowned for her independence, Hepburn was also fiercely loyal and a dedicated caretaker. Often drawn to men whom she could respect for their dynamism and masculinity—John Ford, Leland Hayward, and Howard Hughes among them—Hepburn was in thrall to Tracy for his acting prowess and plainspokenness. By all accounts, she would happily sit at his feet, soaking in his opinions on a variety of matters, rarely questioning or disagreeing, despite her argumentative nature. She provided his life with order and consistency and helped him over his bouts of alcohol abuse and the subsequent withdrawal. Yet this was a relationship that occurred outside the glare of publicity. If gossip columnists knew of it—and surely they did—they said next to nothing. Hepburn biographer William J. Mann challenges this view, saying that "the myth of how respectful reporters had behaved toward Kate and Spencer was largely a latter-day attempt by the press to pat itself on the back," but provides only scattered evidence to refute the myth (383). Perhaps his most convincing argument comes in the form of this comment by Elliot Morgan, head of research at MGM: "Everyone at Metro knew the truth about Kate and Spencer. . . . They knew that they were together but that it wasn't a sexual thing. I always laugh when I hear people say, 'Oh, wasn't it good of Hollywood not to gossip, to be so respectful of their affair.' But nobody was gossiping because they knew there was nothing to gossip about. Everyone knew that they were just good, devoted friends" (382). Rarely has an extramarital affair been treated with such discretion by the media. Whether this was in deference to the tact the couple demonstrated—they were almost never seen together in public—or in response to an edict from MGM studio chief Louis B. Mayer, who wished to see the reputation of two of his biggest stars protected, the fact is that the Hepburn-Tracy relationship was off-limits. Their onscreen coupling was doubtless fueled by the intimacy that had developed between them offscreen, but the latter dimension was one denied to the public at large.

Because Hepburn's personal life during the 1940s remained an unspoken secret, publicists' interest in her remained at a low ebb throughout the period. One searches the pages of *Photoplay* and its ilk in vain for any articles devoted to her, in direct contrast to Grant, whose personal life is chronicled with incessant attention in the fan magazines. Profiles attempt to paint a portrait of the actor by providing accumulated details: his love of British antiques and classical music, distaste for cats and winter sports, his need to shave twice a day because of heavy beard, a penchant for tidiness, and no declared hobbies. He is usually described as being as he appears on screen, jovial and unaffected, but occasionally an insight touching on a possible psychological truth sneaks in, as when it is reported that "he gets sudden periods of depression for no apparent reason" (Joseph Henry Steele, "Portrait of 'U.S.' Grant," *Photoplay*, March 1943, 89) or when another writer suggests that "it is odd that such a reputably 'gay man' should give an impression of sadness—perhaps it is because he does not seem to be anchored anywhere" (Sheila Howarth, "Cary Is Hard to Know," *London Daily Graphic*, 24 May 1947). When one pieces together the information provided from multiple sources, a contradictory composite emerges: while reports from the sets of films indicate a strong-willed perfectionist who frequently clashed with directors, Grant also developed a reputation as an actor who championed first-time filmmakers (as his contracts typically granted him approval of directors for his films). His negotiations for salary and other terms (said to be handled by Grant himself; his long-time agent, Frank Vincent, died in 1946) reveal a hard-headed businessman. Anecdotes concerning his penny-pinching ways also circulated freely, but at the same time he donated generously to the war effort, gave the entirety of his sizable *Philadelphia Story* salary to the Red Cross, and devoted considerable time to entertaining servicemen. During the wartime years, Grant was the president and chairman of a group called The Masquers (whose hostess was his friend and recent co-star Rosalind Russell), which provided dinners for those in the armed service. Though he never served in the U.S. military, as many of his generation of stars did, Grant did acquire American citizenship on 26 June 1942, at which time he also officially changed his name from Archibald Leach to Cary Grant. In a 1950 overview of various stars' contributions to community service, Grant was described as "quietly philanthropic" and "considered very cooperative" by the Hollywood Coordinating Committee, an organization that arranged for public appearances by stars to aid in "good causes" ("The Other Side of the Hollywood Story," *Photoplay*, August 1950, 33).

Befitting his onscreen persona, Grant's romantic travails during the decade received the lion's share of the press's attention, from a failed romance with RKO contract player Phyllis Brooks carrying over from the late 1930s, to a mid-decade involvement with socialite Betty Hensel, and culminating in a marriage at the end of 1949 to Betsy Drake, his co-star in *Every Girl Should be Married*, released a year earlier. Most celebrated was the high-profile marriage to heiress Barbara Hutton, one of the wealthiest women in the world, that lasted from 1942 to 1945. Hutton's extravagant lifestyle and ill-chosen marriages to two different European men of noble birth but limited means had invited widespread revulsion from Depression-era America, and by the end of the 1930s she was engaged in a public relations campaign to restore her reputation. Whether embarking on a romance with Grant, a beloved and financially independent celebrity, was a calculated move on Hutton's part or not, it was two years after their initial meeting before they were actually wed. Once married, the couple submitted to a profile by Louella Parsons to prove they did not live a privileged life available only to the extraordinarily wealthy, as this (ostensible) quote from Hutton demonstrates: "Can you imagine Cary coming home tired, dead tired, from the studio, or from one of the war committee meetings, or back from a swing around the country on one of the camp tours, and then dashing upstairs to put on a dinner jacket?" ("The Married Life of the Cary Grants," *Photoplay*, February 1944, 77).

One article in *Photoplay* from May 1944 names Grant as "the most liked" star by the press, and his cooperation with those involved in promotion and publicity explains in part the extensive (and sympathetic) coverage his activities, both professional and personal, receive. Hepburn, in direct contrast, was notoriously hostile to the press, and though she adopted a somewhat more conciliatory posture after her move to MGM, relations remained chilly. Worse for Hepburn, her reputation as a committed liberal caused her considerable grief during the postwar period, when HUAC investigations put the reputations and careers of those on the political left at peril. While her membership in such organizations as the Committee for the First Amendment was apparently a function more of goodwill than commitment, she did provide one infamously public gesture that raised conservative ire. In May of 1947, incensed that presidential candidate Henry Wallace, former vice president to FDR and running under the Progressive Party banner, had been denied the use of the Hollywood Bowl for a political event, Hepburn agreed to speak at an anti-censorship rally on the candidate's behalf. Dressed in a fiery red dress that would immediately be interpreted as symbolizing allegiance to communism, Hepburn delivered an equally impassioned speech disparaging the activities of HUAC and arguing for the rights of the artist: "The artist since the beginning of time has always expressed the aspirations and dreams of his people. Silence the artist and you have silenced the most articulate voice the people have." Her speech invited a firestorm of criticism that persisted into the fall, coinciding with the time that the first unfriendly witnesses were called before the HUAC investigation. While Hepburn was never asked to testify, the negative publicity further damaged her already shaky box-office status.

Hepburn had encountered potentially damaging publicity before, and in this she shared something in common with Cary Grant. Both stars had been subject to innuendo during the 1930s concerning their sexual orientation: Hepburn was known to prefer the companionship of women; Grant engaged in a longstanding and unorthodox living arrangement with fellow actor Randolph Scott. The brief marriages each experienced during the early 1930s (resulting in divorce for Hepburn in 1934 and for Grant one year later) did little to dispel the gossip. Speculation about the sexuality of each star continues to pervade contemporary biographies, and the prospect of homosexuality becomes just one more layer of complexity in both their star personae. Here, for example, is Richard Schickel on Grant: "And if he had really been homosexual that would have been all right, too. We would have been out of the realm of the merely magical and into that of the patently miraculous. Splendid, really, to be alive and witness to so prodigal and ironic a transcendence: the most enrapturing star in the history of the movies, turns out to be gay" (145). But if the vehicles of the 1940s generally worked to blunt the transgressive potential of the most enterprising of the stars' films from the previous decade, they also succeeded in recuperating those dimensions of Hepburn's and Grant's personae that chafed against socially sanctioned norms. In this, the late-decade films of each represent the successful completion of a project designed to make the stars acceptable for the decade to come. Grant becomes a star self-consciously examining the significance and limitations of his own attractiveness, to the point where the denial of sexual contact either becomes the film's primary conceit (*The Bishop's Wife* [1947], in which Grant plays an angel) or the source of its humor (*I Was a Male War Bride*). Hepburn, for her part, becomes the wife as moral conscience (*State of the Union*, in which she helps political candidate husband Tracy speak out against corruption) or the wife as ideological straw man (*Adam's Rib*, in which she and Tracy are opposing lawyers in a case involving a young woman who has shot her husband; Hepburn's defense of the young woman is shown to be "wrong"). Though there is still pleasure to take from the performances, and pleasure expressed in their realization by the actors, the loss is palpable, manifest in the whacks on the bottom Hepburn endures at the hands of Tracy in their two last films together this decade and the dewy-eyed benevolence with which Grant's angel forsakes earthly delights in *Bishop*. Ultimately, and with unfortunate success, the 1940s made Katharine Hepburn and Cary Grant safe for America. In their own ways, then, both Hepburn and Grant, stars of the 1930s who survived the 1940s, experienced the inevitable punishment meted out to Tracy Lord, the knowingly superior protagonist of *The Philadelphia Story*—an enforced disavowal of distinctiveness required to earn full acceptance.

NOTES

1. Any textual citations on Grant with an incomplete reference are from scrapbooks on Cary Grant held in the Margaret Herrick Library of the Academy of Motion Picture Arts and Sciences in Beverly Hills.

2. Any uncited quotations on or by Hepburn are from folders on Katharine Hepburn held in the Margaret Herrick Library of the Academy of Motion Picture Arts and Sciences in Beverly Hills.

10 ✩✩✩✩✩✩✩✩✩✩✩

John Wayne
Hero, Leading Man, Innocent, and Troubled Figure

EDWARD COUNTRYMAN

John Wayne had a distinct 1940s, different for him from the decades that preceded and that followed. His forties began in 1939, with John Ford's *Stagecoach*, the film that promoted him from Poverty Row to major stardom. It ended with Ford's *Rio Grande* (1950), which elaborates a troubled, complex Wayne persona that began to unfold not long after *Stagecoach* allowed Wayne to leave Monogram, Mascot, and their like behind. Wayne's enduring image appears simple. In both his films and his life, he provided an icon of strong American masculinity, rugged individualism,

Portrait of John Wayne as Captain Nathan Brittles in *She Wore a Yellow Ribbon* (1949), his greatest character role. Copyright 1949, Argosy Pictures Corp.

contained capacity for violence, and unashamedly "conservative" public values. But Wayne's performances between *Stagecoach* and *Rio Grande* are more complex than his stereotype. During the course of his 1940s Wayne brought out and solidified his iconic persona, particularly in his war films and his westerns. Even in those films, which sum up his meaning for the problem of "being American," he did more than play to his emerging stereotype, and in other genres a different "John Wayne" appears. His cultural power by the end of the decade stems not only from his enduring "John Wayne" qualities, but also from the complexity that he brought to many of his roles.

In this decade Wayne worked under many directors. They included Ford and Howard Hawks, who between them brought out the actor's richest performances over his career. Between *Stagecoach* and *Rio Grande* he worked with Ford seven times. Hawks directed him just once, in *Red River* (1948), the film that supposedly caused Ford to say that he never knew "the big son of a bitch could act." Ford was overstating. Wayne had been "acting" effectively for years, several times for Ford himself, and not always onscreen. Wayne also worked once with Cecil B. DeMille (*Reap the Wild Wind* [1942]). He made his other 1940s films with supposedly lesser directors on studio contracts, and the difference shows. But understanding what he accomplished in front of their cameras adds richly to understanding the films that conventionally rank among his major achievements.

Wayne's enduring image cannot be separated from the western genre. So much is that the case that when he died in 1979 the French Communist Party newspaper *L'Humanité* published a deeply moving eulogy-cartoon, showing his by-then huge bulk from the back, in western garb, disappearing into the frame, with badges on him that read "Ford" and "Hawks." But during the 1940s, Wayne made films in genres as diverse as romantic comedy, comic-action, seafaring adventure, and war. Two of his lighter films, *Lady for a Night* (1942) and *Flame of Barbary Coast* (1945), include several onstage production numbers and might qualify as musicals.

Onscreen he was many things during the decade: an innocent ill-fitted to a nasty world, a leading man in the conventional Hollywood sense, an individualist struggling against all restraint, a leader by example, a leader by force, a betrayer, a redeemer, a drunk, and, memorably, a character actor playing roles that ranged far from his usual image. He lost many women. He retreated from other women's company. He won a few. He played against strong women actors, including Joan Crawford, Jean Arthur, Marlene Dietrich, and Claudette Colbert. He became adept at portraying inner anguish that can be far worse than physical suffering. He touched on many of the major themes in American history, sometimes in ways that showed sophistication that a professional historian can admire, sometimes in ways at which that same historian might sigh with frustration. In some films his developing right-wing political stance is clearly visible. But in one of them the Communist Party membership of the director is clear. John Wayne's 1940s films defy any simple John Wayne stereotype.

By the end of the decade, John Wayne possessed a complex screen persona, vastly richer than what he brought to the famous introductory shot in *Stagecoach*, when the camera dollies in on his Ringo Kid until his face fills the screen. But from his pre-*Stagecoach* 1930s films to such later great achievements as Ethan Edwards (*The Searchers* [1956]), John T. Chance (*Rio Bravo* [1959]), Tom Doniphon (*The Man Who Shot Liberty Valence* [1962]), the Oscar-winning Rooster Cogburn (*True Grit* [1969]), and John Bernard Books (*The Shootist* [1976]), his enduring, expanding role was as "John Wayne." Understandably, the young man who had begun life in Iowa as Marion Michael Morrison left that name behind when his screen career began. As biographer Ronald Davis notes, the name that he inhabited thereafter was simply "Duke." "When I started, I knew I was no actor," Duke confessed, "and I went to work on this Wayne thing. It was as deliberate and studied a projection as you'll ever see. I figured I needed a gimmick, so I dreamed up the drawl, the squint, and a way of moving meant to suggest that I wasn't looking for trouble but would just as soon throw a bottle at your head as not. It was a hit-or-miss project for a while, but it began to develop" (Davis 68). "Develop" may be the operative word.

★★★★★ John Wayne Plays John Wayne

One major feature film (Raoul Walsh's *The Big Trail* [1930]) and dozens of serials and Saturday-afternoon fillers lay behind Wayne's image by 1939. He had been too young and inexperienced when Walsh gave him *The Big Trail*'s lead, but between it and *Stagecoach* he learned a lot. In *The Big Trail* and the Poverty Row films alike, his screen persona was uncomplicated and naturally good. So is *Stagecoach*'s Ringo Kid, who has been in prison because of false testimony, not wrongdoing. Though he has broken jail, Ringo is a natural gentleman, with no scorn for the drunken Dr. Josiah Boone (Thomas Mitchell) and with the grace to love bar girl Dallas (Claire Trevor) despite her past. The actor's physical beauty would morph into dignified bulk as Duke aged, but the theme of uncomplicated natural goodness runs the whole length of his career.

Both dimensions of Wayne's persona, the affable, increasingly avuncular, more or less innocent Good Man and the figure tormented by pain and

Wayne (Jim Smith) embraces Claire Trevor (Janie McDougall) in *Allegheny Uprising* (1940), Wayne's first major frontiersman role (and a box office failure). Copyright 1940, RKO Pictures, Inc.

sometimes by hatred, emerged during the 1940s films. The innocent (though not necessarily unworldly) appears as Jim Smith (*Allegheny Uprising* [1940]), Lieutenant Dan Brent (*Seven Sinners* [1940]), Jack Morgan (*Lady for a Night*), Duke Hudkins (*A Lady Takes a Chance* [1943]), Duke Fergus (*Flame of Barbary Coast*), Wedge Donavan (*The Fighting Seabees* [1944]), Joseph Madden (*Back to Bataan* [1945]), Rusty Ryan (*They Were Expendable* [1945]), Kirby York (*Fort Apache* [1948]), and John Breen (*The Fighting Kentuckian* [1949]). In both *Allegheny Uprising* and *The Fighting Kentuckian*, Wayne's figure is buckskin-clad and coonskin-capped, pointing straight toward his David Crockett in *The Alamo* (1960), which he directed. Perhaps buckskin brought out Marion Michael Morrison's Iowa-childhood lessons about American innocence, goodness, and heroism, whether he wore it in 1940 as a Pennsylvania rebel, in 1949 as a Kentucky Indian fighter, or in 1960 to play a myth-sized Texas hero.

The more complex John Wayne began to appear in his first film with Ford after *Stagecoach*, *The Long Voyage Home* (1940). Adapted from a series of plays by Eugene O'Neill, *The Long Voyage Home* follows the crew of a rusty tramp steamer across the war-torn Atlantic, from a vaguely threatening Caribbean, through U-boat danger, to the journey's end in a malevolent, festering London docklands. The driving device is the same that Ford used in *Stagecoach*: a motley crew of people, all male this time, thrown together in a confined place as they cross a vast, dangerous distance. Threats surround them, on the vaguely exotic West Indies island from which they depart, in Philadelphia where they take on a cargo of explosives, at sea, when they finally arrive in London, and, throughout the film, among themselves.

In the shadowed world of the ship's forecastle, Wayne's Ole Olson is indeed an innocent, but he has complications that were not to be found in Ringo. The character is a Swedish farm boy who has gone to sea. Playing opposite Ford's favorite comic Swede John Qualen, Wayne mastered a convincing Swedish accent that betrays no comic qualities at all. He must escape the sea before it steals him from the land permanently, as it has the others. He has a flaw: when he drinks, he cannot stop. He has tried repeatedly to get back to Sweden, but each time a journey's-end binge has sent him back to sea. He does escape at the end of *The Long Voyage Home*, but only by sheer luck when the crew falls into the clutches of conniving Docklanders. Though Wayne had star billing, Ole Olson is more a character role than a lead. Ringo had not been a man of many words, but Olson is stumblingly and movingly inarticulate.

Wayne brings the same inarticulate confusion to Pat Talbot in *Reunion in France* (1942), particularly in the character's early scenes. Talbot is exhausted, frightened, and at the end of endurance when he enters. Like *The Long Voyage Home*, the film is dark and shadowy. Talbot is no blustering American rising above European corruption. A true American *naïf* in occupied Paris, he is ill at ease, completely outside his element, and Wayne's performance shows it.

Ole Olson and Pat Talbot are complex but admirable. His Captain Jack Stewart in DeMille's *Reap the Wild Wind* develops during the film into the actor's first genuinely dark character. The film is set in Charleston, Cuba, Key West, and the western Caribbean before the Civil War. Opulently realized in the DeMille fashion, it draws on but also undercuts *Gone with the Wind*–style Old South imagery. Its aristocratic men are elegantly costumed and its white women's frocks are lavish. But the film shows what all the wealth and glamour rests on, the pain of slavery. At one poignant moment we see black workers toiling in silhouette, as they sing of the burden they must bear. At another, the main black female character Maum Maria (Louise Beavers) steps out of her loving Mammy role with the sharp statement that she can be sold at somebody else's whim. Wayne's own character is offered (but refuses) a chance to take part in the illegal slave trade from Africa to a labor-hungry Mississippi Valley.

This Old South is broken within itself, and the handling of slavery suggests why. Wayne's Jack Stewart breaks as well. He enters as the victim of barratry (wrecking a ship for its value), carried out by his corrupt mate on behalf of a far more corrupt Charleston lawyer who heads a criminal ring. Stewart sets out to clear his name of suspicion in the sinking, but he falls into the master criminal's clutches. He himself sinks the steam-driven pride of the merchant fleet, which leads to an innocent young woman's drowning. She is the cousin of a woman (Paulette Godard) whom Stewart pursues but whom he loses to another Charleston lawyer (Ray Milland). With Wayne's figure gone bad, Milland's rises from effete indolence and leads the campaign against the ring. After a courtroom melodrama, the now-corrupt Stewart and his victorious rival in love dive to the wreck together to find the woman victim's body, fighting off a giant squid and dislodging the wreck from its precarious place on a reef. Stewart redeems himself by sending his rival back to the surface, going down with the wreck when it plunges into the deep. It is the first time a Wayne character dies onscreen.

Jack Stewart, in his turn, points toward a series of troubled Wayne figures. They begin with "Pittsburgh" Markham in *Pittsburgh* (1942), a businessman who loses everything (including Marlene Dietrich) to his ambition. His Quirt Evans in *Angel and the Badman* (1947) enters the film fundamentally flawed. Evans is a cattle thief on the run who reaches the end of possibility at the desert home of a Quaker family. Like Ole Olson and Pat Talbot, he is beyond coherence with privation and suffering. The Quakers take Evans in and heal him, physically and emotionally. He falls for their daughter Penelope (Gail Russell) and she for him. He helps them in trouble. Like *Reap the Wild Wind*'s Jack Stewart, Quirt Evans moves uneasily back and forth between Wayne's well-established good-man persona and the actor's growing ability to deal with inner turmoil. Unlike Stewart, Evans does not die, but he owes more to Jack Stewart than to the Ringo Kid. The film was "A John Wayne Production," an early sign of the actor's growing power in the industry that would culminate in Batjac Productions and in Wayne's directing projects.

In 1948, Wayne made four films, each monumental in its way. They were *Fort Apache, Red River, Three Godfathers*, and *Wake of the Red Witch*. *Red River*'s Tom Dunson, Robert Hightower in *Three Godfathers*, and *Red Witch*'s Captain John Rawls all prefigure Ethan Edwards. Dunson is one of Wayne's great roles. Rawls is truly irredeemable.

Tom Dunson's flaws are clear from the start. Driven by individualist greed, he abandons his love (Coleen Gray) in the film's first moments, condemning her to die in an Indian raid that follows. When he finds good land in Texas, his only justification for claiming it is his own say-so, and he shoots two Mexicans who assert their *jefe*'s lawful title to it. Fourteen years later, when the main action opens, he orders his cowboys to rustle other ranchers' animals and brand them with his own mark, before his great drive to the railroad begins.

During the drive all his faults emerge. Dunson has a grand vision, but it becomes an *idée fixe*. He drives his cowboys harder than they drive his cattle. He drinks. He cuts rations (though it would be easy enough to slaughter a few of the steers along the way). He will not alter his plan to get to Missouri, despite learning that there is a better, safer route to a railhead in Kansas. When his men start to desert, he has them recaptured as if they were under military discipline, and sets out to hang one without the pretense of a trial. At that point he alienates his adopted son Matthew (Montgomery Clift), who deposes him and takes the herd to Kansas safely. Driven now by hunger for revenge, Dunson assembles a private posse of thugs, pursues the herd, and confronts Matthew with intent to kill, even though the $50,000 check for the herd's value is in Dunson's name. They fight. Finally, Dunson's rage is spent and the two reconcile. Nominally the first John Wayne has returned. Whether or not Dunson's demons are exorcised, the film has laid bare the price that building the West has extorted from men, like Dunson and his underlings, who did it.

Three Godfathers is a Christian allegory, writ very heavy. Wayne's Robert Hightower is avuncular, but he and his two companions (Pedro Armendáriz and Harry Carey Jr.) are thieves, bent on robbing the bank in a small desert town. Their heist is pathetically, badly done and they escape into the desert without the water they need. When they reach a sump they find not water, but rather an abandoned, dying woman who is about to give birth. It is Christmas time. She commends her son to them, and the three not-so-wise men set off with the child for the town of New Jerusalem. Hightower alone survives their waterless desert ordeal, and, captured by the sheriff who has pursued him (Ward Bond), faces trial for his crime. But saving the child has transformed him from an unthinking thief into something like an older, wiser Ringo Kid. He will serve his one-year sentence and return to New Jerusalem to raise the boy. Hightower is no Tom Dunson. He is wrong, but there are no demons within him.

Wake of the Red Witch is entirely another matter, at least in terms of Wayne's persona. From the start, John Rawls is vile, running his vessel by

Wayne as the tormented, sadistic Captain Ralls with Gail Russell as the equally troubled Angelique Desaix in *Wake of the Red Witch* (1948). Copyright 1948, Republic Pictures, Inc.

terrorizing the crew. "Strange, sadistic, and cold" is how his mate Sam Rosen (Gig Young), who tells the story in voiceover, describes him. Rawls is not Wayne playing a bad man; he simply is bad and Wayne's hard performance shows it. We meet him first as he presides over the flogging of a sailor. Falsifying the log, he scuttles the ship, which is carrying millions of dollars in gold, thus willfully carrying out at the film's beginning the barratry that Jack Stewart committed late in *Reap the Wild Wind*. Rawls plans to return for the gold. But the film's main story leads through the tortured relationship between Rawls and the vessel's owner Mayrant Ruysdaal Sidneye (Luther Adler), an equally vile, equally corrupt figure whose shipping company is called Batjac Ltd. (Batjac, of course, is the name that Wayne later gave to his own production company.) The hatred between the two turns on a woman (Gail Russell); the gold is a secondary matter. She dies.

Rawls dives to the sunken *Red Witch* for the gold and disturbs the wreck. As in *Reap the Wild Wind*, the sunken vessel teeters off the reef on which it is impaled into the deep, taking Rawls with it. We have learned what made this man Rawls "to wander" the Pacific, but there is no redemption for him, no purging his soul of its demons. At the end the ghosts of Rawls and of Russell's character journey the sea together, straight out of Wagner's *Flying Dutchman*. If anything, Rawls is a darker, more troubled character than even Ethan Edwards was to be. As Wayne plays him, the good-man side of the actor's persona never comes through and his ghostly redemption seems spurious.

Nathan Brittles in Ford's *She Wore a Yellow Ribbon* is, like Ole Olson, a character role. Brittles is a gray-haired, widowed cavalry captain who is approaching retirement, about a quarter-century older than the actor was at the time of filming. Wayne was only forty-one; to carry off Brittles he needed more than makeup wrinkles and dyed gray hair. He had to learn how to walk, talk, and behave like a man more than half again as old, lost in reminiscence for his past and completely uncertain about his future after the army forces retirement upon him. He also had to learn to look with bemusement on the love triangle of two junior officers (Harry Carey Jr. and John Agar) and the woman they pursue (Joanne Dru, who played opposite Clift rather than Wayne in *Red River*). Driven not by demons but rather by loss, Brittles is complex in a different way than Jack Stewart, Tom Dunson, John Rawls, or Ethan Edwards. But as with them, the role shows that Duke could act, not just be (or play) "John Wayne."

★★★★★ The Leading Man and His Women

In his life, Duke's relationships with women were tangled and difficult. He married three times, failing at all three, and reportedly had many flings. But he preferred the company of men when he wanted to relax, often at sea with the hard-drinking crowd on John Ford's yacht *Araner*. By his full maturity, no woman actor could upstage him except, perhaps, for Angie Dickinson's young, intensely sexual Feathers in *Rio Bravo* and Kim Darby's fourteen-year-old Mattie in *True Grit*. In some of his forties films, however, he faced strong female leads. Thus Joan Crawford's Michelle de la Becque ("Mike") in *Reunion in France*; Marlene Dietrich's Bijou Blanche in *Seven Sinners* (1940), her Cherry Malotte in *The Spoilers* (1942), and her Josie Winters in *Pittsburgh*; Jean Arthur's Molly J. Truesdale in *A Lady Takes a Chance*; and Claudette Colbert's Christopher "Kit" Madden in *Without Reservations* (1946). Wayne took lower billing to the female lead in all these films, as well as to Claire Trevor in both *Stagecoach* and *Allegheny Uprising*. His two performances with Trevor may have been stronger than hers, but against Crawford, Dietrich, Arthur, and Colbert he was outmatched. The films he made with them belong to their characters, not to his.

Dietrich's Malotte, Arthur's Truesdale, and Colbert's Madden all show how. Set in Nome during the Alaskan Gold Rush, *The Spoilers* presents Dietrich completely within her own spectacular persona. Her glorious costumes dominate the screen in almost every shot in which she appears, particularly during a strip in which we see only her feet as each garment falls. Her sexuality is bold. Ultimately her hold on Wayne's Roy Glennister, a mining entrepreneur, is unshakeable, though early in the film he falls for a modestly dressed conventionally good woman (Margaret Lindsay), who has arrived on the boat from Seattle. Nicely reversing good woman/bad woman imagery, Lindsay's figure in fact is part of a ring centered on a corrupt judge, which is bent on despoiling the miners. The film closes with a spectacular fight between Wayne's figure and another member of the ring (Randolph Scott, also billed above Wayne), but the real clash is between the two equally knowing women, one of them open about being "bad," the other subverting the normal iconography of "good."

Jean Arthur's Truesdale has no rival within *A Lady Takes a Chance*. She is a New Yorker who sets out on a bus tour to escape the men pursuing her, see the West, and perhaps find adventure. She finds it with Wayne's Duke Hudkins, a rodeo cowboy whose job is to balance Arthur's manic comedy. So too with Wayne's Marine Captain Rusty Thomas facing down Colbert's best-selling (but incognito) novelist Christopher Madden in *Without Reservations*, a screwball comedy that takes them through one misadventure after another between New York and Los Angeles.

Forties Wayne characters do have complex relationships with women in *Reap the Wild Wind, Lady for a Night, A Lady Takes a Chance, Flame of Barbary Coast, The Fighting Kentuckian, They Were Expendable*, and *Wake of the Red Witch*. Some of those films play gender games. *Reap the Wild Wind* puts Wayne's nightshirt-wearing Jack Stewart in the Paulette Goddard character's boudoir when he is recovering from the first shipwreck, and costumes

Gabby Hayes, Wayne, and Jean Arthur in *A Lady Takes a Chance* (1943), a light comedy during the darkness of World War II. Copyright 1943, RKO Pictures, Inc.

her in trousers and a tight, functional sweater rather than southern-belle frills when she goes to sea. *The Spoilers* wraps the hyper-masculine Wayne figure in one of Cherry Malotte's boas. Arthur's Molly Truesdale ties a frilly apron around Wayne's cowboy so he can help with the dishes after she has tried to seduce him with a dinner. In *Lady for a Night* and *Flame of Barbary Coast*, Wayne's character is a dapper man-about-town, at home in the bars of Memphis or San Francisco. He can form a strong friendship with women of the same sort, but he neither needs nor seeks their love.

But in 1940s war films and the westerns, from *The Long Voyage Home* through *Flying Tigers* (1942), *Reunion in France*, *The Fighting Seabees*, *Back to Bataan*, *They Were Expendable*, *Fort Apache*, *Red River*, *Three Godfathers*, *She Wore a Yellow Ribbon* to *Sands of Iwo Jima* (1949), Wayne's character either is alone throughout the film or loses a woman during its course. The same is true of *Reap the Wild Wind* and *Wake of the Red Witch*. Wayne's mature persona as unquestionably heterosexual but also as troubled by and about women, of which his Ringo Kid gives no hint, is nearly fully formed by decade's end.

★★★★★ John Wayne at War

One might expect Wayne's 1940s World War II films, which, with one exception, were shot while combat still raged, to be outright propaganda. One might expect his westerns, particularly John Ford's so-called "Cavalry Trilogy" (*Fort Apache*, *She Wore a Yellow Ribbon*, and *Rio Grande*) to be much the same, given both the large cultural function of the classic western genre in defining and celebrating American identity and, for the cavalry films, a continuation in western garb of the military theme. But in both the World War II films and the cavalry films, Wayne's character and his performance are not simple at all.

Made in rough synchronicity with the actual war, the earlier World War II movies present a running dramatization of the day-before-yesterday's newsreels. The dramatization starts with Ford's *The Long Voyage Home*, released more than a year prior to Pearl Harbor, while war already was raging in both Europe and Asia. The Eugene O'Neill plays that are the film's source are set during World War I, but the film updates them to the time of its own making. Its storyline is cruel and its ending is bitter, with one of the ship's crewmen dying as a ship onto which he has been shanghaied goes down in the U-boat-infested English Channel. Wayne made *Flying Tigers* and *Reunion in France* during the first year of American involvement in the war. Like *Long Voyage Home*, both films are set prior to Pearl Harbor. Unlike *Long Voyage Home*, both of them offer tales of prescient individual heroism, as if to encourage the mass mobilization that was underway as the films were in production. *The Fighting Seabees*, *Back to Bataan*, and *They Were Expendable* all reconstruct the war's history in the Pacific, each of them also meditating on its complexity. By the final forties war film, *Sands of Iwo Jima*, the actual war was four years in the past and patriotic propaganda was less necessary. Wayne's character is a complex, troubled man who finds refuge from his own problems in war's legitimate violence, both against the enemy and against the marines he leads.

In *Flying Tigers*, Wayne's Jim Gordon is a hired gun, flying for the beleaguered Chinese against Japan, as part of a unit of mercenaries. Gordon understands the primacy of the unit over the individual flyer. He has to deal with fellow mercenary Blackie Bales (Edmund MacDonald), who is in the fight strictly for money and personal glory, until news of Pearl Harbor arrives. At that point, in disgrace and about to be sent home, Bales sacrifices himself to save Gordon's life. The historical Flying Tigers were not mercenaries at all, but rather volunteers detached from the American military to serve with Chinese forces prior to Pearl Harbor. They flew with direct White House approval. But their service *was* voluntary and the film explores the relationship among selfish motivation, commitment to a unit of one's fellows, and larger commitment to a historical cause. *Reunion in France* deals with similar material, this time in a European setting. Wayne's Pat Talbot is an innocent young man from Wilkes-Barre, Pennsylvania, who has flown with the RAF, has been shot down, escapes from a concentration camp to occupied Paris, and seeks to flee with the help of the Resistance so that he can fight again. There were, in historical fact, many such figures, premature American entrants into a war that began in both Europe and Asia long prior to 7 December 1941. Taken together, *Flying Tigers* and *Reunion* raise most of the issues of individual self-preservation, public emergency, and commitment that combine with huge force in *Casablanca* (1942).

Perhaps the most propagandistic of the war films, *The Fighting Seabees* celebrates a marriage of capitalism and military virtues, but it also meditates on the relationship between martial and civilian virtues. Wayne's Wedge Donavan is a contractor based in New York whose construction crews in the Pacific cannot fight back against the Japanese, because they are civilians. He joins forces with a naval love rival to create the navy's Construction Battalions (CBs, hence the nickname), takes a commission himself, forgets his real purpose in the larger effort, and hinders the effort rather than aiding it when he leads his men away from their actual task of building an airfield in order to shoot Japanese. He dies as a consequence of his own gung-ho mistake. *Seabees* has a deeper point: the industrial might of the United States underpinned not only its own successful war efforts against the Axis Powers, but also the far bloodier contributions of the European allies, including communist Russia.

Back to Bataan acknowledges both that the United States did not win the war alone and that problems could and did emerge between it and its allies. Wayne's Colonel Joseph Madden stays in the Philippines after the Japanese conquest of the islands in 1942 to lead a guerilla movement. The film teeters uneasily between a more or less explicit position that mere "natives" needed a (white) leader like Madden, and repeated assertions that freedom has to be seized, whether from the Japanese invaders or, through repeated historical references, from the American occupiers who had driven Spaniards out four decades earlier, only to impose their own dominion. Balancing Wayne's Madden, Anthony Quinn's not completely convincing Filipino Andrés Bonifacio (the fictional grandson of a historical Filipino freedom fighter) forcefully makes that point, that the Americans had been occupiers rather than liberators. Early in the film we see Filipino children celebrating American history. By its end we have good reason to think they should celebrate their own. By no means was this Wayne's only populist film; the theme of a good community threatened from the outside returns repeatedly in his work with Ford. But none of Ford's films state so explicitly that freedom cannot be granted from above. On the contrary, despite revealing a deeper story behind one legend after another, they repeatedly insist that the legend, not the deeper story, needs to be endorsed. Wayne realized during production that Dmytryk was a communist, a point that is quite apparent in the film's Popular Front–handling of the alliance between the Americans and the Filipino guerillas. Apparently the director's politics did not bother him at the time.

As an actor, John Wayne wore many uniforms during his film career. He was a marine sergeant, a naval lieutenant, an army captain, a naval commander, and a cavalry colonel. But he never donned one for actual service. The reason was medical rejection on the grounds of injuries suffered during his high school and college football career, and in the many film stunts that he had insisted on doing himself. Biographer Ronald Davis suggests that being rejected may not have bothered him deeply at the time: this was his moment for A-stardom (Davis 101–02). Quite possibly Duke, who had not served, was deeply bothered to see his director and his co-star in *They Were Expendable* get credit as John Ford, Captain, U.S.N.R, and Robert Montgomery, Commander, U.S.N.R. Apparently Ford, who was notorious for hounding his actors, ragged Wayne heavily during production of that film for his non-service during the war.

They Were Expendable is the most complex, the most fully realized, and the most historically accurate of the war films. Based on the memoir of a PT-boat skipper, the two leading figures are lightly fictionalized versions of officers who served in the Philippines between Pearl Harbor and the American defeat there in 1942. Wayne's Lieutenant Rusty Ryan (real name, Robert Kelly) aches for action and gets it, from Manila Bay to his character's evacuation as the Japanese take over. He and Montgomery's character John Brickley (based on Medal of Honor Winner John D. Bulkeley, who wrote the memoir) prove the worth of their small vessels, take a heavy toll on Japanese ships, and start General Douglas MacArthur toward Australia before the Japanese can capture him. Despite stirring action sequences (in which, of course, the PT boats win against heavy odds), the film is a bitter tale of retreat and ultimate defeat, though with the solace of knowing that MacArthur would return and the Japanese victory in 1942 would be temporary, leading to their overall defeat in 1945.

Wayne made *Sands of Iwo Jima* four years later, in a changed historical time. His Sergeant John Stryker is a by-the-book marine. Psychologically

Stryker is the most complex of Wayne's war figures, a tough, troubled, deeply embittered man, venting his passions against the marines he leads as much as against the Japanese enemy, and often unable to control his rage. Stryker has held higher rank but has been busted to squad sergeant. He drinks hard and loses his tight self-control. His handling of new arrivals is sadistic, though he claims it will be for their good when they see combat. Stryker's wife has left him (understandably), and he is estranged from his son. He finds a suitably alienated substitute for his son in PFC Peter Conway (John Agar), whose deceased father had been an officer in Stryker's own style. Stryker dies during the final assault that leads to the famous planting of the Stars and Stripes on Mount Suribachi (using the actual flag from the event and three of the five marines who planted it). Reconciled, Agar's Conway takes on not just Stryker's role as the squad's leader but his identity, signified by his use of Stryker's signature phrase "Saddle up" to stir the remaining marines into action. John Ford already had used that same device when Wayne's Captain Kirby York succeeds Henry Fonda's martinet Lieutenant Colonel Owen Thursday, donning Thursday's signature desert cap at the end of *Fort Apache*.

Wayne's 1940s war films, then, are not simply adventure tales. They lead from the uncomplicated Jim Gordon of *Flying Tigers* to the torn, ravaged soul of John Stryker. They also lead to a fresh reading of Ford's cavalry films. Conventionally, these present a retreat in Ford's western oeuvre from bright optimism about America's possibilities (*Drums Along the Mohawk* [1939] and *My Darling Clementine* [1946]) to a darkening view that finds community and redemption from civilian corruption among the outnumbered, beleaguered, isolated denizens of threatened army posts scattered across the post–Civil War Southwest (all of which seems to look like Monument Valley). The device of a small American force (reduced to one man in the case of Pat Talbot in Nazi-occupied Paris) facing an overwhelming enemy runs through the war films and the cavalry films alike. In historical terms it is justified in the cases of *Flying Tigers*, *Reunion*, the early parts of *Bataan*, and *Expendable*. But by the Battles of Leyte Gulf (October 1944), which ends *Bataan*, and Iwo Jima (February-March 1945), Japan's material ability to fight was far smaller than its will to continue fighting.

In the cavalry films this device is just a convention. "Custer is dead. Another such defeat," announces the opening voiceover in *She Wore a Yellow Ribbon*, "and it will be a hundred years before another wagon train dares to cross the plains." In reality, the plains wars of the late 1860s and 1870s were the last gasp of resistance by a few thousand ill-equipped but determined Native Americans against the millions of people of the United

States and their industrial machine, as overwhelming against them as it later would be against Japan. The military narratives and Wayne's specific characters in *Fort Apache* and *Yellow Ribbon* turn on the futility rather than the glory of war.

Fort Apache offers a meditation on the well-known Indian victory over George Armstrong Custer (1876). Its Custer figure is Henry Fonda's Lieutenant Colonel Owen Thursday, a former Civil War general, bitter about being transferred from a military-diplomatic post in Europe to this remote command. A martinet (despite denying it when he addresses his officers after arrival), Thursday disrupts the fort's community, invokes spurious class distinctions to frustrate the young love of his daughter (Shirley Temple) for an Irish lieutenant (John Agar) whose father is the post's wise sergeant major (Ward Bond), fantasizes himself as "the man who brought Cochise back" from an escape into Mexico out of a corrupt reservation, breaks faith with the Indians, and leads his regiment into a futile charge that brings its and his destruction. Wayne's Captain Kirby York has none of those faults, but cannot dissuade his commander's foolishness. Through his character we see through Thursday's heroic imagery. Nonetheless, York endorses Thursday's imagery, rather than the reality, when he assumes command.

Both *Fort Apache* and *Yellow Ribbon* celebrate the cavalry as spectacle, the latter in Academy Award–winning Technicolor. Each film celebrates the cavalry as community, probing the relationship among a regiment's officers, its enlisted men, and its women. Despite the spectacle and the Technicolor, *Yellow Ribbon* undercuts what *Fort Apache* asserts, that the imagery of heroism must prevail over less than heroic military realities. Wayne's Nathan Brittles is at the end of his military career. Faced with the prospect of war against angry, united Natives, he seeks to avoid it. He tries to negotiate with his Indian counterpart Pony-That-Walks (Chief John Big Tree), but the Indian leader's power is spent. Finally, in his last military action, Brittles has his troops run off the Indians' pony herd. There will be no war for anybody to turn into heroic myth.

In both films the Wayne figure is partially outside the community. He is unattached in *Fort Apache* and widowed in *Yellow Ribbon*, conversing with his dead wife in luridly lit evening visits to her grave. The contrast between the grave sequences—obviously shot on a sound stage—and the vivid outdoors of Monument Valley is striking. Nathan Brittles's actual world of the post and the desert, which he is about to lose through retirement, and his remembered world of a woman and perhaps children are utterly separate from one another, even though she is buried in the post's cemetery. Wayne's Ringo Kid and Claire Trevor's Dallas had escaped "the blessings of civilization" together in 1939. A decade later Wayne's Nathan Brittles can do nothing save remember a time when such blessings had been his.

★★★★★ Coda: Kirby Yorke at the Rio Grande

Rio Grande is a fitting film to end an account of Wayne's 1940s. Perhaps John Ford did not intend to complete a self-conscious "Cavalry Trilogy" when he made it. But all three of the cavalry films reduce American history to a tale about soldiering. All three use the cavalry device to deal with issues of family and man-woman relationships. Wayne's Colonel Kirby Yorke in *Rio Grande* bears nearly the same name as his Captain Kirby York (no "e") in *Fort Apache*. Colonel Yorke brings together themes and developments in "John Wayne" that reach back across the whole decade since he played the Ringo Kid.

Like D. H. Lawrence's take on James Fenimore Cooper's Leatherstocking, Colonel Kirby Yorke is (by character) hard, stoic, isolated, and (by profession) a killer. Wayne's Captain York had a joshing, knowing relationship with the people around him, officers, men, and women alike. His artificially aged Nathan Brittles has his men's love, teases his youthful lieutenants, flirts with two women, and joshes with Victor McLaglen's stage-Irish Sergeant Quincannon. But Colonel Kirby Yorke is a man alone. When his own son (Claude Jarman Jr.), expelled from West Point for academic failure, comes to the post as a trooper, Yorke insists on military etiquette and treats him harder than all the rest. But Wayne's Yorke is a commander, not a martinet. Following the rules is less important than achieving the goal, whether the goal be his regiment's cohesion or a mission accomplished.

Into Yorke's bare-bones borderland outpost, the aptly named Fort Stark, come not only his son but also his long-estranged wife Kathleen (Maureen O'Hara), who plays her half of a broken couple as perfectly as Wayne plays his. Unlike the convoluted (and highly improbable) stories that "explain" the isolation of Wayne's Jack Stewart and John Rawls from the women they sought, the mutual alienation of this couple is easy to comprehend. She is of the Virginia gentry. Serving with the Yankee cavalry during the Civil War, he had obeyed orders to sack his own wife's plantation. Nobody makes a speech, but she does tell him that he has destroyed "two beautiful things: Bridesdale and us." He has not seen her or their son since that time. But unlike his analogue John Stryker, Colonel Yorke is not bitter. As another character puts it to Kathleen when she asks what kind of man her long-lost husband has become, Yorke is simply "a lonely man, a very lonely man."

In contrast to most of the contract directors with whom Wayne worked in the 1940s, John Ford was a master at telling a tale cinematically. No dialogue, or voiceover storytelling, is needed to explain Yorke's loneliness. Wayne brings intense self-control to the effort of masking Yorke's deep emotion when he first sees his son. When the regimental singers serenade his wife after an officers' dinner with "I'll Take You Home Again, Kathleen," he comments to her that he did not ask for that. She responds that she wishes he had. Neither needs to talk about the pain that binds them. Still later, as some of the soldiers sing together around a fire (the curiously titled "My Girl Is Purple"), Yorke wanders alone along a riverbank. A montage of shots leads to Yorke walking toward the camera, until he fills the frame with his haunted face, reversing the movement of *Stagecoach*'s dolly-in on Ringo and showing without words how much the actor had learned, how much his skill had grown since then.

Yorke is wounded during the final action sequence, when his regiment (illegally) rescues the fort's children from their Apache captivity in Mexico. He returns to the fort on a travois. Kathleen searches for him as the troop returns, echoing the search by Lana (Claudette Colbert) for Gil (Henry Fonda) in Ford's *Drums Along the Mohawk*. Yorke's injury prefigures the wound that Ethan Edwards suffers toward the end of *The Searchers*. Both wounds bring out the (literal) vulnerability of Wayne's stoic, suffering figure. Each wounding seems to drain away a deep abscess of moral poison. Yorke and Kathleen do reunite, a happier resolution than Ethan Edwards's return to the desert. But most of the themes that Ford brought to *The Searchers* and all of the acting skills that John Wayne brought to Ethan Edwards are present.

In strict calendar terms, both *Stagecoach* and *Rio Grande*, which provide the immediate frame for this reading of Wayne's 1940s films, are outside this volume's temporal framework. But they do denote the beginning and the end, respectively, of a decade of intense development on Duke's/John Wayne's part. Raoul Walsh took his chance too early on promoting the former Marion Michael Morrison. As *The Big Trail*'s Breck Colman, Wayne simply did not have the gravitas or the acting skill for so major a part. Duke mastered his craft during his decade-long traverse through the purgatory of Poverty Row. He brought what he had learned during that time to the Ringo Kid, as Ford knew he would. He learned a great deal more about himself and the making of films during the thirty-seven projects that separate *Stagecoach* and *Rio Grande*. By the end of his 1940s, Duke had made John Wayne into a mature, accomplished actor of depth, complexity, and skill, not just a persona or a star.

In the Wings

SEAN GRIFFIN

Intriguingly, a sizable number of performers who became major stars just before and during World War II would see their popularity barely survive into the 1950s, including many of those discussed in this volume. On a basic level, the sudden and precipitous decline in fortunes for all of Hollywood during the postwar period would impact the durability of various A-list performers (see Kinder 319). As Milton Berle triumphantly demonstrated, television was capable of making stars too. As a result, certain stars responded by switching to the small screen, including Gene Autry, Roy Rogers, and Lucille Ball. Furthermore, beyond the economic woes of the industry, the ways in which a star's persona resolved social dualities during the war may have no longer matched the cultural shift of the country and the new contradictions that developed as a result. For example, what may have been considered an acceptable image during the war might suddenly seem suspicious with the onset of the Cold War. The effort to place women back in subservient roles contributed to the sense of scandal around Ingrid Bergman and Rita Hayworth toward the end of the decade as well.

Those stars who managed to survive and thrive past the 1940s somehow found new ways to mediate their image to this shift in outlook. Yet the most successful stars have always managed to adapt themselves across the years. While a number of new stars emerged during the 1940s, many others had risen to prominence during the 1930s and discovered how to maintain their popularity under new circumstances. James Cagney, Errol Flynn, Bette Davis, Joan Crawford, Barbara Stanwyck, Claudette Colbert, Ginger Rogers, Fred Astaire, Gary Cooper, Bing Crosby, Spencer Tracy, Katharine Hepburn, and Cary Grant were all top draws during the Depression but maintained relevance during the 1940s as well. Many would continue to do significant work in the ensuing decades also, as would certain of those who emerged as stars during the 1940s (such as James Stewart, Ingrid Bergman, Gene Kelly, Humphrey Bogart, and John Wayne). The Hollywood studio system might have been fading at the end of the decade, but the American public would still need stars.

While the studio system was facing restructuring, most executives still did not realize exactly how far such restructuring would reach, and thus discovering, grooming, and developing talent under contract carried on as the 1940s came to an end. A number of individuals who had not become full-fledged stars were nonetheless on various parts of the metaphorical conveyor belt. By 1949, some were already being positioned as stars, but were still in the process of solidifying the personae that would bring them greater success, such as Doris Day at Warner Bros., or the new comedy team of Dean Martin and Jerry Lewis at Paramount. Day's first films often seem modeled on the vehicles created by Paramount for Betty Hutton, and many early Martin and Lewis comedies show them in the military—a strategy borrowed from Abbott and Costello. In the ensuing decade, these stars would etch out their own unique images.

Similarly, other contract artists had gotten some notice but were not yet being positioned toward stardom. For example, MGM noticed that child star Elizabeth Taylor was blossoming into a remarkably beautiful woman, but they had not yet found the right part to define her as a personality. Others had knocked around without much notice, but finished the decade by taking steps to alter their trajectory and get studio attention.

William Holden, for example, had been in films throughout the 1940s, playing variations of male ingénues. Shifting into a more cynical persona, including a slightly more gruff outward appearance, would pay off right as the 1950s began in Billy Wilder's *Sunset Blvd.* (1950). Judy Holliday had tried to break into pictures in the 1940s but gotten nowhere. In response, she went back to New York and triumphed as the star of *Born Yesterday*. When Columbia bought the screen rights to the property, she returned to Hollywood with a star contract.

Various other performers were slowly gaining attention during the late 1940s but doing it without studio support. Rather than placing themselves under contract, a new generation of stars began as and stayed independents. Susan Hayward, much like the roles she would eventually become famous for playing, climbed the ladder to stardom in Hollywood slowly but surely—from such B-pictures as the musical *Hit Parade of 1943* (1943) to Academy Award nominations at the end of the decade for *Smash-Up: Story of a Woman* (1947) and *My Foolish Heart* (1949). Burt Lancaster alternated between noir and derring-do adventure pictures, an odd mix that possibly kept audiences from getting a solid sense of his persona. Similarly, Kirk Douglas bounced from role to role until landing a showcase part (followed by an Oscar nomination) in *Champion* (1949) that would make him a bonafide star as the 1950s began. Like Holden, Lancaster and Douglas blended a sense of sturdy masculinity with more troubled anti-hero aspects.

While such emerging stars heralded a new image of the American male, one younger actor seemed ready to push these developments even further. Montgomery Clift had strong ties to the emerging "Method School" of theater and brought this intensity and emotionalism with him as he began a career in film. Watching Clift alongside John Wayne in *Red River*, or as a potential suitor to Olivia de Havilland in *The Heiress* (1949), audiences seemed taken not only by his incredibly handsome face, but also a sense of depth of feeling that was new onscreen. Clift was arguably the harbinger of a new sense of what stardom meant. He was the first of an avalanche of Method actors and actresses who would populate Hollywood films in the next decade. Their connections to the "legitimate" stage and avowed commitment to their craft would lead to actors making names for themselves through their extraordinary performances rather than their glamour. Like Clift, this new generation of stars would tend not to tie themselves to a studio contract—and increasingly would disdain the trappings of stardom by wearing grubby clothes, going unshaven or without makeup, and refusing to play along with the industry publicity machine.

While much attention would be focused on this new type of star, not all younger aspirants would forsake the old Hollywood system. Two performers who began working in Hollywood in the late 1940s would stand as epitomes of the last great gasp of the studio star-making machine. Neither seemed initially destined for stardom: her first small role in *Scudda-Hoo! Scudda-Hay!* (1947) ended on the cutting room floor, his first one-line part in *Fighter Squadron* (1948) took thirty-eight takes. Yet, as the decade ended, Norma Jean Baker had rechristened herself Marilyn Monroe and changed her hair from strawberry to peroxide blonde. Similarly, Roy Fitzgerald had changed his name to Rock Hudson. Both would be molded and promoted by their studios (Twentieth Century–Fox and Universal, respectively) into enduring screen icons.

Thus, as the 1940s ended, that sense of divide discussed at length at the start of this volume would remain. On one side were the traditionally studio-crafted stars—those who fit the molds yet made them their own, and who behaved as they were advised. On the other were stars who stood out precisely by breaking the molds and becoming notorious precisely for not behaving in a manner that was considered appropriate. Furthermore, stars like Hayward, Lancaster, Douglas, and Holden seemed to straddle these two extremes—hanging onto some of the aspects of conventional Hollywood stardom, but also moving into some of the newer possibilities being carved out by rebels like Clift. Clearly, what it meant to be a star, and what being a star meant to audiences, would continue to evolve as the 1940s came to an end.

WORKS CITED

☆☆☆☆☆☆☆☆☆★

Fan magazines and other primary or archival materials are cited in the text of individual essays.

Alicoate, Jack, ed. *The 1943 Film Daily Yearbook*. New York: Film Daily, 1943.

Autry, Gene, and Mickey Herskowitz. *Back in the Saddle Again*. Garden City, N.Y.: Doubleday, 1978.

Bacall, Lauren. *Lauren Bacall by Myself*. New York: Alfred A. Knopf, 1979.

Barton, Ruth. *Acting Irish in Hollywood: From Fitzgerald to Farrell*. Dublin: Irish Academic Press, 2006.

Basinger, Jeanine. *The Star Machine*. New York: Knopf, 2007.

Bego, Mark. *The Best of Modern Screen*. New York: St. Martin's, 1986.

Bergman, Ingrid, with Alan Burgess. *Ingrid Bergman: My Story*. New York: Delacorte, 1980.

Blaetz, Robin. *Visions of the Maid: Joan of Arc in American Film and Culture*. Charlottesville: U of Virginia P, 2001.

Britton, Andrew. *Cary Grant: Comedy and Male Desire*. Newcastle upon Tyne: Tyneside Cinema, 1983.

———. *Katharine Hepburn: Star as Feminist*. New York: Columbia UP, 2003.

Buehrer, Beverley Bare. *Cary Grant: A Bio-Bibliography*. New York: Greenwood, 1990.

Buscombe, Edward. "Inventing Monument Valley: Nineteenth-Century Landscape Photography and the Western Film." *Fugitive Images: From Photography to Video*. Ed. Patrice Petro. Bloomington: Indiana UP, 1995. 87–108.

Casper, Drew. *Postwar Hollywood, 1946–1962*. Malden, Mass.: Blackwell, 2007.

Ceplair, Larry, and Steven Englund. *The Inquisition in Hollywood: Politics in the Film Community, 1930–1960*. Garden City, N.Y.: Anchor/Doubleday, 1980.

Clarke, Gerald. *Get Happy: The Life of Judy Garland*. Thorndike, Me.: Thorndike, 2000.

Cogley, John. *Report on Blacklisting*, Vol. 1, *Movies*. New York: Fund for the Republic, 1956.

Cohan, Steven. *Incongruous Entertainment: Camp, Cultural Value, and the MGM Musical*. Durham, N.C.: Duke UP, 2005.

Damico, James. "Ingrid from Lorraine to Stromboli: Analyzing the Public's Perception of a Film Star." *Star Texts: Image and Performance in Film and Television*. Ed. Jeremy G. Butler. Detroit: Wayne State UP, 1991. 240–53.

Davis, Ronald. *Duke: The Life and Image of John Wayne*. Norman: U of Oklahoma P, 1998.

———. *The Glamour Factory: Inside Hollywood's Big Studio System*. Dallas: Southern Methodist UP, 1993.

Deans, Mickey, and Ann Pinchot. *Weep No More, My Lady*. New York: Hawthorn Books, 1972.

Deming, Barbara. *Running Away from Myself: A Dream Portrait of America Drawn from the Films of the Forties*. New York: Grossman, 1969.

Dick, Bernard F. *The Star-Spangled Screen: The American World War II Film*. Lexington: UP of Kentucky, 1985.

DiOrio, Al. *Little Girl Lost*. New Rochelle, N.Y.: Arlington House, 1973.

Dixon, Wheeler Winston, ed. *American Cinema of the 1940s: Themes and Variations*. New Brunswick, N.J.: Rutgers UP, 2006.

Doherty, Thomas. *Projections of War: Hollywood, American Culture, and World War II*. New York: Columbia UP, 1993.

Dyer, Richard. "Judy Garland and Gay Men." *Heavenly Bodies: Film Stars and Society*. 2nd ed. London: Routledge, 2004. 137–91.

———. *Stars*. London: BFI, 1979.

———. "White." *Screen* 29 (Autumn 1988): 44–65.

Eames, John Douglas. *The MGM Story*. London: Octopus, 1975.

Eckert, Charles. "Shirley Temple and the House of Rockefeller." *Jump Cut* 2 (July-August 1974): 1, 17–20.

Edwards, Anne. *Judy Garland: A Biography*. New York: Simon and Schuster, 1975.

———. *A Remarkable Woman: A Biography of Katharine Hepburn*. New York: William Morrow, 1985.

Elkin, Frederick. "Popular Hero Symbols and Audience Gratifications." *Journal of Educational Psychology* 29.3 (November 1955): 97–107.

Everson, William K. *Claudette Colbert*. New York: Pyramid, 1976.

Finch, Christopher. *Rainbow: The Stormy Life of Judy Garland*. New York: Grosset and Dunlap, 1975.

Flynn, Errol. *My Wicked, Wicked Ways*. London: Heinemann, 1960.

Foertsch, Jacqueline. *American Culture in the 1940s*. Edinburgh: Edinburgh UP, 2008.

Fontaine, Joan. *No Bed of Roses: An Autobiography*. New York: William Morrow, 1978.

Fordin, Hugh. *The World of Entertainment: Hollywood's Greatest Musicals*. New York: Frederick Ungar, 1975.

Frank, Gerold. *Judy*. New York: Harper and Row, 1975.

Frayling, Christopher. *Mad, Bad and Dangerous?: The Scientist and the Cinema*. London: Reaktion Books, 2006.

Freedland, Michael. *Gregory Peck*. New York: William Morrow, 1980.

Fricke, John. *Judy Garland: World's Greatest Entertainer*. New York: Holt, 1992.

Fuller-Seeley, Kathryn. "Shirley Temple: Making Dreams Come True." *Glamour in a Golden Age: Movie Stars in the 1930s*. Ed. Adrienne L. McLean. New Brunswick, N.J.: Rutgers UP, 2011.

Furmanek, Bob, and Rob Palumbo. *Abbott and Costello in Hollywood*. New York: Perigee Books, 1991.

Gabor, Mark. *The Pin-Up: A Modest History*. New York: Bell, 1972.

Gallafent, Edward. *Astaire and Rogers*. New York: Columbia UP, 2002.

Gelley, Ora. "Ingrid Bergman's Star Persona and the Alien Space of *Stromboli*." *Cinema Journal* 47.2 (Winter 2008): 26–51.

George-Warren, Holly. *Public Cowboy No. 1*. New York: Oxford UP, 2007.

Giles, Nell. *Punch In, Susie: A Woman's War Factory Diary*. New York: Harper, 1943.

Glancy, H. Mark. *When Hollywood Loved Britain: The Hollywood "British" Film 1939–45*. Manchester: Manchester UP, 1999.

Gomery, Douglas. *The Hollywood Studio System: A History*. London: BFI, 2005.

Griffin, Sean. "The Gang's All Here: Generic versus Racial Integration in the 1940s Musical." *Cinema Journal* 42 (Fall 2002): 21–45.

———. "The Wearing of the Green: Performing Irishness in the Fox Wartime Musical." *The Irish in Us: Irishness, Performativity, and Popular Culture*. Ed. Diane Negra. Durham, N.C.: Duke UP, 2006. 64–83.

Harmetz, Aljean. *Round Up the Usual Suspects: The Making of* Casablanca—*Bogart, Bergman, and World War II*. New York: Hyperion, 1992.

Harris, Warren G. *Cary Grant: A Touch of Elegance*. New York: Doubleday, 1987.

Harvey, Lynn. *Gregory Peck: A Charmed Life*. London: Robson, 2005.

Hedling, Erik. "European Echoes of Hollywood Scandal: The Reception of Ingrid Bergman in 1950s Sweden." *Headline Hollywood: A Century of Film Scandal*. Ed. Adrienne L. McLean and David A. Cook. New Brunswick, N.J.: Rutgers UP, 2001. 190–205.

———. "The Welfare State Depicted: Post-Utopian Landscapes in Ingmar Bergman's Films." *Ingmar Bergman Revisited: Performance, Cinema and the Arts*. Ed. Maaret Koskinen. New York: Wallflower, 2008. 180–93.

Hiney, Tom, and Frank MacShane, eds. *The Raymond Chandler Papers: Selected Letters and Non-Fiction, 1909–1959*. New York: Atlantic Monthly Press, 2000.

Hout, Michael, and Joshua R. Goldstein. "How 4.5 Million Irish Immigrants Became 40 Million Irish Americans: Demographic and Subjective Aspects of the Ethnic Compositions of White Americans." *American Sociological Review* 59.1 (February 1994): 64–82.

Hurst, Richard. *Republic Studios: Between Poverty Row and the Majors*. Lanham, Md.: Scarecrow Press, 2007.

Jewell, Richard B. *The Golden Age of Cinema: Hollywood, 1929–1945*. Malden, Mass.: Blackwell, 2007.

Johansson, Stefan. "Ingmar Bergman at the Royal Opera." *Ingmar Bergman Revisited: Performance, Cinema and the Arts*. Ed. Maaret Koskinen. New York: Wallflower Press, 2008. 51–63.

Johnston, Sheila M.F. *Let's Go to the Grand!: 100 Years of Entertainment at London's Grand Theatre*. Toronto: Dundorn, 2001.

Kael, Pauline. "The Man from Dream City" (1975). *When the Lights Go Down*. New York: Holt, Rinehart and Winston, 1980. 3–32.

Kanin, Garson. *Tracy and Hepburn: An Intimate Memoir*. New York: Viking Penguin, 1971.

Kendall, Elizabeth. *The Runaway Bride: Hollywood Romantic Comedy of the 1930s*. New York: Anchor/Doubleday, 1990.

Kinder, Gorham. "SAG, HUAC, and Postwar Hollywood." *Boom and Bust: American Cinema in the 1940s*. Ed. Thomas Schatz. Berkeley: U of California P, 1997. 285–312.

Kobal, John. *People Will Talk*. New York: Alfred A. Knopf, 1985.

Koppes, Clayton, and Gregory Black. *Hollywood Goes to War: How Politics, Profits and Propaganda Shaped World War II Movies*. Berkeley: U of California P, 1987.

Kracauer, Siegfried. "National Types as Hollywood Presents Them." *Public Opinion Quarterly* 13.1 (Spring 1949): 53–72.

Leamer, Laurence. *As Time Goes By: The Life of Ingrid Bergman*. New York: Harper and Row, 1986.

Leaming, Barbara. *If This Was Happiness*. New York: Viking, 1989.

Lewis, Jon. *American Film: A History*. New York: Norton, 2008.

Light, Alison. *Forever England: Femininity, Literature and Conservatism between the Wars*. London: Routledge, 1991.

Lugowski, David M. "Ginger Rogers and Gay Men? Queer Film Studies, Richard Dyer, and Diva Worship." *Screening Genders*. Ed. Krin Gabbard and William Luhr. New Brunswick, N.J.: Rutgers UP, 2008. 95–110.

Madelbaum, Howard, and Eric Myers. *Forties Screen Style: A Celebration of High Pastiche in Hollywood*. New York: St. Martin's, 1989.

Mann, William J. *Kate: The Woman Who Was Hepburn*. New York: Henry Holt, 2006.

Marx, Arthur. *The Nine Lives of Mickey Rooney*. New York: Stein and Day, 1986.

Mast, Gerald. *Howard Hawks, Storyteller*. New York: Oxford UP, 1982.

Maxtone Graham, Ysenda. *The Real Mrs Miniver: The Life of Jan Struther*. Stroud, U.K.: Tempus, 2007.

McBride, Joseph. *Hawks on Hawks*. Berkeley: U of California P, 1982.

McDowall, Roddy. *Double Exposure: Take Three*. New York: William Morrow, 1992.

McElhaney, Joe. "The Object and the Face: *Notorious*, Berman and the Close-up." *Hitchcock: Past and Future*. Ed. Richard Allen and Sam Ishii-Gonzalès. New York: Routledge, 2004. 64–84.

McGilligan, Patrick. *Ginger Rogers*. New York: Pyramid, 1975.

McLean, Adrienne L. *Being Rita Hayworth: Labor, Identity, and Hollywood Stardom*. New Brunswick, N.J.: Rutgers UP, 2004.

———. "The Cinderella Princess and the Instrument of Evil: Revisiting Two Postwar Hollywood Star Scandals." *Headline Hollywood: A Century of Film Scandal*. Ed. Adrienne L. McLean and David A. Cook. New Brunswick, N.J.: Rutgers UP, 2001. 163–89.

———. "Feeling and the Filmed Body: Judy Garland and the Kinesics of Suffering." *Film Quarterly* 55.3 (March 2002): 2–15.

———. "Putting 'Em Down Like a Man: Eleanor Powell and the Spectacle of Competence." *Hetero: Queering Representations of Straightness*. Ed. Sean Griffin. Albany: SUNY Press, 2009. 89–110.

Melzer, Richard. *Buried Treasures: Famous and Unusual Gravesites in New Mexico*. Santa Fe: Sunstone Press, 2007.

Meyerowitz, Joanne. "Beyond the Feminine Mystique: A Reassessment of Postwar Mass Culture, 1946–1958." *Not June Cleaver: Women and Gender in Postwar America, 1945–1960*. Ed. Joanne Meyerowitz. Philadelphia: Temple UP, 1994. 229–62.

Naremore, James. *More than Night: Film Noir and Its Contexts*. Berkeley: U of California P, 1998.

Negra, Diane, ed. *The Irish in Us: Irishness, Performativity, and Popular Culture*. Durham, N.C.: Duke UP, 2006.

Palmer, R. Barton. *Hollywood's Dark Cinema: The American Film Noir*. New York: Twayne, 1994.

Parish, James Robert. *Katharine Hepburn: The Untold Story*. New York: Advocate Books, 2005.

Polan, Dana. *Power and Paranoia: History, Narrative, and the American Cinema, 1940–1950*. New York: Columbia UP, 1986.

Renov, Michael. *Hollywood's Wartime Woman: Representation and Ideology*. Ann Arbor, Mich.: UMI, 1988.

Rogers, Roy, and Dale Evans, with Jane and Michael Stern. *Happy Trails: Our Life Story*. New York: Simon and Schuster, 1994.

Schatz, Thomas. *Boom and Bust: American Cinema in the 1940s*. Berkeley: U of California P, 1997.

Schickel, Richard. *Cary Grant, A Celebration*. New York: Applause Books, 1999.

Shipman, David. *Judy Garland: The Secret Life of an American Legend*. New York: Hyperion, 1993.

Smit, David W. "Marketing Ingrid Bergman." *Quarterly Review of Film and Video* 22 (2005): 237–50.

Soila, Tytti, Astrid Soderbergh Widding, and Gunnar Iverson. *Nordic National Cinemas*. New York: Routledge, 1998.

Spencer, Nicholas. "Movies and the Renegotiation of Genre." *American Cinema of the 1940s: Themes and Variations*. Ed. Wheeler Winston Dixon. New Brunswick, N.J.: Rutgers UP, 2006. 117–39.

Sperber, A. M., and Eric Lax. *Bogart*. New York: William Morrow, 1997.

Spoto, Donald. *Notorious: The Life of Ingrid Bergman*. New York: HarperCollins, 1997.

Stacey, Jackie. *Star Gazing: Hollywood Cinema and Female Spectatorship*. New York: Routledge, 1994.

Stanfield, Peter. *Hollywood, Westerns and the 1930s: The Lost Trail*. Exeter: Exeter UP, 2001.

———. *Horse Opera: The Strange History of the 1930s Singing Cowboy*. Urbana: U of Illinois P, 2002.

Steele, Joseph Henry. *Ingrid Bergman: An Intimate Portrait*. New York: David McKay, 1959.

Third, Amanda. "'Does the Rug Match the Carpet?': Race, Gender, and the Redheaded Woman." *The Irish in Us: Irishness, Performativity and Popular Culture*. Ed. Diane Negra. Durham, N.C.: Duke UP, 2006. 220–53.

Thomas, Helen. *The Body, Dance, and Cultural Theory*. London: Palgrave, 2003.

Thomson, David. *The Big Sleep*. London: BFI, 1997.

Troyan, Michael. *A Rose for Mrs. Miniver: The Life of Greer Garson*. Lexington: UP of Kentucky, 1999.

Vermilye, Jerry. *Barbara Stanwyck*. New York: Pyramid, 1975.

Warren, Doug. *Betty Grable: The Reluctant Movie Queen*. New York: St. Martin's, 1981.

Watson, Thomas J., and Bill Chapman. *Judy: Portrait of an American Legend*. New York: McGraw-Hill, 1986.

Wood, Robin. *Hitchcock's Films Revisited*. New York: Columbia UP, 1960.

CONTRIBUTORS

★★★★★★★★★★

ROBIN BLAETZ is associate professor and chair of film studies at Mount Holyoke College. In addition to publishing widely in journals internationally, she edited the anthology *Women's Experimental Cinema: Critical Frameworks* (2007) and wrote *Visions of the Maid: Joan of Arc in American Film and Culture* (2001).

EDWARD BUSCOMBE is the editor of *The BFI Companion to the Western* (1988) and has written three volumes on westerns for the BFI Film Classics series. His most recent books are *100 Westerns* (2008) and *Injuns! Native Americans in the Movies* (2006).

EDWARD COUNTRYMAN is University Distinguished Professor of History at Southern Methodist University. He is co-author with Evonne Von-Heussen Countryman of *Shane* in the British Film Institute Film Classics Series, and was a consulting editor and contributing editor of *The BFI Companion to the Western* (1988). His main scholarship is on colonial and Revolutionary America. His interest in westerns developed when he had the chance long ago to join Robin Wood in a course at the University of Warwick on westerns as history and myth.

SEAN GRIFFIN is an associate professor in and chair of the Division of Cinema-Television at Southern Methodist University, author of *Tinker Belles and Evil Queens: The Walt Disney Company from the Inside Out* (2000), and co-author of *America on Film: Representing Race, Class, Gender, and Sexuality at the Movies* (2002) and *Queer Images: A History of Gay and Lesbian Film in America* (2006). He also edited *Hetero: Queering Representations of Straightness* (2009) and co-edited *Queer Cinema: The Film Reader* (2004).

HANNAH HAMAD is a Lecturer in Media Studies at Massey University in New Zealand. She was awarded a Ph.D. in Film and Television Studies from the University of East Anglia in July 2009.

CHARLIE KEIL is director of the Cinema Studies Program and an associate professor in the History Department at the University of Toronto. He is the author of *Early American Cinema in Transition: Story, Style and Filmmaking, 1907–1913* (2002) and co-editor, with Shelley Stamp, of *American Cinema's Transitional Era: Audiences, Institutions, Practices* (2004). With Ben Singer he co-edited *American Cinema of the 1910s* in the Screen Decades series. In addition to numerous essays on early cinema, he has published on documentary and contemporary cinema.

DAVID M. LUGOWSKI teaches cinema and media studies as an associate professor of English and chair of Communication Studies at Manhattanville College. He has written on an international range of film topics for *Cineaste*, *Cinema Journal*, *Senses of Cinema*, *Baseline*, *Arizona Quarterly*, *The Encyclopedia of Documentary Film*, and *The International Encyclopedia of Queer Culture*, and his essays have appeared in such anthologies as *Screening Genders* (2008), *Film and Sexual Politics* (2006), *American Cinema of the 1930s* (2007), *Looking Past the Screen: Case Studies in American Film History and Method* (2007), and *Hetero: Queering Representations of Straightness* (2009). He serves on the editorial board of *Cinema Journal* and is currently writing a study of James Whale's complete oeuvre for the University of California Press.

ADRIENNE L. McLEAN is a professor of film studies at the University of Texas at Dallas. She is the author of *Dying Swans and Madmen: Ballet, the Body, and Narrative Cinema* (2008) and *Being Rita Hayworth: Labor, Identity, and Hollywood Stardom* (2004), and is co-editor, with Murray Pomerance, of the Star Decades series.

DAVID SEDMAN is an associate professor in the Division of Cinema-Television at Southern Methodist University and has taught classes on film and television comedy. He has published articles related to radio and television and authored book chapters on topics ranging from video production to television programming.

RICK WORLAND is a professor in the Division of Cinema-Television at Southern Methodist University, where his teaching includes courses in film/TV theory, documentary, popular genres (the western, film noir, the horror film), and the films of Alfred Hitchcock. His research has concentrated on popular film and television of the Cold War period. His work has been published in *Cinema Journal*, *The Journal of Film & Video*, *The Journal of Popular Film and Television*, and *The Historical Journal of Film, Radio, and Television*, among others. He is also the author of *The Horror Film: An Introduction* (2007).

I N D E X

★★★★★★★★★★★

Note: Featured stars in boldface; page numbers for illustrations in italic.